Melissa Sweet is a journalist who spec[...]
and medicine. Her work appears in a wide range of publications, and
she has worked for the *Sydney Morning Herald*, the *Bulletin* and Australian Associated Press. She is co–author, with Judy and Les Irwig, of
Smart Health Choices, which provides some tools for assessing health
information and advice, and is an Adjunct Senior Lecturer in the
School of Public Health at the University of Sydney. Melissa lives
near Sydney.

INSIDE MADNESS

How one woman's passionate drive to reform
the mental health system ended in tragedy

MELISSA SWEET

MACMILLAN
Pan Macmillan Australia

First published 2006 in Macmillan by Pan Macmillan Australia Pty Limited
1 Market Street, Sydney

National Library of Australia
cataloguing-in-publication data:

Sweet, Melissa.
Inside madness.

ISBN-13 978 1 4050 3708 2.
ISBN-10 1 4050 3708 3.

1. Tobin, Margaret. 2. Murder – South Australia – Adelaide.
3. Murder victims – South Australia – Adelaide.
4. Trials (Murder) – South Australia – Adelaide.
5. Mental health services – South Australia. I. Title

364.1523

Every endeavour has been made to contact copyright holders to obtain the
necessary permission for use of copyright material in this book. Any person who
may have been inadvertently overlooked should contact the publisher.

Typeset in 12.5/14 pt Bembo by Midland Typesetters, Australia
Printed in Australia by McPherson's Printing Group

Papers used by Pan Macmillan Australia Pty Ltd are natural, recyclable products
made from wood grown in sustainable forests. The manufacturing processes
conform to the environmental regulations of the country of origin.

For Jeff Sweet

Contents

Foreword

This is an important book for the Australian community. It does not simply detail the circumstances surrounding the loss of one of our most valued members but also seriously questions the adequacy of our professional, legal and personal responses. Most importantly, it recognises the outstanding contribution that Margaret Tobin made to the lives of people with mental illness and their families.

Every family in Australia will at some stage need to understand the nature of mental illness and the affects that these disorders can have on our lives. That understanding is significantly advanced by this book. It forces all of us to look carefully at those who develop illness, those families who provide support and care and those professionals who attempt to relieve that suffering.

Professor Ian Hickie
Executive Director, Brain & Mind Research Institute

1

Another life

This day, pale and grey as it is, has been so slow in arriving. But now that the long wait is ended, Jean Tobin is not sure what she feels. She dresses carefully, to keep out the chill. She is also dressing for protection. It will help to feel that she looks smart. Jean does not know exactly what the day will bring but knows it will deplete yet more of her reserves. She is far stronger than most people realise but she is also far closer to her limit than is comfortable. Her confidence is gone and she often finds herself worrying that something will happen to another of her children. She has already lost two. She couldn't bear to lose another one.

Jean knows all about grief. It was her job for so long – helping people through all the traumas that arrive with a cancer diagnosis. She knows that she has been stuck for almost two years, frozen by loss and anger. She knows, too, that there is so much more sorrow waiting for her when she unfreezes. Today, Jean hopes, might mark the beginning of a thawing. She wraps herself in an olive green coat of heavy, fine wool, and pushes her small hands into a pair of smart leather gloves. When she bought the coat four years earlier, she worried that it was too expensive for her modest budget. Don't be silly, Mum, her daughter had forthrightly reprimanded her, you should have bought two. That was just so typical of her first-born, to say something like that.

But it is another daughter who is by her side this day: Bernadette, her fourth child. Bernadette has left behind her husband, children and patients to stand by her mother's side in a strange city. She has seen something of her mother's struggles, and knows she is needed. Bernadette also has her own reasons for being here. Her last visit to Adelaide was for her sister's funeral. Amid all the pomp and ceremony, Bernadette had felt left out. Murder had transformed her big sister into a celebrity. In death, she had belonged to others – the politicians, the television cameras, her colleagues. A public death leaves little room for private grief. Bernadette has come to Adelaide because she needs to reclaim her sibling. *She was my sister too.*

After passing themselves and their bags through the machinery of the security guards, Jean and Bernadette enter the grandeur of the Sir Samuel Way Building, wherein lies the Supreme Court of South Australia. They climb the wide marble staircase to Court Room Two. There they find the man they want. Peter Brebner is tall, and has to stoop and bend in close to catch Jean's tiny voice. She always speaks with this reserve. She is naturally a quiet person but it is also a way of exerting control, over herself and others. I just want to know what happened to my daughter, she says. Gentle and tough Jean. In her long coat, she looks like a neat little bird, with her fine, smooth chest and delicate legs. Brebner, with a prominent beak, piercing blue gaze and a touch of hauteur, as befits his position of a crown prosecutor of more than 25 years' standing, is more of a hawk.

Some of the evidence might be upsetting, Brebner warns. The forensic pathologist who did the autopsy will be explaining exactly what those bullets did to Margaret's body. Brebner doesn't mention the other traumas that will emerge – that her daughter knew what had happened. Margaret's last few seconds of consciousness were filled with that terrible knowledge.

Jean is undeterred. She is tired of learning about the horrors second-hand. She doesn't want to read about the trial in the news-papers or hear the latest gruesome details from her neighbours. She wants to know for herself. And she wants to see the man responsible for this terrible crime against her family. Behind the big glasses, tears suddenly rise. He is a monster, she says.

Another family has been waiting for this day too, with mixed emotions. In the last 21 months, Xavier and Maud Gassy have gained years and lost much. It seems that they have shrunk inwardly as well as outwardly. They hobble up the stairs, their small figures bent by age and suffering. Xavier's limp, old bones seem to be held together by the belt holding up his jeans. The Gassys have produced such good-looking children, they must once have been a striking pair themselves. But it is difficult to picture them like that now. In the streets outside, when they shop at the bustling Central Market flanking the court building, Xavier often throws an arm over Maud's shoulders for comfort. Sometimes they walk hand in hand. They came to this country so their children could have a better life. Their first-born, their wonderful son, did them proud. He was not just any doctor; he was clever enough to be a specialist. His success made their own sacrifices easier to bear.

Xavier and Maud have a clear view of their son across the court room. They christened him Jean Eric, but he has always answered to Eric. He is neatly dressed, as usual, in a white collared shirt and dark trousers. He is still a handsome man, though not as handsome as he was before piling on some pounds. His body and neck are thicker and coarser now, his face more fleshy. A belly pushes at his shirt. But still his features are striking, his eyebrows outlining fine bones and dark eyes. His thick, dark hair is neatly cut and his curved lips are well defined. His photo would not look out of place in the social pages. Eight weeks and two days ago, Maud stood in this room, at the end of another monotonous day of pre-trial legal argument, and asked if she could speak to her son. Permission granted, she reached over the Perspex barrier and held his hand as she wished him happy birthday. It was his second in custody. He doesn't look anything like 48 though. He has never looked his age. A smooth, honey complexion holds its youth well.

Jean and Bernadette find their seats in the public gallery, as far from the door as possible. They feel a strong need to keep a distance from the Gassy family. A police officer tells them that the judge, Ann

Vanstone, is a former prosecutor and this is her first big trial. Some of the judge's relatives are in the gallery today, the officer says. The front benches are packed with journalists, who are joking, gossiping and passing around lollies. There is an undercurrent of excitement to their banter. This day, Thursday, 8 July 2004, has been a long time coming for them too; the pre-trial hearings and legal argument seemed to go on forever. The first day of a murder trial like this is guaranteed to win the journalists a good splash in their newspapers and news bulletins. It also makes a welcome change from the gruelling days that some have spent in a nearby court room, hearing stomach-turning details of torture, mindless cruelty and decomposing bodies in barrels – the Snowtown case.

Beth, the judge's associate, stands to face the six women and eight men who have been empanelled as jurors. There are fourteen, rather than the usual twelve, because this is expected to be such a long trial. This way, if a few jurors get sick, it won't mean the end of the trial. On first glance, they seem a motley crew. If they are taken as representative of the community, then the typical Australian must be an ageing, grey man of unspectacular dress and poor eyesight. Beth, however, has the face of an angel. Her skin is as pale as alabaster, accentuating the dark arches of her brows and the tendrils of dark hair that escape around her forehead. She keeps her face carefully blank as she instructs the jury: the accused is now in your charge.

It is just before midday by the time Brebner finally stands to begin his opening address. The journalists have been waiting for this. It will sum up the prosecution case and deliver them plenty of good copy. Brebner rocks lightly on his heels as he speaks, outlining the evidence that implicates Dr Jean Eric Gassy in the murder of Dr Margaret Tobin. His voice is gentle as he explains to the jury that circumstantial evidence is 'a process of logical reasoning that everyone uses in normal everyday life' and that it can be more reliable than eyewitness evidence. Brebner often pauses to straighten and adjust his long black gown with a flourish. It has become a habit, as it is also a habit to throw a sudden glance back over one shoulder. He is inspecting the time shown on the wall clock behind him but those sitting in the public gallery feel they, too, are being scrutinised.

As Brebner weaves his story, Maud strokes her head and Xavier jiggles in his seat. Sometimes the old man shakes so hard that the vibrations pass along the length of the bench. But their son sits impassively on his chair in the dock. He could be waiting for a train; there is so little to read in his face. By now it is almost an automatic reflex for Gassy to hide his thoughts under the cover of a smooth face and brow. He knows that most people cannot be trusted, that he must keep himself to himself. Gassy doesn't give away much, but he takes in plenty. He observes the journalists sitting in the front rows. He notices the pretty, young girls on the jury, and he takes note of the court reporters who sit in front of the judge, recording the proceedings. One, in particular, catches his attention.

In the break, Bernadette is upset. I am not as strong as Mum, she says. Jean says that when she can't bear what she is hearing, she focuses on her favourite memories of her daughter. She thinks of Margaret when she was a diligent young girl, studying hard for exams, and of her wonderful, warm laugh. Jean remembers the joy of her first baby, the exciting initiation to motherhood. Jean and Margaret had their moments, like any mother and daughter. Margaret could be cutting at times. But Margaret was more than a daughter to Jean. She was like a sister or friend, she was the one who prodded Jean into making a second life for herself. Margaret had been firm; of course you can go to university at your age, she told her mother. She had pushed Jean into a career, after a life of child-rearing and household duties, even though the head of the household, Joseph, hadn't liked the idea.

Some journalists take the opportunity of the break to compare notes. They want to make sure they have the same versions of the key quotes from the opening address. In the media world, as in any harsh environment, cooperation is as important as competition for survival. One journalist congratulates Brebner on the 'fantastic opening'. It's like a children's book, the journalist says drily: the same words over and over again. Brebner had repeatedly mentioned Gassy's 'anger and resentment' towards his former boss.

Witnesses are not usually permitted to sit in court before they have given evidence. But Xavier and Maud are watching the case even though they may be called as witnesses. The judge is anxious to ensure that the defendant suffers no disadvantage as a result of his decision to represent himself. If it will help to have his family in court, then so be it.

Don Scott is not in court today, however, as he may be called as a witness. He is sitting alone at home. Since that morning when his wife kissed him goodbye for the last time, Don has been on an emotional roller-coaster. It has been a rough ride, and he has struggled to stay on board. There have been far more lows than highs. The highs have been powered by anger, drink, or by satisfaction in achieving some new memorial to Margaret's memory.

Don felt a load lifted when Gassy was arrested, but since then he has been waiting in no-man's-land for the trial. His buddy Deirdre has been there for him, keeping him company, keeping him busy, laughing at his jokes. She is his own private social worker. But still it has been so terribly lonely. Margaret was the centre of his universe, she was his world. He has lost his core. Often he talks to Margaret. He looks to heaven and says, what would you think? Sometimes he has caught himself sitting on the sofa, waiting for her to come home. He was used to waiting for her, she was away so much with work. There were so many spaces in their time together. After she had been away for a few days, he'd tackle her as soon as she came through the door. Let me tell you about the trip, she'd say. Yeah, Don would reply, giggling. After. It was one of their rituals. In all their years together, it was as if the honeymoon had never ended. There was always the anticipation and excitement of a reunion. Theirs was, he is fond of saying, a mutual admiration society.

Don keeps close a sentimental Valentine's Day card. He likes to show it to people, to make them understand what he had and what he has lost. 'For the one I love' is embossed on the front. Inside the card, a heart contains a couple walking into the sunset. 'Donny,' she had written. She only called him that in private. 'All my life I have looked for someone who would respond to my love and caring by giving me warmth and security and love in return; I will always try to be worthy of what you give me and to care for you as I feel you care for me; all my love to you, sweet sexy man. The wind beneath my wings. I love "u". Meggets xxxx'

As Don waits for news from the first day of the trial, he cannot keep still. It is cold outside but he feels the heat of rage. The house which he once kept so tidy has become a bachelor's pad. Margaret would have had something to say about the mess. But some things are unchanged. It is almost two years since she died, but Margaret's clothes still hang neatly in her wardrobe. Her scarves, carefully arranged according to colour, remain in the chest of drawers. Other drawers hold neatly folded underwear and stockings. Her shoes are packed away in boxes in the cupboard, each carefully labelled and cleaned from when she last slipped them off her small feet. Her make-up and toiletries still clutter the sink in her bathroom. The home office is lined with her books and medical certificates. Leaning against her desk are the large, framed colour photographs of the beautiful gardens that she and Don once had on a property near Ballarat.

Margaret's presence is still strong in her home, but it is noticeably absent from the court room. This trial, like any other, reflects where the law's focus lies. It is preoccupied with providing a fair trial to defendants rather than with ensuring justice or dignity to the victims of crime. Margaret was violated when she was shot from behind as she walked to her office, and her memory will be violated again in court. Before the judge and jury, a professor of psychiatry will concur with the defendant's descriptions of Margaret as someone who could be abrasive, arrogant and insensitive to the impact of her behaviour on others. Her loved ones will be given no opportunity to defend or explain or present another view; their memories are not relevant to the court's considerations. On another day, Don Scott will sit outside the court room, waiting to be called to answer questions about whether his wife was a closet lesbian.

In life, Margaret Tobin treasured her privacy, but death has stripped it away. In this room strangers will hear intimate details of her under-wear, as it was seen in her dying moments. Will they appreciate the awful poignancy of the image of Margaret's slip? It was left lying in the foyer of her workplace, after she was raced to hospital. Margaret loved clothes, and was always smartly, immaculately dressed, even on weekends. In life, she never would have let her slip show.

Margaret was a woman of many parts and was passionate about so many things, most particularly her work, striving to improve the care of some of society's most neglected, the mentally ill. But in this impersonal court room, she will be reduced to her vital statistics. The jury is told that on the autopsy slab, her naked corpse weighed 75 kg or 11 stone and 11 pounds. She measured 65 inches or 165 cm.

In life, she had seemed so much larger than that.

2

The good girl

Jean Bond was not yet eighteen when she met Joseph Tobin at an Irish dance in a church hall in Birmingham, England. He was thin, had a soft Irish accent and was smartly groomed in a suit and tie. He spoke to the small, shy girl with smooth skin and pretty blue eyes, and asked her to dance. It was the beginning of a long courtship.

Joseph had left his family's dairy farm near the small village of Grangemockler in Tipperary to seek work in England, as his older brother had done before him, and was now working in a creamery. After his father died, he had left school young, when he was about fourteen, and his mother died several years later.

Jean already had a sense that life was not for the faint-hearted. As a young girl, she had run for shelter from planes bearing bombs bound for Birmingham, the industrial centre of the Midlands. Her father, William, a painter and decorator, had refused to evacuate the family, saying if they were going to die, they would all die together.

William died not long after Jean left school at fifteen. He fell from a ladder, broke some ribs, and succumbed to complications, including pneumonia. He was twenty years older than Jean's mother, Jennie, who was his second wife. Jennie then took lodgers into their large

9

home, and Jean helped look after them. A pianist and music teacher, Jennie held great hopes that her daughter would become a classical singer. She sent Jean for elocution lessons and voice training, which erased all traces of the distinctive 'Brummie' accent. No longer would Jean say ''e was ever so poorly' like her sister did.

Jean loved singing but her voice wasn't big enough to sustain a career. Instead, she found work in an office and then a grocery shop. She was taking instruction in Catholicism when she met Joseph, having decided that the Baptist church of her schooldays was not for her, not least because a fear of water put her off being baptised as an adult. She had tried a number of different churches, in search of something she couldn't really describe. Perhaps it was Joseph's strength that drew her attention. He was nine years her senior, and she wondered later if she had been looking for a father figure. They became engaged when she was eighteen and married more than a year later, on 6 October 1951.

Jean was terrified when she went into labour early on 23 September 1952. She had no idea what to expect, and Joseph tried to reassure her. 'Don't worry,' he said, 'I have delivered lots of cows.' He called the ambulance, and she waited while he shaved and put on a collar and tie for the trip to hospital. But he was left at the hospital door, allowed no further. Jean found herself among strangers and with little understanding of what was to follow. She laboured for about twelve hours, hearing her little girl's first squawks just before 1 pm. Afterwards, the young intern who delivered her baby offered tea and some bread and butter with strawberry jam, a treat after years of rationing.

Jean caught a brief glimpse of the baby's head as she was wrapped and taken away, and didn't see her again for some hours. When Joseph finally was allowed to visit that evening, he could see his new daughter through the nursery window, but was not allowed to hold her. Ten days later, Jean was released from hospital with a baby who cried constantly. A week later, at her wit's end, she put little Margaret Julia into her pram with a hot-water bottle for the hour-long walk to the welfare centre. The nurses found that the baby was failing to thrive, and switched her from the breast to the bottle. Margaret then blossomed into a chubby, happy baby who brought much joy. Jean always remembered those early months, her first foray into motherhood, with a special fondness.

Joseph was a man of his times and of a strict Catholic background. He was the unchallenged head of the household, and held strong views. When he said the family would migrate to Australia because he was sick of city life and miserable weather, little heed was paid to Jean's protests that Canada would keep them closer to family. In August 1954, the young couple packed up their radio, the satin eiderdown that had been a wedding present, two religious statues, the bassinet that a blind man had made for Margaret, and which was to bounce many Tobin babies, and the wooden cot that Joseph had made for Margaret. It now held her baby sister Helena. Thus equipped, they paid their £10 fares and sailed on the SS *Strathnaver*. Another 25 years would pass before Jean and Joseph could afford to return to visit their families. For Jean, the month-long voyage was a blissful break from household chores. The only cloud was Margaret's illness – probably seasickness, the ship's doctor thought.

But Margaret's troubles continued after their landing in Melbourne on 7 September 1954. Joseph had intended to go sharefarming but was set to work in a factory. Life in a migrant hostel, with shared bathroom and communal dining, was difficult enough without the worry of Margaret's constant vomiting. Mashed potato and pumpkin were the only foods that she seemed able to tolerate. Jean was used to thinking of pumpkins as fit only for feeding pigs. But she didn't torment herself with dreams of the old country. She knew she just had to get on and make do.

About three weeks after the family's arrival in Melbourne, Margaret was admitted to the children's hospital and treated for gastroenteritis. She had just turned two. Not long after, she was admitted again for several weeks of tests. Every day, Jean made the long bus trip, with Helena in the pram, for the strictly enforced visiting hours. From 2 to 4 pm, she sat and read to Margaret, who was wearing the regulation hospital nightie in her old steel cot. Jean wasn't allowed to hold her daughter or take her outside for a walk. That was standard practice in children's hospitals at the time. Parents were not encouraged to be involved in their children's care.

One day, Jean teased Margaret that the nurses reported she was a chatterbox. 'I am not a chatterbox,' the toddler retorted indignantly. 'I am a letterbox.' Jean was amazed by Margaret's stoicism. She didn't seem upset by the invasive tests, or cry and scream when it came time to say goodbye. But for years after, Jean relived her own distress at those farewells, and wondered what mark they had left on the little girl. Margaret had just left her home, travelled across the seas, and now she was separated from the only people she really knew in a strange country – her parents and her little sister.

Eventually, Jean was told that Margaret had coeliac disease. This meant she would never be able to eat foods made of wheat or other gluten-containing grains without suffering health problems. Jean had not heard of the disease before, but learnt to bake without flour and to make new recipes for food that didn't contain gluten. The doctor told Jean that if Margaret hadn't been diagnosed, she would have suffered restricted growth. Jean realised then why Margaret's feet had remained so small. She had been wearing the same size shoe for some time.

For more than two decades, Jean was either pregnant or caring for little ones. There were nineteen years between the first and last of the eight Tobin children. Reciting their names was like an Irish Catholic rollcall – Margaret, Helena, Gerard, Bernadette, Patrick, Mary Catherine, Peter and Damian. The oldest children helped look after the youngest and everyone was expected to pitch in. For years after Helena left home she would automatically say, 'Shhh, you will wake the baby' whenever voices were raised.

As the family grew, so did its acquaintance with the medical world. Bernadette was born with kidney troubles, and was often in and out of hospitals and operating theatres. Jean became skilled at home nursing, tending Bernadette's wounds. Margaret was eight, and a conscientious pupil at Our Lady of Perpetual Succour school in Ringwood, when her parents became concerned about her baby brother Gerard, their third-born. He was a bright, loveable boy, but was having trouble walking, and sometimes ignored his surrounds. Jean wondered if he might be deaf. On yet another visit to the children's hospital, she learnt of another disease with an unfamiliar name.

Gerard was at her side when Jean learnt that he had muscular dystrophy, an incurable disease causing progressive muscular deterioration. Gerard wouldn't see his eighteenth birthday, the doctor told Jean. It would stand in her memory as one of the two worst days of her life.

Jean found strength and solace in prayer. The Church was an integral part of the family's daily life. When the family sold their bush block at Ringwood – Joseph was forced to abandon plans of building his dream home there because of a heart murmur – they moved to Croydon, then a developing suburb on Melbourne's eastern fringes. Their new home was a short drive from the Tarrawarra monastery, where the Cistercian monks tended dairy and beef cattle, made hay and grew vegetables as part of their devotion to lives of work and prayer. The order was proud of its hospitality, and kept an open door to visitors. The Tobins were familiar faces at the monastery, where they were known as a happy, close-knit unit, and some of the monks stopped at the Tobin home for a cup of tea and chat on their journeys to and from the city.

The family said the rosary every night after dinner, without fail. The children's knees often ached from the kneeling, but they knew better than to complain. In later life, Patrick could still picture the lines left on his knees by the seagrass matting. Jean was allowed to sit only when a pregnancy was well advanced. Some of the children cringed when Joseph came out to the street to call them away from cricket games for rosary. Like many migrant families, they felt theirs was somehow different from those around them, that they weren't part of the Aussie barbecue culture. Apart from his love of all things Irish, Joseph felt a close affinity with the French. He cycled, wore a beret when working around the house, and was mad about French cars. He was sure the Tobins were of French lineage, descended from the Saint Aubin family.

Joseph found work as a technician at Telecom's Box Hill exchange, a job he held for almost 30 years until his retirement. The pay was barely enough to keep his family. Jean ran a tight ship. She didn't need to raise her voice often to exert control. She baked, she sewed and she nursed. There was always a dessert on the dinner table, and her daughters were always beautifully dressed. She had not been allowed to have

13

long hair or a ribbon as a child, so all her girls had plaits and ribbons. Jean insisted the children make their beds and keep their rooms neat. She was self-conscious about having a large family, and felt that some in the neighbourhood looked down on them. She made sure the house was always tidy.

Margaret was the dutiful eldest child, and glowing school reports reflected her diligence. She learnt piano, went to Mass on Saturday mornings before tennis as well as on Sundays, and sat opposite her mother at the dining table. Everyone had their places – it was always an awkward moment when a visitor unknowingly sat in Joseph's chair – and mealtimes were strictly conducted with grace, good manners and minimum noise. No wonder some of her children grew up to be so opinionated, Jean would later joke. Not allowed to have a voice when they were young, they made sure they did in later years.

Invisible lines divided the busy household. In a big family, you have to fight for privacy and Margaret was quick to claim hers. She curled up in her bedroom with a book or schoolwork when the other children were playing or watching telly, and jealously guarded her space in the bedroom shared with Helena. Jean and Joseph also valued their privacy. The children were not allowed into their parents' bedroom, though Joseph would allow them to bring in a cup of tea when Jean was sick during pregnancy, as she so often was.

Joseph was free with his opinions – he followed politics and was an instinctive supporter of the underdog – but kept his emotions close to his chest. He was affectionate to Jean in private but the children rarely saw them kiss. Nor did daily life allow much space for sentimentality or vulnerability. Jean made it a rule not to intrude into her children's lives. If they wanted to discuss something with her, they would, she thought. She loved her children dearly but didn't put them on a pedestal. She knew their little foibles well.

As Gerard deteriorated physically, moving into a wheelchair at thirteen, the load on his parents and older siblings increased. In the days before home nursing and community health services, Jean was his primary carer. She turned him every few hours every day for many years, and was proud that he never had a bedsore, although her own back suffered. Joseph's sleep was disrupted for years, as he rose to turn Gerard regularly during the night and carry him to the toilet. It was not unusual for people outside the family to talk down to Gerard because they saw only the wheelchair, and not the smart, funny boy sitting in it. 'It's only my body that can't move,' Gerard complained to his mother when this happened. But mostly he was in good spirits. He loved listening to the races on his prized radio, and betting on the horses with his benefits money.

One of the Tarrawarra monks, Bryan Gillard, visited Gerard regularly for several years, sometimes bringing with him a box of fresh produce from the monastery. The monks were aware of the family's financial struggles. Gillard was impressed by Gerard's intelligence, and the family's obvious affection for him. He and Gerard played chess and laughed often. Once Gillard took Gerard to the races, where he was given special odds on the favourite. When his horse came in, Gerard joked to Gillard, his voice slurring but his delight obvious: 'I will break that bookie yet.'

Jean often looked worn and exhausted. She and Joseph had little time or energy to spare, and Margaret and Helena helped fill the parents' places with the younger children. The youngest ones looked up to them. Patrick, the fifth-born, left early for school in the mornings so he could share the 25-minute walk to the train with Margaret. As they walked, Margaret talked about her school lessons. Patrick understood not a jot but was content to have her attention. In years to come, he often measured himself and his progress by what Margaret might think.

Among the neighbours, Joseph was known as someone who always helped out. He didn't drink or smoke. He gave more money to the Church than he could afford. He mowed lawns for the nuns, did voluntary work at St Vincent de Paul, and managed the school fete. Joseph loved to chat, tell a joke – especially if it was at the expense of the English – and to dance, preferably to Irish music. He was proud of his handiwork around the home. He always had a project going – making furniture, or adding on a room here or there. Margaret's father was a skilled and enthusiastic mechanic, and was often to be found working on his car. He was proud of his old Rovers and, in later years, Peugeots.

The family also knew another side. Joseph was from an era which believed that sparing the rod spoilt the child. Like many fathers of his generation, he was not effusive with praise or cuddles. When one of the children got into a scrape, Joseph told Jean it was because she hadn't insisted on their praying regularly. 'Like most fathers he just wants his kids to be perfect,' Jean wrote many years later to Patrick. 'I would like it if they were too, but I know it isn't possible. There are no Perfect People.' No matter how well Margaret did at school, it was never good enough. When Margaret got 95 per cent for a subject, Joseph asked what happened to the other 5 per cent. Years later, Margaret wrote to Patrick: 'In our family, it certainly seemed to be the rule that what came easily, what was not a challenge – was not worth having. That to be worthy of anything, the end had to be achieved at great cost.'

Joseph rarely allowed himself to show his pride in his family's achievements. But he couldn't suppress his anger. Patrick, the first son to follow Gerard, often bore the brunt of his father's fury – and his belt. Patrick escaped home as soon as he could, leaving to join the air force. The beatings left a deep mark not only on him, but on some of those who witnessed them. In later years Patrick felt sorry for his father, believing Joseph had had no other outlet for his rage at Gerard's fate. He also felt sorrow for the man who signed letters 'yours sincerely' when writing to thank his adult son for sending money home.

Margaret and Helena often acted as intermediaries between their father and brothers. As she grew older, Margaret began to challenge Joseph more often. She also became frustrated at her mother's subservience. With the forces of illness, poverty and Catholicism shaping the children's early years, it was not surprising that the healing professions beckoned. As a young girl Margaret toyed with becoming a dental nurse – her illness had meant she needed a lot of dental work as a child. Then she thought of nursing. By high school, she was determined to become a doctor. Her sisters would make careers in nursing, psychology and social work.

The girls who went to Mount Lilydale, the school where Margaret had won a scholarship in year 7, were known as 'brown cows' because of their unattractive uniforms. It was also appropriate given the school's picturesque situation, on a hillside overlooking idyllic countryside. Pretty though it was, the school wasn't up to scratch in the subjects Margaret would need to get into medicine. Eventually, it was agreed that during years 11 and 12, Margaret and two of her classmates would make the fifteen-minute train trip to the Aquinas boys' school at Ringwood for chemistry and physics classes. Most days they spent half of their time at the boys' school. This was a mini-revolution for the Christian Brothers, who had never taught girls before.

At first it was overwhelming for the girls, strangers in a sea of several hundred boys. But Margaret seemed to settle in quite comfortably, and years later would reflect that the experience helped prepare her for working in senior management situations surrounded by men. At the school, she soon struck up a connection with Tony Cotter, a tall, handsome lad with an engaging smile. He was also the eldest in a large Catholic family struggling to give their children an education. Margaret and Tony understood each other's situation instinctively. In later years, Tony didn't mind when she asked if Gerard could accompany them on drives in his prized Rover, despite the effort of getting him in and out of the car.

Tony liked Margaret's pixie Irish face, determination and dry sense of humour. You could tell she was alive from her bright eyes, he thought. She confided in Tony how difficult it was to find enough space and peace for her homework. He was shocked when she declared she would never have children. She didn't want to pass on the muscular dystrophy gene, she said.

Margaret was a good student – it was a big deal for the whole family when she became president of the school's Young Catholic Women's Association and flew to Sydney one weekend for a conference. But she also enjoyed a touch of mischief. One friend who went with her on the train to the boys' school was surprised when Margaret admitted telling Tony what colour ribbons would be on her pigtails the next day, so that he could win the bet with the other boys. Margaret also had the idea of her and Bernadette sneaking Mary Catherine onto the train after school, so they could buy fish and chips with her fare. When Margaret asked Tony to partner her at a debutantes' ball at Kew Town Hall during their final year of school, it meant them giving up months of Sunday afternoons for ballroom dancing classes at the Lilydale convent. He saw that the serious, deter-mined student also enjoyed dancing.

No-one was surprised when Margaret won a scholarship to Melbourne University; she had worked hard enough for it. Such scholarships were highly prized, offering a passport into the otherwise unaffordable world of tertiary education. The surprise lay in how difficult those years proved. Margaret struggled to balance the demanding studies with the long train trip into university and family duties. She was moving away from her childhood certainties, ques-tioning the Catholic dogma and her family relationships. The power balance at home began to shift. She and Joseph argued more often and more heatedly. Over politics, how she dressed, how he treated his sons. Margaret began to blame the Catholic Church for her father's hardness and her mother's suffering. I will never forgive the Church for what it did to my family, she would later say.

Margaret found being a medical student 'very lonely, alienating from former friends and not at all rewarding', she wrote to Patrick some years afterwards. She wouldn't have been the first young idealist to find medical studies a rude shock. It was perhaps inevitable that a young woman from a working-class background would have difficulty finding her place in a world dominated by the graduates of private boys' schools. Margaret was studying anatomy, biochemistry and pathology, amongst other things, when Melbourne University's appointment of Priscilla Kincaid-Smith as the first female professor of medicine created some furore. How outrageous, a woman in the job – she should be home looking after her children, spluttered many in the medical establishment. Kincaid-Smith, whose work in kidney disease became internationally recognised, wasn't deterred. It was nothing compared with her shock when she first migrated to Australia in 1958, after growing up in South Africa and working in England, to be told that she couldn't have a hospital job because she was married. Even worse, she would later joke, was having to give up golf, after discover-ing that women weren't allowed on the greens on Saturdays.

At the end of 1971, Margaret's first year at university, she was dev-astated to discover she had failed chemistry. It was a terrible blow to her pride. She was unused to failure, especially as she had received top marks in year 12 chemistry. Her friends thought her pragmatic about the setback, but she sobbed and raged at home, and contemplated what other jobs she might be able to do. When she applied to repeat the year, a member of the university's interview panel asked what was the point? You will only get married and have babies, he said. I don't intend to have a family, Margaret replied firmly. She was furious. The anger stiffened her will to persevere.

After repeating first year, this time achieving second-class honours in chemistry, Margaret made the break from home. One of her sisters sobbed as Margaret packed her bags for the move to St Mary's College, a Catholic residence for young women. There she revelled in having her own room, freedom, privacy. She tried to throw off the shackles of her coeliac disease, ignoring the dietary restrictions that had been part of her childhood, perhaps hoping that she had outgrown the problem. Her college friends were impressed by her gusto for food, and teased her for being the only one prepared to tackle the thick skin on the custard in the dining room. The illness caught up with her eventually, however, and she returned to a gluten-free diet after becoming seriously unwell.

The 1970s was a rebellious time for many on campus, but not for Margaret and her St Mary's friends, most of whom were the first women in their families to reach university. They studied hard and met in each others' rooms for hot chocolate. They listened to Cat Stevens, Nana Mouskouri and Neil Diamond, and thought themselves wicked if they stole a rose from the gardens to perfume their rooms.

Margaret struggled with some subjects, and her friends, who were studying music and science, sometimes coached her for exams. She once invited them to an anatomy lecture where a female volunteer's intimate anatomy was broadcast live onto the screen. She wanted them to see her classmates ogling. The group came to know her kindness, brisk practicality, good humour and bluntness. Margaret was not known for mincing words. If she didn't want to do something, or needed her space, she had no difficulty saying so.

She organised for her friends to go to the Irish Ball some years running but didn't dwell much on family matters in her conversations with them. They knew about Gerard and that Margaret didn't want a life like her mother's. But none of them wanted that sort of life. They were young women absorbed in their dreams and ambitions for the future. They felt they were doing something different from their mothers, and breaking the mould. Even then, Margaret gave the impression that she was determined to make the most of her life.

In university holidays, Margaret and some of her friends worked as nursing aides at Caritas Christie, a hospice for the terminally ill. They emptied bedpans, washed patients and made beds. There Margaret struck up a friendship with Brendan Kelly, a sincere, earnest young man who had left Hobart in order to study for the priesthood. He had joined the Catholic Order, the Missionaries of the Sacred Heart, and was doing a short placement at the hospice as part of his training when they met in 1971, during Margaret's first year of medicine.

Margaret and Brendan liked similar music and had much else in common, including the Christian Brother, Terry Burke. Burke had known Brendan at St Virgil's College in Hobart, before moving to Aquinas College in Melbourne, where he'd met Margaret. Burke had been a tad nervous about having Margaret and the other girls attend his physics lessons; he was more used to teaching boys and wasn't quite sure how to handle the girls. But he soon developed a rapport with Margaret, who struck him as a quiet, shy girl although he also saw the mark of determination in her face and came to appreciate her warmth. As the years passed, he heard news of her now and then. He often told other students who were struggling with their studies of how Margaret had made a great success of her career after failing some of her medical studies.

Brendan enjoyed Margaret's company and conversation. He also liked spending time with her family, and sometimes dropped in to the Tobin home for a cup of tea on his way back to the Sacred Heart Monastery. After Brendan moved to Canberra in 1972 to continue his studies, he and Margaret didn't see each other for nearly two years but kept in touch by letter.

As Brendan began to question what he wanted for his future, the life of a priest started to hold less appeal. He was frustrated by the lack of professional training available to help him develop the counselling skills that he could see were required for priestly work. His friendship with Margaret was evolving, but it was only one of the factors influencing his unrest. He knew that Margaret didn't want to be responsible for his leaving the seminary, and also felt it was important for himself to make that decision independently.

For quite a while, Margaret's friends at college didn't realise the significance of the relationship. Eventually Margaret confided in an old friend that she didn't know what to do, as she didn't want to be the reason for Brendan leaving the seminary. They talked it through and decided that life was too short to let it go; that if it's meant to be, it's meant to be.

In late 1974, Brendan left the seminary in Canberra with $50 in his suit pocket and a train ticket. It said a lot, he thought, that the Missionaries of the Sacred Heart could not bring themselves to provide more support and assistance for someone in his situation. He delayed his return to Melbourne for another two months, finding casual work as a gardener in some of the embassies, because Margaret had asked him to leave his return until after her exams. Anatomy and physiology had been a struggle all year, and they defeated her at its end. Again, she would have to plead to the university powers to be allowed to repeat a year. This time around, however, she had other, happier things on her mind. Brendan had proposed.

Margaret wanted the ceremony held in her family's local church, St Edmond's at Croydon, so Gerard could attend in his wheelchair. She and Brendan worked hard on their wedding plans, and put together a booklet for their guests. Joseph lent the couple his pride and joy, his old Rover, to use as their wedding car. Jean crocheted a beautiful, close-fitting dress, and would remember Margaret telling her that Brendan did not want her to wear a veil because it reminded him of nuns. After some last-minute nerves, the bride looked absolutely radiant on her wedding day, 18 January 1975. A friend who was a tenor gave a guest solo and Brendan sang in a small choir with some of Margaret's girlfriends. Guests were strictly instructed not to throw confetti in case it stained the dress. One of Margaret's friends protested, half-heartedly, when a priest pinched her bottom at the reception, held in the bride's childhood backyard. 'You can't do that, you are a priest,' she said. 'I am retired,' he laughed.

The newlyweds had a motoring holiday for their honeymoon, making the first of many visits together to Adelaide and the Barossa Valley. Their first year of married life was a financial struggle, with Brendan studying counselling and Margaret determined to succeed in her course. But there was also time for Irish dancing, swimming and tennis. They were frequent visitors to the Tobin family home. They often had friends over for dinner parties, and Brendan appreciated Margaret's culinary skills. On holidays, they packed up the car and explored the countryside. Many of their friends saw Brendan as a rock for Margaret. He seemed to give her confidence to tackle her studies, and clearly adored her.

Finally, the inevitable phone call. It woke Margaret and Brendan in the early hours of Saturday, 31 July 1976 and hurried them out of bed and into the car. They rushed to Croydon, but Gerard had died by the time they arrived. On the Friday evening, he had placed his bets on the horses as usual and told Jean, as she turned his wasted frame, that he would go into respite care soon to give her a break. He could see she was desperately tired. He died just six weeks before his twenty-first birthday.

At the funeral at St Edmond's, some of the younger Tobins were surprised to see their usually self-contained big sister so distressed. Margaret wept and wept. Some university friends, however, had the impression that she was very stoic and matter-of-fact about it all. Brendan knew otherwise. He saw how much she was hurting.

Gerard's death left an enormous hole in the family, especially for Jean. He had been the central figure, governing so much of their daily routines. He was so good-humoured and gentle, he had been easy to love. After Gerard's death, Margaret told one of her sisters that she could no longer believe in God.

Not long after the funeral, Margaret rang her mother and asked what she was doing. 'I thought I might come and visit you, Mum,' she said. 'Margaret, I am okay,' Jean replied. 'But I'm not okay,' said Margaret. 'I need my mum.' It was one of the few times Jean saw her daughter express such vulnerability. She was more used to seeing Margaret as a source of strength.

Margaret's strength was also obvious to her fellow students. She was the only woman in a study group of eight, whose members spent long hours together during the final three years of the course. She was the only one who was married and was a few years older than most. Relations were sometimes strained. One of the group, John Gallichio, saw Margaret as a mother hen. She was polite but firm in organising them, and expected the others to be as focused and hardworking as she was. She made it clear that sexist jokes would not be tolerated in her presence. Gallichio felt Margaret was more mature than the rest of them. She was also better dressed, and took an obvious pride in her presentation. Decades later, he would still remember one of her typical summer dresses for its bright colouring – red with white polka dots. Other members of the group would not have such kind memories. One student, who went on to become an orthopaedic surgeon, would clearly remember Margaret telling the group at the end of their final year together that she hoped never to see any of them again. He was not particularly taken aback by this pronounce- ment. He thought it was quite in character, and adopted his usual policy of ignoring her.

After eight years of undergraduate study, Margaret finally finished her medical course at the end of 1978. Fewer than one-third of her graduating class were women. Early in the following year, Margaret and two other young women, Elizabeth Benson and Mary Anne Holland, spent three months as residents at Gippsland Base Hospital at Sale, east of Melbourne. It was quite an event for the hospital, which had never seen so many young women doctors before. Some weeks passed before the trio realised that they had not been extended the privilege usually accorded to visiting resident doctors – honorary membership of a local men's club.

The three women worked closely and supportively, helping each other through a stressful period of adjustment. Like many young doctors before and since, they endured the brutal initiation rites which mark the transition from being a medical student to a junior doctor. They worked horrendous hours, were constantly on call and faced daunting responsibilities with little backup. Margaret's pager often went off just as she stumbled into sleep in the doctors' accom- modation in the hospital grounds.

Margaret was enjoying the work and came across as serious, efficient, self-confident and well organised. Holland thought Margaret a great doctor; she wrote comprehensive, clear notes about patients and obviously went to some effort to obtain a detailed history from them. Benson thought she detected an almost naive streak in Margaret. She clearly was an altruist, who was doing medicine because she believed she could make a difference. Benson would have been surprised if Margaret ended up working anywhere other than in the public health system. The three women were so busy they rarely had a chance to chat about personal issues.

Despite the long hours, Margaret found time to dash off quick letters. In 1979, she raised herself out of a full-body exhaustion to write to Patrick that she had worked 130 hours the previous week. She was forthright that she expected a prompt reply. 'Hope you will acknowledge last week's letter soon – otherwise I won't be sending any more,' she said.

Work commitments kept Brendan in Melbourne but he made the four-hour trip to visit whenever possible. He was horrified by Margaret's working conditions but also felt she was thriving on the challenges. She had been thrown in at the deep end, and had found she could swim. She seemed to blossom as her confidence grew. And she was delighted, at last, to be earning a salary after so many years of financial struggle.

Margaret sent regular cheques home to provide pocket money to the two youngest siblings, Peter and Damian. In a birthday card to Patrick, she joked:

I was thinking of buying you a present but that has been a fiasco in the past. I nearly bought a white shirt with grey, lemon and pink stripes but if you had not liked it, Brendan would not have wanted it. I almost bought you a decanter and then I remembered that you have gone off all booze.

The only thing left after eliminating household items, booze, clothes and books was a plastic inflatable woman, and then I couldn't choose a colour. So plain old cheque comes instead.

As time went on, Jean and Joseph looked more and more to Margaret for advice. To her younger brothers and sisters, it seemed their parents held Margaret as the expert on absolutely everything. Nor was she slow to give advice to her siblings – about how they dressed, their partners, their gardens, what they should do with their lives. After she and Brendan had some trouble getting a home loan, Margaret advised Patrick 'for goodness sake don't make our mistake, start saving a little now, even $10 a week will at least put you in favourably with the Bank . . .'

When Margaret moved back to Melbourne to work at St Vincent's and the Royal Children's hospitals, the pace did not let up. Again Brendan was appalled by the working conditions. It was not unusual for her to work around the clock, putting in up to 100 hours a week. He thought the young doctors were treated like slaves, but Margaret was too busy and too tired to make much complaint. She was also preoccupied with what to do next. She knew she wanted to be a specialist but in her discussions with Brendan wavered between the two extremes of the specialist spectrum. Maybe she would apply for surgical training. Or psychiatry.

Why don't you do psychiatry, Brendan suggested as she prevaricated again one day. You're interested in people and you've got good people skills, he told her. In 1981 Margaret began training in psychiatry at the Heidelberg Repatriation General Hospital, where she spent the next three years working mainly with veterans of World War II and Vietnam, observing the damage that war inflicts on its survivors. In years to come, the suffering of many of these men would be given a name: post-traumatic stress disorder. But at this time, they were more likely to be diagnosed with depression, anxiety, personality disorder or alcoholism.

Paul Debenham, a senior lecturer in psychiatry who supervised Margaret's work on the wards, thought her conscientious and noticed how she mixed firmness with kindness in her dealings with patients. She attended to one of his private patients, who had been admitted to the ward and was causing mayhem. Margaret made it clear she would brook no nonsense from the woman. Behave or I will certify you, was the message she gave. The patient responded well, and seemed glad to have some limits set. Debenham also observed Margaret effectively manage other difficult situations with patients. She would make a competent psychiatrist, he thought.

At times Margaret felt the stress of being constantly on the receiving end of other people's troubles. 'I feel as if I need a psychiatrist myself sometimes,' she wrote to Patrick. She surprised at least one colleague at the hospital by showing an early interest in management. Clinicians, then as indeed now, are not famous for having a high regard for managers, whom they tend to see as the enemy. But Margaret recognised early that if she wanted to have an impact, she could affect more people as a manager making decisions about policy and resources than as a clinician seeing one patient at a time.

Margaret was 30 when she finally went for her driver's licence in 1982. Brendan was delighted, having for some time encouraged her to overcome her anxieties about driving. For years he had driven her around, waiting all hours of the night and day outside hospitals for her to finish work.

When Margaret began driving herself around town, at least one of the couple's friends saw her new independence as symbolic of a broader shift in her relationship with Brendan. As Margaret had become more and more absorbed in psychiatry, Brendan was becoming increasingly impatient. He was also studying and working long, hard hours, running a family counselling and support service. He wanted to start a family, but Margaret remained lukewarm on the topic. He was also tired of the impact of her long working hours on their life together. For Margaret, the relationship, once so passionate and exciting, had begun to feel stifling. Her career was becoming her real passion.

Margaret and Brendan were heading in different directions. They separated in early 1983 when Margaret moved out into a flat near her work.

3

The road to hell is paved with good intentions

Good intentions* are well known for causing great suffering, and this is as clear in the history of medicine as anywhere else. The insidious consequences of worthy works often become obvious only with the passage of time and the benefit of hindsight. Perhaps it is also true that good intentions are particularly vulnerable to corruption. Most sensible people don't expect to find a wolf when grandmother comes knocking.

In the late 1700s and early 1800s, the plight of the mentally ill began to excite public attention in various places of the world. Social reformers envisioned a better future than the brutal conditions under which the mad were then held, whether in their families' homes or in madhouses. The visionaries' dreams were grandiose, of majestic settlements in idyllic surrounds. They foresaw that the mentally ill would learn self-discipline if put in a structured community away from family influences. They would reap the benefits of a pleasant situation,

---

* The chapter title was also the title of a talk in 2005 by Dr Bill Barclay, one of the architects of deinstitutionalisation in New South Wales.

27

preferably one with fresh air and views over surrounding countryside. They would follow routines, undertake useful work and develop healthy relationships as part of their 'moral therapy'.

But the vision was quickly overwhelmed. The asylums which proliferated in many countries in the nineteenth century soon became dumping grounds for society's rejects, and places of misery and horror. Their inmates were, according to the parlance of the times, incurables, idiots, imbeciles, inebriates, defectives and lunatics. In Australia, the history of asylums was 'chillingly consistent', one academic account noted, with the experience throughout the Western world. Patients suffered from overcrowding, loss of connection with families and the community, and oppressive practices, countered by 'earnest but often thwarted attempts' to improve conditions.

Dr Fred Stamp, a 40-year-old psychiatrist with startling blue eyes and a trim physique from his years as a British Army medical officer, was well acquainted with the corrupting influence of institutions when he became superintendent at Willsmere Hospital in Melbourne in 1981. He had seen their mark on both inmates and staff. Even so, he was aghast at what awaited him atop the hill at Kew. Many years later he would have difficulty confronting his memories of the place, beyond repeating, 'It was a total bloody disgrace.' He was horrified by the impact of longstanding political and public indifference, and how humanity had been stripped from staff and patients alike.

For most of its history, Willsmere, grandly situated with a prominent outlook over the city, was known as the Kew mental asylum. It was modelled on the notorious Colney Hatch Lunatic Asylum in England, and within five years of being completed in 1872, it housed 1,000 people including the mentally ill, epileptics, drunkards, the criminally insane and the senile. Its Italianate architecture was much admired as one of Victoria's largest and most striking examples of public works from that era. But critics were vociferous in demanding its closure from even before its opening, and several unsuccessful attempts had been made to shut it down. Uncertainty over its future contributed to Willsmere's neglect over many years. It was difficult to attract staff, and the place was starved of even basic maintenance.

Stamp was not the first to think that the place which looked like a palace from a distance was more like a jail up close. He was horrified by what he found as he investigated the decaying buildings, where years of damp and poor ventilation had done their work. The stench was the first thing most people noticed, as decades of filth and neglect permeated the senses. Toilet facilities were crude and insufficient for the hundreds of frail, confused elderly who accounted for the majority of patients by the 1980s. Most no longer had any medical reason for being in a psychiatric facility, if indeed they'd ever had one. What they needed now was geriatric care. Some wards had more than 30 people but access to only one toilet. Entrance to the wards was often through the ablutions area. Floorboards were rotting, hand rails were coming away from the walls, the kitchens were filthy, and outbreaks of diarrhoea were frequent.

Stamp saw patients who were fed, sheltered and clothed but afforded little dignity or humanity. The environment exacerbated their confusion and distress, rather than relieving it. Old women walked around muttering to themselves, their gowns open at the back. They did not know what it was to have privacy, or a quiet space to sit or receive visitors. Their clothes were stored in common clothing rooms. Many of the staff had migrated from war-torn Europe. It was the displaced caring for the dispossessed.

Stamp saw how Willsmere, as is the nature of all institutions, had evolved to suit those in control, with patients firmly consigned to the bottom of the hierarchy. He was horrified to see patients tricked into signing voluntary admission forms by being told they were signing for their pensions. The 'two days on, two days off' roster suited the nurses, many of whom held second jobs, but was to the detriment of patient care. The place was also a firetrap. The long, narrow wards with a single exit were designed to contain people, not to ensure their safety or wellbeing. Six patients had died in a fire in 1968, and the ongoing hazard had been documented many times. In the space of twenty years, fire officers attended 38 blazes at the hospital.

Willsmere was tough even on experienced psychiatrists, and Stamp's health deteriorated over the next several years. For young doctors, it must have been a nightmare, like stepping back to another, crueller century.

Margaret Tobin was 32 and in the fourth year of a five-year training program for psychiatry when she started at Willsmere in 1985. After struggling for some years to find her niche in medicine, she really only began to enjoy her career after starting psychiatry. 'I discovered within myself an interest in "why" people do certain things . . . what are their motivations,' she later reflected when talking to a journalist. 'This interest was fostered during my residency years by my finding fascination in the social and psychological issues for patients with medical illnesses. My fellow residents were frequently only too happy to direct patients with emotional problems my way, knowing I was interested in them.'

But Willsmere horrified her. She was upset when telling Jean and Joseph of two elderly women who had been there since their teenage years without knowing what it was like to have a private toilet. Her younger brother Damian was frightened by the oppressive atmosphere when Margaret took him and their parents on a tour one weekend. She told them that the peacocks in the grounds had been kept in years past to cover the screams of people undergoing shock therapy.

In the year that Margaret started at Willsmere, a Victorian parliamentary inquiry highlighted the place's shocking conditions, and gave politicians the resolve and the ammunition to act, finally. Margaret became closely involved in what was to become a landmark decommissioning of such a facility. Registrars at Willsmere took on responsibilities far beyond their experience, and Stamp quickly realised that he could rely on Margaret. He asked her to become his deputy, even before she 'had her letters', the professional slang for Fellowship of the Royal Australian and New Zealand College of Psychiatrists (FRANZCP). Once she became a fully fledged psychiatrist, Margaret came to Fred Stamp to renegotiate her conditions. She would continue in the deputy's job, she said, so long as she could do a Master of Business Administration. She laughed when he replied: 'I can see you finishing up one day being my boss.'

In years to come, the closure of Willsmere in December 1988 would be described as being of international significance. Unlike the closure of many other such institutions, there was sufficient planning and resourcing to ensure that its demise was attended by the birth of many replacement facilities in the community. However, the transition was difficult for all concerned. Many staff were as institutionalised as the patients, and the move aroused huge anxiety and antagonism. There were endless rounds of exhausting negotiations – over the 'decanting' of patients and staff to other facilities, over logistics and union deals. Acid was thrown over the car of one staff member involved in the closure, and Stamp's car tyres were deliberately punctured. He heard reports of a firebomb being thrown at another staff member's home. When Stamp was off work for three months because of illness, Margaret became acting superintendent. He was impressed that she managed so well in his absence, rarely disturbing his convalescence.

One subsequent research paper said the enormity of the decommissioning project could not be overemphasised, and described it as a bigger, more complex task than the building of Loyang Power Station, one of the largest construction jobs ever undertaken in Victoria to that time. Margaret's work at Willsmere brought her to the attention of senior Victorian health department bureaucrats. John Rimmer, a former academic and self-described 'policy entrepreneur', was impressed by the assertive, articulate young psychiatrist who he had seen thrust into the eye of the storm. He was surprised when Margaret asked him to mentor her in developing management skills. It was an unusual request coming from a doctor, especially one so early in their career. But it was not unwelcome, and the pair had many discussions about strategies for implementing change in the health sector, with all its entrenched practices and rivalries.

As well as throwing up professional challenges for Margaret, Willsmere also marked a time of self-reflection. As part of her training, she undertook psychoanalysis and began to seriously question what she wanted from life.

For Margaret, the end of her marriage was also a beginning. She told some of her old friends, from school and university days, that she was moving on and did not want to keep up contact with them. Some were hurt about this for years after.

Her divorce from Brendan came through in May 1985, not long after Margaret had started at Willsmere. About that time, she wrote to

Patrick, who was grappling with career choices, of the importance of taking responsibility for one's own happiness.

I wonder if you are in danger of doing what I did – that is, putting off actually getting down and enjoying living because of a future goal. I now realise it is more important to work out why me [sic] is not happy in the present and do something about that. Chasing rainbows of any sort, even very justifiable goals such as careers only puts off the fatal moment, when me has to take responsibility for me's own happiness . . .

I am currently working with old people and I am seeing very clearly that the ones who look back with satisfaction and happiness are the ones who have had contented lives, good relationships and a sense of creativity. Not all those who were professional successes are having happy old ages. Knowing our family conflicts as I do, and having had to work through all the difficulties I carried from my family into the outside world, I encourage you to look at these issues from your perspective – work out what you are trying to prove to Dad, what you are trying to get from Mum, who are you attempting to achieve success for?

It is terribly important to work at being a fun and caring person to be with – to give lots of yourself, to be open to other people and the possibility that by studying all the time – you are avoiding getting to know yourself, simply because you don't have time or energy. From all this philosophy, I am trying to say that it won't matter which career choice you make – if you know and like yourself you will be happy and successful and if you are unhappy now – chances are you will remain so until you take charge and start enjoying whatever you do . . . Hope I have made some of the pain that I have been through in reaching these beliefs clear without actually saying so, in so many words – maybe some of what I said will be helpful to you if you pick your way through it.

Am having a happy and satisfying life myself – difficulty in actually accepting the adult 'specialist' 'buck stops here' role completely, but enjoying the process at long last. Have a fantastic garden for relaxation. I see lots of movies and making new friends.

Margaret signed the letter with 'much love and concern'.

Margaret's time at Willsmere also coincided with a chance meeting that would change much. Margaret was not a confident driver, and confided this once to Fred Stamp in a conversation that would stick in his memory because it was unusual for her to discuss life outside work. Sometime later, her car broke down one morning on the Eastern Freeway.

Don Scott, a mechanic by trade, pulled over to help the well-dressed stranded motorist before realising who it was. He had found her attractive when they had met some years earlier at a daytime classical music performance at the Melbourne Town Hall but, at the time, had thought her out of his league. He remembered thinking that because she'd been 'done up to the bloody nines' that time too.

Margaret gave no sign of remembering their previous encounter. After fixing the problem on the old car, Don decided to make the most of fate's gift. He asked Margaret out, one thing led to another, and he didn't need to think twice when she delivered the ultimatum: give up smoking or me. About six months after their roadside encounter, Don and Margaret moved into their first home together, a modest 1960s brick house in North Balwyn. When Margaret told friends the story of their roadside meeting in the years to come, some gained the impression that she enjoyed portraying herself as the damsel in distress who had been rescued by a white knight.

It was a relationship that would intrigue many. What could they have in common, the focused, ambitious professional and the knock-about bloke with a withered arm? Don was eight years older than Margaret, in his early forties, and in a bad space when they met. He was on a disability pension, unable to work after a traumatic injury ten years earlier. His arm was caught and mangled in a conveyer belt when he was working in a quarry. Years of painful surgery and rehabilitation followed. Don was a working-class man who had lost much more than just his job. He had left a part of himself on the conveyor belt. The accident was the cream on the cake, he would say years later. He already had plenty to be upset about: a divorce; his time in a war that he didn't like talking about; and the loss as a young boy of his baby sister. When told she had gone to heaven, he blamed God.

Don was angry with the world when he met Margaret. She made him laugh, and she calmed him down. They had fun together. He liked that Margaret took her job seriously but not herself. She laughed like a child, from the belly up, at a funny movie or an everyday absurdity, while Don was more of a giggler. He liked how she always had a coin for the buskers on the streets. He saw that she had also done some hard yards, and each drew strength and support from the other. They enjoyed flirting with each other. He opened the car door, and bought her flowers. Don had never felt as comfortable on the dance floor as he did with Margaret. Theirs was an easy and natural chemistry. Watching their favourite television shows in the evenings, Margaret snuggled her head under Don's arm and said, 'I just fit, don't I?'

She encouraged him to work in their garden at North Balwyn, and he regained some confidence in his wounded body. He realised he could still shovel, and plant and build, and set to creating the first of many gardens for Margaret. She liked having a man around who could fix things. They were worlds apart but had much in common. They shared an almost childlike enthusiasm for everyday things – the people they met on the street, a cake in a particular shop, a new tree for their garden, going to the movies, discovering a bargain in a junk shop. They also shared a strong work ethic, a sense of social justice and a straightforward vocabulary. Neither had any difficulty calling a spade a bloody shovel. Don was happy to tell anyone who asked that he thought the sun shone out of Margaret's bum. He was a petrol-head who stayed up half the night watching motor racing and who vented his aggressions behind the steering wheel. But he was just as happy to spend hours shopping with Margaret for clothes, sharing his opinions on colours and fabrics with her and anyone else who might be in the shop. She was book smart, and he was streetwise.

On more than one occasion, Margaret gave friends and family some pragmatic advice about how to manage men. She cautioned against expecting a relationship to meet all your needs. It was important to make men feel valued, she said, and there was no point focusing on their inadequacies. If you can't find everything you want in the relationship, look to other people – your girlfriends and family – for your other needs, she said. At least one recipient of this advice thought Margaret seemed to have no difficulties in compartmentalising her life so neatly.

Don was the youngest of six children, and he and Margaret valued their privacy. Never, ever play your full hand of cards – that was his philosophy. Margaret's family did not know much about her new relationship for some time, and its beginning also marked a shift in Margaret's connection with them. Perhaps she did not want a repeat of the situation of Brendan becoming so enmeshed in her family. Perhaps she had grown tired of the complexities of family dynamics, and had decided to move on. Perhaps it was just because there were some things that she and Don decided to keep to themselves.

Never short of a quip, Don's response was ready when he attended work functions with Margaret. 'And what do you do?' would come the inevitable query from the inevitable suit. 'Pretty much like you,' was Don's standard reply. 'Whatever Margaret tells me.'

Their roles were clearly and happily defined from the outset. Her job was all-important. And his job was to support her – to tend to Margaret and their home and garden. He shopped carefully, checking labels for gluten-free products, and cooked, and made sure Margaret had the rest she needed.

Don was in full protector mode when Margaret came home one day, her face swollen and bruised after being badly bashed by a patient at Willsmere. He pestered to know who had done this. He wanted revenge. But Margaret refused to divulge. She did tell her family, though, that the patient had been a doctor unhappy about his medication. Don was certain the culprit was a psychiatrist. Bernadette was shocked when she went to visit. Margaret was sitting in Don's dressing gown, looking like a little old woman with her face smashed in. She needed several weeks off work, but felt the effects for far longer, jumping whenever a car backfired. Her hearing was never quite the same afterwards.

No-one would have been surprised if Margaret's assailant was a psychiatrist, of course. Then, as now, the accepted wisdom among both the medical profession and the general public was that psychiatrists are as crazy as their patients. Hence the joke, repeated in one journal article, that the difference between good and bad psychiatrists is that the former merely sleep with their patients; the latter also kill them.

Psychiatry's image problem reflects the fear surrounding mental illness, as well as the specialty's historic separation from the rest of medicine. One of the more significant advances in modern medicine was made by an Australian psychiatrist, John Cade, who discovered the benefits of lithium salts in treating mania. It is perhaps a telling comment on the relative standing of psychiatry within the medical hierarchy that Cade is not nearly as well known as he deserves. Psychiatry's isolation – indeed, psychiatrists working in asylums were once known as 'alienists' – fostered stigma and misunderstanding, and the ideal conditions for abuses. Margaret's formative years as a psychiatrist coincided with far-reaching reforms aimed at ending this system of apartheid between mental health and the mainstream health system. In the late 1980s, a coalition of psychiatrists and mental health advocates joined forces with the aim of putting the appalling state of mental health care on the radar of the public and the politicians. In years to come they would call themselves the 'issue entrepreneurs', who helped build momentum for a hugely ambitious project – the first National Mental Health Strategy – which would have as its goal an unprecedented shake-up of mental health services around the country.

It could be said that Margaret hit her straps during a time of historic reform in mental health but indeed the same could have been said of mental health many times in the previous century. The history of mental health is woven with recurring motifs: the march of change in the face of resistance, and punctuated by scandals and periods of inertia. In the 1950s, the appointment of Dr Eric Cunningham Dax as director of the Mental Hygiene Authority had led to huge changes in Victoria's asylums. Locked wards were opened up, the fences and divisions between the male and female quarters came down, and the huge dormitories of 50 patients or more were divided into smaller units. Throughout the 1960s and 70s, the policies of deinstitutionalisation, driven by the impact of new medications and the passion of the human rights movement, began sending patients back to the community. The irony, of course, was that most patients had always been in the community; the big institutions only ever cared for a minority of people with mental illness. Most people with mental health problems had difficulty accessing care because the resources were tied up in institutions.

The challenge for Margaret's generation of reformers was to redirect resources to where they were most needed – to the communities where patients lived and sought help, most often from general practitioners rather than specialist mental health services. Margaret was finding her professional feet during difficult, uncomfortable times for psychiatry, which was beset by internal and external pressures, including the awkward questions raised by scandals such as Chelmsford and Ward 10 B.★ 'Nobody is very critical of their peers' was the explanation one insider gave historians for the Royal Australian and New Zealand College of Psychiatrists' failures to act against psychiatrists at Chelmsford.

No longer the superintendent emperors of their own kingdoms, many psychiatrists struggled to find their places amid the new jargon of multidisciplinary teams, and to cope with the emergence of notions such as patients' rights. Legislative changes brought their management of patients under unprecedented external scrutiny. Many fled the stresses of the public sector for the refuge of private practice, which generally offered both a higher income and an easier life. A festering split arose between public and private psychiatry. The latter tended to look down on those in the public sector as the dregs – surely only the desperate would take such desperate jobs. Public psychiatrists, on the other hand, complained they had been left with the hardest and most thankless work, looking after the really sick, and

---

★The deaths of patients who underwent deep sleep therapy at Chelmsford Hospital in Sydney between 1965 and 1979 was the subject of a royal commission in New South Wales from 1988 to 1991. In 1990, the Queensland Government held an inquiry into the care of patients in Ward 10 B at the Townsville General Hospital between 1975 and 1988.

accused their private colleagues of catering for the 'worried well'. Private psychiatry, with its long waiting lists and reluctance to engage in providing support to GPs or to areas outside its metropolitan comfort zone, was also bagged for being unresponsive to the needs of the broader community. The battle, according to one psychiatric wit, was between those who looked after patients with unmet needs and those who catered for 'met unneed'. Or between the doctors of psychoses and the doctors of neuroses.

The irrational, fractured nature of health funding in Australia only reinforced the divisions and imbalances. Psychiatrists in private practice could make almost unlimited claim on the public purse through the federally funded Medicare, while treating patients according to their own particular ideologies and idiosyncrasies, whereas those working in state-funded hospitals and services were subject to ever-increasing rationing of resources and pressures. The gap between public and private psychiatry was reflected in the first National Mental Health Strategy, endorsed by Australian health ministers in 1992, which failed to engage or even acknowledge the role of the private sector in providing services. The profession also fractured between those convinced of the biological basis of mental illness versus those whose ideology and livelihoods were firmly founded in the psychoanalytic model. The emergence of a more holistic view, encompassing all aspects of humanity, was slow and painful.

Amid all these chasms, Margaret's position was unambiguous. She was committed to public psychiatry and to the care of the seriously mentally ill. Some years later, she would put her name to an academic article noting that half of the people with serious mental illness went untreated while many with less serious illnesses were overserviced. After Willsmere, she spent a year in the late 1980s in the Victorian health department's head office, watching and learning from the messy interplay of politics, personalities and policy. As she became more active in professional circles, Margaret irritated not a few peers by suggesting that psychiatry had abrogated its responsibilities, and needed to become more accountable and to develop better management and leadership skills. In some circles she became known as a street fighter because of her willingness to pick a fight with her colleagues.

Margaret would need the steel of a street fighter in her next job, helping to push through changes at two old-fashioned psychiatric hospitals at Ballarat and Ararat in the goldfields of rural Victoria. Aradale Hospital and Lakeside Hospital, originally known as the Ballarat Asylum, were institutions trapped by their history when Margaret arrived as their new director of clinical services in May 1989. That Aradale Hospital, on a hill outside the town, still held both psychiatric and intellectually disabled patients was a measure of its old-fashioned practices. To take on one of these hospitals would have been tough enough; that Margaret was asked to tackle both was a measure of the difficulty of finding psychiatrists to work in the country. When she arrived, the two hospitals had a total of four psychiatrists for 600 patients. She knew it would be a difficult job and was anxious about whether her management skills were up to the task. Time would reveal it to be far more gruelling than she could then have imagined.

Much had changed at Lakeside and Aradale since the days when patients tore their clothes to shreds, paced the hours away in the 'airing courts', or sat with nothing to do other than pass pebbles from one hand to the other, until the pile shone brilliantly. Since the advent of effective medications, patients no longer spent long hours each day confined by straitjackets or kicking pants, a strip of moleskin sewn between their trouser legs to stop them lashing out with their feet. Nurses no longer hosed down patients en masse in the evenings, or searched them closely, including inspecting their anal passages, to make sure no cigarettes or matches were smuggled into their rooms at night. Patients were no longer lined up every evening to be painted with a white goo, and then put to bed without pyjamas. The goo, a mix of oil and zinc oxide lotion, was to protect them from the effects of bed-wetting. People were no longer confined to hospital because they had been found masturbating or because they were homosexual or because they had had a child out of wedlock. No longer were they held for decades without review of the necessity for their containment.

Yes, much had changed. Dr Steele Haughton, the superintendent at Lakeside from 1968 to 1988, and described by one researcher as 'a memorable personality of patriarchal proportions, immeasurable commitment and generally benevolent disposition', had overseen a reduction in Lakeside's inpatient numbers from 1,100 to 350. He once described how difficult this had been in the face of opposition from staff who did not want 'their' patients moved. 'I would wait until the particular consultant went on annual leave and I would roster myself in his ward and when he or she came back from leave, they would find that patient numbers had been reduced considerably in their absence,' Dr Haughton told a researcher. 'It was devious but it was the only way I was able to do it.'

But many attitudes lingered from those earlier times. This was not surprising. The environment itself – scatterings of decaying buildings across sprawling grounds – was symbolic of another time. Many staff were second- or third-generation employees. Their views about the way things should be done were set in concrete. Newcomers quickly learnt that little good came out of reporting colleagues who drank on duty or were rough with patients. There was, one researcher subsequently observed, a culture of collusion.

By the time Margaret arrived, both hospitals were close to dysfunctional. They had been poorly managed and their budgets were in the habit of blowing out. Staff and their unions were suspicious of the push to community-based care, and fearful for their jobs and their patients. They had not been helped to feel part of the changes, or to understand them. Local community leaders, conscious of the hospitals' substantial contribution to the local economy and employment (Lakeside's annual budget was then about $20 million), were vigorous in their opposition to deinstitutionalisation. Many locals were uncomfortable coming face to face with patients who had previously been kept out of sight and out of mind behind Lakeside's big iron fence.

The bureaucrats in head office had Lakeside in their sights, and were looking for an excuse to act. They knew they needed to shut down the big 'bins' if funds were to be found to modernise and redistribute the state's mental health services in line with the needs of the broader population. They also knew this could be politically explosive, given the depth of opposition.

A confidential departmental briefing paper noted there were serious concerns about patient care. Lakeside consistently reported among the highest death rates of any psychiatric institution in Victoria, even after taking account of the age of its mainly elderly patients. The paper also noted that Lakeside staff numbers had remained stable despite falling patient numbers, and that the movement of patients into the community was not being accompanied by staff or funding. 'The challenge over the next 12 months is to determine how long structural inefficiencies and anomalies such as Lakeside can continue at the expense of more responsive and accessible services,' the paper said.

4

Transformation

On her first day in the big old office at Lakeside, Margaret unpacked her medical library and surprised Lesley Hopkins, her new secretary and one of the unofficial keepers of the hospital's history, by doing two things. 'Do you think you can get used to calling me Margaret?' she asked.

'Yeah,' replied Lesley drily. 'But it will take a few days.' Lesley, a woman of large, slow physique and a quick mind, had worked for the hospital's former superintendent, Dr Steele Haughton, for more than twenty years without attaining first-name familiarity. She had rarely heard anyone, not even his psychiatrist colleagues, use his first name.

Margaret then asked for a pair of scissors. She put them to immediate work, hacking up the centre of a pair of heavy cream wool drapes which had been recently installed. She wanted to let in the light.

'What have we got here?' Lesley wondered to herself. Then she rushed out to buy some braid to tidy up the job. Lesley, a keen observer of life's little oddities, soon became used to her new boss's quirky requests. What a circus, she thought to herself when asked to take two pieces of gluten-free bread, home-made by Don, up to the sandwich shop for filling at lunchtime. She chuckled when Margaret sent her to a local car dealer to buy a handbook after Don had taken the car to bits and needed some help putting it back together again. She was sent to retrieve credit cards left in stores and once drove many kilometres to fetch a bag of knitting that Margaret had left in a cafe.

Lesley became used to messages being left on her answer phone at 1 am or 2 am with requests for the next morning's work. She chortled at her new boss's straightforward language. She had heard Dr Haughton tell nurses their hair needed a trim in the past, but had never before had a boss who told nurses to stop 'piss-farting' around. Over time, an enduring friendship developed. Lesley, who once worried about what she would say to her boss while driving her to the airport, found they had plenty to chat about. Margaret always had a book on the go or a shopping story to tell. She confided to Lesley that her ambition was to be a professor. One year, Margaret told Lesley that she and Don had had the best Christmas ever. They had stayed home, cleaned windows, and not seen a soul.

The friendship with Lesley was one of the few supportive relationships Margaret could count on at work. Many staff regarded her with suspicion and hostility. She had been sent by head office to do 'another Willsmere', they thought. Nor did her manner encourage friendships. Margaret knew what she wanted and expected others to be equally efficient and focused. She was ready to criticise and challenge the old-fashioned practices of the nurses and her psychiatric colleagues. She didn't mince words, disguise her anger, or indulge in niceties. She had little time for the status quo or chitchat. 'It was hard to start a conversation with her about what you had done on the weekend,' observed one senior colleague. A bloody pushy woman, concluded others. 'Might as well be speaking to a brick wall,' sighed one senior nurse after trying to argue the demerits of deinstitutionalisation. He thought she was a woman on a mission.

One of Margaret's bosses in head office, Dr Peter Eisen, director of psychiatric services for Victoria, also became familiar with her forthright ways. Unlike many of her colleagues, Margaret told Eisen to his face when she didn't like something he had done. He didn't always agree with her feedback but sometimes it was on the mark, uncomfortably so. Eisen also became used to Margaret's late-night calls. He sometimes groaned when he realised who was on the phone. He knew it would mean a problem that he'd have to do something about.

When Margaret started at Lakeside, an investigation was under way into a spate of recent patient suicides. She soon realised that staff wars were a contributing factor. 'It was clear that there was a problem of communication of medical concerns about a patient suicide risk and nursing action on it – but because the medical/nursing staff weren't talking to each other in a professional sense, people weren't able to take that as an incident which highlighted a problem and solve it in a general large-scale way,' she concluded. 'The psychiatrist would say to me, "The problem is that the director of nursing and the nursing executive are hopeless" . . . The nurses would say to me, "The problem is that the psychiatrists are obnoxious and arrogant and won't talk to us".'

Locals were not impressed when Margaret began to bring in changes. She was told she was mad and stupid to be pursuing community-based care. She felt many of the concerns were paternalistic and also reflected resistance from services which did not want to be bothered with the mentally ill. 'You're discharging these people into the community and it's not fair,' was the message she received. 'We shouldn't have to provide for them. It's always been your problem. Why should we have to worry about them?'

'Lakeside provided everything to everybody before I came,' Margaret later told a government inquiry. 'If you were old, if you were cold or had no money or you had a drinking problem or you had a fight with your wife, I mean there was a whole myriad of reasons you could get into Lakeside and of course when I came I just stopped all of that . . . I said the only people that can come into Lakeside from now on are people with psychiatric illness or a suggestion of psychiatric illness that might need assessment.'

For some of those bent on reform, however, Margaret's changes did not come quickly enough or go far enough. They felt she was floundering. She agreed the job was too big for one, and began to lobby for an offsider, who could at least take responsibility for Aradale, an hour's drive away.

In conversations with John Rimmer in head office, Margaret shared some of her difficulties, wondering if she was up to the task. She found time to write to Fred Stamp, saying she now had a better appreciation of his troubles at Willsmere. He was touched to receive her note. Margaret was frank about her fears and frustrations in a formal learning group that had been set up to assist several relatively junior psychiatrists who had been thrown out of their depth into senior management positions, often without good organisational or political backup.

The group was facilitated by a psychologist turned management academic, Geoffrey Prideaux, who believed in teaching management skills through 'action learning' rather than theory. This meant sharing and learning from each other's battle stories at their regular meetings. Prideaux also brought in a variety of experts to give some practical tutoring for the typical problems the group's members faced – how, for example, to decipher creative accounting to discover when money allegedly under their control was being diverted elsewhere in a hospital or a service.

Margaret had joined the group while still in head office, and Prideaux watched her development at Ballarat. He saw that she was extremely determined and felt deeply about the importance of good mental health services. It really mattered to her, it was not only ambition that drove her, he thought. Prideaux also saw that Margaret was desperately unhappy and lonely at Ballarat at times. She became the meat in the sandwich, caught between those who felt she wasn't pushing reform fast enough and those who thought her a bulldozer. She went to Ballarat as a reformer but in the eyes of some became tainted by her association with the problems she was trying to change.

The psychiatrist managers in the group felt extremely isolated and exposed in their positions; they were responsible for systems plagued by problems they could not fix. They were vulnerable to being scapegoated. They knew the intense frustration of being forced into actions they did not support. When Margaret became distressed, one colleague saw her tears as an expression of enraged frustration rather than plain upset. They all knew what it was like to be instructed to do something they believed was detrimental to their services or patients. At times Margaret joked about the career she had chosen; at other times she wondered whether she should resign.

Margaret later reflected on the group's discussions in a thoughtful journal article, describing their discomfort, stress and fear at moving into new territory of managing budgets, working with complex health bureaucracies and dealing with staff. 'Psychiatrists are trained in the rational scientific view of problem solving, together with adopting an understanding and empathic relationship with patients,' she wrote.

> Management, however, even in health care, is not particularly rational and empathy is a most unhelpful tool in any power struggles with non-clinical managers.
>
> The realisation of the need to adopt yet another perspective to our world view in order to compensate for the deficiencies of our previously cherished value systems was quite a dissonant experience for us all. We painfully reached the conclusion that the management world is frequently illogical and chaotic, functions within a complex, open system often governed by power struggles and personal loyalties and is too often concerned with the protection of hierarchy and the control of resources.
>
> It became apparent to us that the day-to-day management of a health care system is only partially occupied with the provision of good patient care. Without this knowledge the psychiatrist who, for example, expends all of his or her energies on the counselling of a suicidal patient and then rushes late to a management meeting, can be at a decided disadvantage, especially when the non-clinical managers may have spent most of the previous 24 hours collecting damaging material about the psychiatrist's difficulties in managing his or her component of the service system.

She wrote that clinicians who join management can find themselves identifying with patients in feeling bewildered, despondent and powerless. 'However, all psychiatrist-managers must realise that the powerless patient is not in a position to influence the system,' she cautioned. 'We are powerless ourselves if we can only take a clinical view and lose battles over the resourcing and direction of service delivery to the more politically astute, non-clinical manager. It behoves us then to be influential members of the executive, and to use our newly acquired influence to change the system for the better.'

The doctor who made a successful transition to manager would also undergo an image change, she said. 'The constantly empathic clinician will have been superseded by a person with the ability to be a tough negotiator in the appropriate settings.'

On Sunday, 23 September 1990, Margaret celebrated her thirty-eighth birthday. She knew a difficult week lay ahead thanks to a state-wide union campaign against the reforms occurring in mental health. Bans on garbage collection and linen washing had begun the previous week.

That evening, a frail elderly patient who had been at Lakeside for more than 30 years and who was known among staff as a 'king hitter' because of his aggressive tendencies, became involved in an altercation with a nurse after helping himself to an extra cup of tea. The man was variously named in reports at the time as Keith Murie or Murrie. The nurse, who had been drinking, shoved Keith backwards violently and assaulted him. The patient fell and hit his head. He was patched up and put to bed. When the charge nurse came to work next morning, he was told that poor old Keith Murie had been found dead in bed the previous evening, and that all the usual procedures were under way. He thought nothing more of it, until an angry patient stormed into his office alleging murder and cover-up.

The stone had been cast into the pond. What began as a small ripple quickly built into the wave that would engulf Lakeside and Aradale. For those determined on ending an era, there would be no turning back now. News of Murie's death hit the press and triggered a series of crisis meetings in head office. Eventually an announcement was made: a major investigation would be held into Lakeside, and an administrator, John O'Neill, was installed to shake up the hospital's management. So began the *annus horribilis* for Lakeside and Aradale.

Staff came to dread the horror headlines of their morning paper. Neighbours began to look at them askance. A retired nurse reprimanded a colleague at the shops one day: 'How did this get out? It wouldn't have in my day.'

Morale sank even lower when nurses walked out on strike for several days in December 1990 as part of a state-wide dispute. Margaret worked around the clock, coordinating volunteers to feed, bathe and care for patients. The local paper photographed her standing at a whiteboard drawing up a roster for volunteers. Her secretary Lesley Hopkins was, of course, put to work, organising the roster of volunteers. At times, there were not enough volunteers and whole wards were left unattended. Margaret was furious with the nurses. She swore about them over the phone to head office and berated their lack of professionalism. It was just the latest in a long series of incidents that insulted her, observed one colleague who thought her 'stressed as buggery'. When the strike finally ended, Margaret told the local paper that it had enabled many patients to strike up friendships with volunteers, and she hoped these relationships would continue.

Meanwhile, the board of inquiry was unable to investigate Keith Murie's death as it was sub judice. The nurse was charged and eventually convicted over the assault. It was not the first time he had assaulted patients. The inquiry instead was asked to examine the death of Patient X, which had occurred several months after Margaret's arrival at Lakeside in 1989, as well as a bus trip which was to become infamous. Eisen briefed the inquiry that these incidents were not isolated examples but reflected broader, longstanding concerns which needed to be urgently addressed.

Patient X, an overweight 41-year-old with a drinking problem, had been rushed to Ballarat Base Hospital late one evening after swallowing what his mother described as a handful of 'truckie pills', which were presumed to have been amphetamines. She had found him thrashing around on his bedroom floor and having flashbacks to his Vietnam War service. He was diagnosed with drug-induced psychosis and transferred to Lakeside. After becoming disturbed, he was put in seclusion, where he became sicker and sicker. After a frightful day, where he sweated profusely and became increasingly agitated and delirious, he died that night of a heart attack.

At the time of his death, Margaret had been humiliated to learn about it from her bosses in head office when in Melbourne for a meeting. It seemed clear to them that she was being deliberately undermined by being kept out of the loop. A colleague who saw Margaret that day was surprised by her appearance. She didn't look her feisty, bouncy self. It seemed the stuffing had been knocked out of her.

The Lakeside inquiry found a multitude of failings in Patient X's care. He had died after taking a potentially lethal overdose of a medication usually used to treat Parkinson's disease, but the inquiry concluded that his death had been avoidable. Some of the treatments had actually exacerbated his poisoning. If he had been correctly diagnosed and treated for the physical problem of poisoning rather than being seen as a psychiatric patient, he might have lived. If he had not been transferred to Lakeside, he might have lived. If the nurses and doctors had been on speaking terms and communicated better about his care, he might have lived. If there had been better communication between Ballarat Base and Lakeside hospitals, he might have lived. If Lakeside had had better policies and protocols in place, he might have lived. When patients suffer at the hands of health services, it is rarely because just one thing has gone wrong.

The news was cold comfort for Patient X's family, who had struggled for months to find out what had happened. No real effort was made to advise or counsel them after his death.

The board also investigated a bus trip by staff and patients to a hotel at Avoca on 31 August 1990. To the nurses, it was just a typical outing. It was custom to use patients' pension money to fund all sorts of excursions, including once taking six patients on a joy flight on a light aeroplane. Staff withdrew $800 in patient funds to cover the bus trip, lunch and wine and beer. The publican was upset by a student nurse's apparent theft of a bottle of Baileys and a glass, and some were not impressed that nurses were photographed standing on a table in the hotel lounge. Money left over from the trip was used to take some other patients to the Melbourne Cricket Ground the next day.

Some of the nurses, even years later, could not understand the fuss. It was no different from many other such outings. Margaret, however, was furious. There was nothing therapeutic about the trip, in her book. The inquiry was similarly scathing, concluding that 'decisions in Lakeside appear frequently to be made with little, if any, reference to the wishes of patients'. It noted that Margaret was 'determined to set a high standard of service to clients and radically update the hospital' and that she 'needs considerable support in her attempts to achieve this task'. Margaret had told the inquiry that she was trying to get a position established for a deputy director to assist her, and its report supported this, calling for a deputy director to be appointed with responsibility for Aradale Hospital.

The Victorian Health Minister, Marie Tehan, called the inquiry's findings scandalous. 'Unfortunately Lakeside is not an isolated example but indicative of the accepted culture in all state-run psychiatric institutions,' she told journalists. The report provided the perfect launching pad for a state-wide audit of all psychiatric institutions.

Lakeside attracted yet more damning headlines when its administrator, John O'Neill, gave evidence to a hearing convened by Human Rights Commissioner Brian Burdekin in Ballarat in April 1991. Lakeside was O'Neill's first job in mental health, after a decade managing public hospitals, and he was appalled by the place.

O'Neill, a tall, lean character, was nicknamed 'Darth Vader' by some staff who saw his as a reign of fear and loathing, but was respected by others as a tough, capable manager. He was rewarded with some wry chuckles when, describing his management techniques to a nurses' meeting, he produced the book, *Leadership Secrets of Attila the Hun*. Meetings with O'Neill left Margaret in tears on more than one occasion. He thought she should have been doing more to combat abuses and improve patient welfare.

O'Neill pulled no punches in his presentation to Brian Burdekin. He said that patients' needs came a poor second to staff and union demands. He had been unable even to change patients' meal times to better suit their daily routines. 'The union involved said that its members have the first choice in deciding meal times . . . the patients are not the primary concern,' he said. O'Neill said staff-to-patient ratios at Lakeside were about three to one, compared with a ratio of closer to one staff member for every 150 seriously ill patients in the community. He estimated that half of Lakeside's patients, who had come from across the state, could be relocated to centres closer to their families if the appropriate facilities were in place.

Not long after his widely publicised presentation to the Burdekin inquiry came the inevitable announcement. Lakeside would close. This would take another six years to achieve, however, and would involve moving patients to nursing homes and other facilities in the areas where they had come from, sometimes 50 years previously. Some families received an unexpected phone call about an elderly relative they had long since thought dead, not realising they had been put in hospital. Some were delighted by the news. Others didn't want to know. Some patients were pleased to move into more independent living; others didn't want to leave the only home they could remember.

Aradale was next to fall under the microscope. Its notorious J Ward, where mentally ill prisoners had been kept under nineteenth-century conditions, closed early in 1991, but more than 200 patients with intellectual disabilities and psychiatric problems remained in its care. When an inquiry was ordered into allegations of prostitution rackets involving staff and patients, Sue Tait, a softly-spoken human rights lawyer, was among those sent to investigate. The brutality of the place would haunt her for years. Tait found patients with unexplained injuries and hostile, intimidating staff.

The entries in one of the ward diaries said everything about the prevailing attitudes to patients, Tait thought. A senior nurse wrote of a patient as a 'fart filled fuck wit'. The same nurse also wrote: 'We are all sick to death of . . . I've checked with the post office, for the price of a $78 stamp we can send the prick to Siberia (second class) . . . Some peoples [sic] relatives are yobbies and greasy, slimy, dirty, low life, fuckin yobbies at that.'

Lynda Stephens, who headed the inquiry into Aradale, was known for her sharp mind and tongue. Having previously worked as a psychiatric nurse, she knew where institutions hid their dirty secrets and how to uncover them. Her inquiry did just that. The investigation did not uncover evidence of prostitution rackets, but its findings were damning enough, documenting a long list of human rights abuses and negligent practices.

Almost one-quarter of Aradale's patients were underweight, while much of the food meant for their plates was pilfered. More than 3,600 chickens went missing from stores over a two-year period. Rumour was that they were raffled at local clubs. Enough fruit was bought for each patient to have a few pieces a day, but they were lucky to get that each week. The investigators found that several hundred pieces of fruit – up to 40 per cent of the amount bought – went missing each week. It was not clear to the investigators whether the large-scale, systematic pilfering involved most staff or only a few. Either way, knowledge about it must have been commonplace.

Nurses had control over a portion of patients' pension money, which was pooled to buy cleaning materials, staff stationery, furniture, meals and drinks. Thousands of dollars were spent on an expensive TV, VCR and sound system for one ward lounge, while funds from a male ward were used to buy pantyhose and nursery wear. In 1990, more than $100,000 of patients' funds could not be accounted for. The report found no evidence patients had agreed to their funds being pooled, or that they were consulted about how it would be spent.

Aradale, where patients often wore pooled underwear, went hungry, had to buy their own furniture and had little meaningful therapy, cost taxpayers $18 million in 1990/91, or the equivalent of $70,000 per client. This, the investigators wrote, compared with charges of $17,000 for the most expensive private boarding school or about $35,000 for 24-hour nursing care for dependent aged. There were 455 staff to care for 245 patients whereas fourteen years earlier, 420 staff had cared for 621 clients. Once admitted to Aradale, there was no easy exit. The average stay was 22 years, or 54 times the international standard then recommended by the World Health Organization.

Lynda Stephens, who boiled with rage at the abuses she found at Aradale and did not have much time for psychiatrists in the best of circumstances, clashed with Margaret. Stephens thought Margaret was trying to make things better, but that her stubbornness and insistence on her own point of view got in the way.

Margaret received unfavourable mention in the Aradale inquiry's report, dated November 1991. 'The director of clinical services partially shares responsibility for this mismanagement with the other members of the executive,' it said.

The fact that the position is off campus does not exonerate the person. Furthermore, findings in relation to programs delivery and length of stay of psychiatric patients reflect poorly on the overall clinical care provided to psychiatric patients. The task force is aware the director of clinical services is alert to these issues and her attempts to relocate some patients in more appropriate community settings have often been undermined by nursing staff.

Few escaped untarred from the Lakeside and Aradale inquiries. 'The year has been, I suspect, the most challenging in the 110 year histories of Lakeside and Aradale,' said the Christmas 1991 newsletter to staff.

Margaret was devastated by the Aradale report. Don thought she had been left carrying the bloody baby and that both she and the baby had been thrown out with the bath water. She was in tears when she went to see her boss, Jim Fletcher, who had taken over from O'Neill in mid 1991, about the report. It was so unfair, she said. How could she have been held responsible given the enormity of the job she was trying to do, without sufficient resources or staff? She had been pushing so hard for so long without the backup that she needed, and now she was being blamed for the problems she had been trying to fix.

Fletcher was amazed that Margaret had turned to him for support as they had not enjoyed an easy relationship. She thought him a bully and had told him that he was pushing change too fast, slashing funds and staffing. He thought Margaret a good clinician but that her management skills were not up to scratch and that she needed to be given direction. He told her that she had to take some responsibility for Aradale because of her position there.

In the two and a half years that Fletcher ran psychiatric services in the area, full-time equivalent staff numbers were reduced from 1,000 to 385 and tens of millions of dollars were cut from the budget. During that time he also had a number of anonymous phone calls relaying death threats, and his hair became noticeably greyer. In his 30-odd years administering hospitals, he would always remember this as one of the toughest jobs he ever had.

The problems identified by the Lakeside and Aradale inquiries were not particularly unique to those institutions, according to the state-wide clinical audit of psychiatric institutions published in March 1992. It painted a damning picture of systematic deficiencies in care, of patients and their families not being respected or involved in decisions, and of patients suffering frequent abuses with limited avenues for complaint or recourse. 'The quality of cleaning and maintenance of wards suggests that many staff have an attitude that psychiatric patients do not deserve to have adequate living conditions,' the audit said.

It also highlighted the difficulties that managers were facing, working very long hours and struggling to juggle oversight of both the closure of institutions and development of new community services. The audit found many managers felt under siege from head office: 'A number felt that their achievements were little recognised and that their supposed failings were the main focus of attention from central office.'

Some years would pass before Margaret made public her reservations about the Lakeside and Aradale inquiries, arguing in a journal article that politically motivated inquiries did not achieve the long-term positive outcomes which might flow from more rigorous and systematic analyses.

She believed that ongoing organisational development was necessary to counter the almost inevitable situation whereby patients in psychiatric institutions ended up as the 'least important person in a complex hierarchy'. The inquiries had failed, she said, to address the lack of support within the system for the ongoing organisational development necessary to provide a productive and satisfying work environment and to ensure good standards of care.

The Health Department of Victoria had long been unwilling to accept its responsibility in supporting and funding such a system of isolated institutional care, she concluded. Instead, it had attacked the system through holding inquiries, without acknowledging 'its own important contribution of negligence'.

No matter how tough Margaret's working days, peace and replenishment were always waiting at home, in the bush escape which Don was creating. The hundreds of native trees and bushes that he had planted on their 5-acre rural block outside of Ballarat were growing and blossoming. Bodie, the Airedale that Margaret had bought Don as a puppy, was also maturing. He was the only one in the place who didn't take Margaret's orders, Don liked to joke. They had settled on getting an Airedale after finding one that was lost when they were out walking the streets around Balwyn one night. By the time the owners came to collect the dog the next day, Margaret and Don had been impressed by the mixture of affection and independence they saw in the breed.

When Margaret heard that her sister Bernadette wanted to move to Ballarat, she kept an eye on the real-estate market, and sent her a clipping about a rural block, not realising it bordered her own place. Knowing Margaret's liking for privacy, Bernadette asked if she would mind if they bought the house. It was agreed that Bernadette's three children would climb over the sty to visit Aunty Margaret only when invited. Margaret often bought books for her nieces and nephews, and would also dispense advice. Don't let the world go by, follow your dreams, she told them. Bernadette worked at Ballarat Base Hospital but she and Margaret rarely discussed work. They talked of gardening, trees and cooking.

Margaret had popped the question to Don not long after moving to Ballarat. He was delighted and responded typically. Whatever you want to do is fine with me, he said, so long as it includes me. They married quietly in their backyard on 2 March 1990. Margaret only told her family about the wedding after the event. She wanted no fuss. Also, she thought it unfair to ask people to buy wedding presents a second time.

Some years later Margaret told her brother Patrick and his wife Natalia, not long after they had married in a town hall in London with two friends as witnesses, that she was delighted they also had chosen a private ceremony. 'I am completely opposed to glamour weddings which have more to do with show than really behaving like adults which is what marriage is supposed to be all about,' she wrote to them.

The number of times that people seem to be more interested in how much the dress cost or what the bridesmaids wore is astounding and I always feel that the two getting married in this way are really playing at adult roles.

So congratulations and don't let anyone tell you different. Make sure however that you both program a balance of work and play into your life together so that you can see both the best and worst of each other in the early stages and then overcome any obstacles whilst it is worth it. The other piece of advice is that you should make sure that you both have friends and life outside of and independent of the relationship. There is nothing worse than a couple who do everything together and have no separate life. It is bound to fail. Unfortunately, most couples don't feel like that they need or want others in the early days and by the time they do it is too late. Enough of the elder sister advice already!!!!

Fuss and fanfare were again absent when Margaret became an Australian citizen a month after her wedding, on 5 April. She'd come home from work one day and told Don that she was going to the ceremony. She didn't want any carry-on, and she didn't expect Don to come along.

Margaret's four and a half years in Ballarat were harrowing and exhausting. But they also brought rapid professional growth. By the end of her tenure, Lakeside was being held up as an example of a recalcitrant institution which had been turned around. She had also been changed by her role in its transformation.

Wedding photos, taken early in Margaret's time at Ballarat, show a sweet, smiling face framed by a thick, soft brown bob. She wears a colourful paisley blouse with a matching skirt. A much stronger, more confident and assertive person faces the photographer a few years later. This time she wears a tailored red shirt, her hair is short and sharply cut with a red tinge, her gaze is firm and direct, and the light in her eyes is bright.

Looking back at the photos in years to come, Don could see the mark of Ballarat on Margaret's face. She had toughened up.

Self-confidence, Geoffrey Prideaux told his protégés, develops out of surviving difficult situations. Margaret had passed through fire. She had been burnt but had also discovered her steel. She had learnt to trust herself and her abilities.

As 1993 drew to its close, she was ready to move on. It was time for a fresh start, a new challenge.

5

Paradise lost

The tourist brochures suggest that Mauritius has much in common with paradise. White beaches, coral reefs and turquoise waters fringe the small island, which lies in the Indian Ocean about 800 kilometres east of Madagascar. At different times, it was claimed by the Dutch, the French and the English. It also became home to slaves brought from Africa and to indentured labourers from India. These days, the divisions of the past are glossed over in tourist brochures. They speak instead of the rich cultural heritage, and of how the fragrances of French, African, Indian and Chinese spices mingle deliciously in the sea breezes.

Mauritius has many historical links to another multicultural island nation, some tens of thousands of kilometres further to its east. These are well described by historian Edward Duyker in his book about the ties that bind Australia and Mauritius, *Of the Star and the Key*. Duyker is formerly the honorary consul for Mauritius in New South Wales and the eldest of eight children born in Melbourne to a Dutch father and a Mauritian mother. He tells in his book how British settlement of New South Wales and Tasmania was encouraged by France's hold on strategically positioned Mauritius.

Many early explorers used Mauritius as a base for exploring the coastline of Australia. Indeed, Matthew Flinders was on his way home from Port Jackson when he was seized and held captive for some years by the French authorities on Mauritius, which was then known as the 'Isle de France'. He was released just before the British took control of the island in 1810, when they changed its name back to the Dutch name of Mauritius. In following years, the ships from Mauritius brought sugar, convicts, and gold-prospectors to Australia. Among those who left Mauritius to make a home in Australia were two women whose sons later became famous: the artist Lloyd Rees and the singer 'Angry' Anderson. But for decades the racist immigration policies of 'White Australia' prevented many Mauritians from making such a journey.

The 1960s were uncomfortable times for those in Mauritius who feared that the end of colonial rule would lead to rule by the Indian majority. Newspapers reported on the inevitability of independence, as well as the exodus of Franco-Mauritians. In 1965, British troops were despatched to the island to quell rioting, which many locals worried was a harbinger of worse violence to come. Duyker reports that in 1967, the year when 56 per cent of Mauritians voted for independence, 1,330 Mauritians sailed for Australia – more than twice as many as in the previous year. In the months leading up to independence on 12 March 1968, further violence erupted. Many people died or were injured, and hundreds of homes and buildings were burnt to the ground. Another 2,038 Mauritians left for Australia that year.

Many on those ships bound for Australia carried with them a fierce pride in their French and Creole heritage, as well as a heavy grief. They had what Duyker would later call a 'refugee mentality'. They felt they were being forced to leave everything behind, their family and friends, in order to give their children a chance for the future.

Jean Eric Gassy was born in Mauritius on 11 May 1956. His formative years coincided with times of uncertainty for his family, who wondered whether their lives could continue as comfortably after independence. Eric was eleven when his parents, Xavier and Maud, joined the Australia-bound exodus. The young boy found it a wrench to leave behind his extended family. He had grown up speaking French at home, but having all school lessons in English. Arriving in

Australia, he met a version of English that was not familiar. Some months passed before he felt comfortable with the speed and accent with which Australians spoke.

Xavier worked as a meteorologist and Maud as a teacher. Life was busy, with one thing and another, not to mention three young children, Eric, Robert and Elizabeth. To outsiders, the Gassys seemed a happy lot. They discussed books, played games and enjoyed their family jokes. Xavier and Maud doted on their oldest son, and Eric was conscious of their expectations. There was no question but that he would succeed. The children of immigrants learn that they must pay for their parents' sacrifices. Fortunately for Eric, academic achievement came easily.

As the Gassys settled into building their new lives, making friendships with other émigrés and within their local Catholic church, the newspapers back home were full of stories of Mauritians making good in Australia. News spread quickly between the Mauritian networks in Melbourne and Sydney and their contacts in Mauritius. Those who had left so much behind wanted to be sure that their effort was justified; just as importantly they wanted it to be seen to be worthwhile. No doubt this holds some truth for immigrants generally, but perhaps even more so for Mauritians. As one expat has observed, Mauritians tend to be very status conscious because their post-colonial culture is so conservative and stratified. On a small island, where everyone knows everyone else's business, appearances are carefully maintained. The lighter shade your skin, the higher your status in Mauritius. 'They are more French than the French,' says Claudie Larose, a psychologist who left Mauritius as a young child and has researched the expat community in Australia. 'In Mauritius, if anything is wrong with you or your family, everybody knows about it.'

Media reports in both countries emphasised the lack of discrimination that Mauritians faced in Australia. But, growing up in Sydney's southern suburbs, a stronghold of WASP prejudices, Eric was conscious of his skin colour. He sometimes blamed it for his difficulties in making friends. At school, some students thought him Aboriginal. He was in year 11 at Sydney Technical High School when the former ALP leader Arthur Calwell insulted Mauritians by saying that they 'lived on the smell of an oily rag and bred like flies', and that he was opposed to a 'chocolate-coloured' Australia. Gassy also felt at a disadvantage in the one place where Australians did not discriminate on the basis of skin colour: the sports field. He had not found much joy in sport as a young boy because he suffered dreadfully from asthma, although this was much better controlled after the family's move.

At Sydney Technical High, a selective school which boasts the aviator Sir Charles Kingsford Smith among its alumni, Eric contributed to the school journal, joined the library group, and was known for his interest in music. At least one schoolmate thought him a bit of a loner and a nerd. But by the time he reached medical school at the University of Sydney, Eric had grown into a good-looking young man. Some fellow students thought he rather enjoyed having an exotic background. Some gained the impression he was French rather than Mauritian. He gave no appearance of struggling with his studies, attaining respectable passes and more than the occasional credit and distinction. But it was music that he loved. Some friends thought that if Eric had a choice, his vocation would have been music rather than medicine.

In 1979, his final year as a medical student, Eric was photographed for the Faculty of Medicine's senior year book. He stared straight at the camera, with the hint of a smile parting his lips and lighting his eyes. With his mop top of black curls, fresh face and dark eyes, he could almost have passed for a youthful member of the Jackson Five. At the time, he was based at the Royal North Shore Hospital in Sydney's affluent northern suburbs, a long journey from his family home in more than just the obvious sense. 'Despite having no visa, Eric, native of the southern St George region, daily sacrificed hours in travel to train at North Shore,' reads his year book entry.

As one of the many compensations, Eric has controlled the Student Quarters' table tennis table for the last three years using an exotic bat worth more than his stethoscope.

Over the last few years he has successfully graduated to tennis and has also taken a very active interest in music. Eric has always worked on the principle that what he wants he gets, and has shown real application over the past year by intermittently doing quite well academically (despite his hairstyle). Eric is respected and liked in the Faculty and should do very well in the future.

The prediction of future success came to be echoed by Eric's supervisors after he began training as a psychiatrist at Bankstown Hospital, in western Sydney, in 1983. He had been drawn to psychiatry while working in general medicine for two years at the prestigious teaching hospital in central Sydney, the Royal Prince Alfred. The senior psychiatrists who supervised Eric's training at Bankstown's inpatient unit, Banks House, thought him a competent, caring clinician. Each morning, registrars presented a patient's case to their colleagues for scrutiny of their management. Eric's comments were generally sensible and revealed a good understanding of both psychiatry and general medicine, his seniors felt. They also enjoyed his company socially. Eric was known as a fine cook and a convivial host, who took his enjoyment of good food quite seriously.

He also was serious about tennis, spending many hours on the staff courts, where competition was intense. Eric liked to win, more than one observer noted, and had a knack of spinning his serve so that it was very difficult to return. When the tennis was on the television, he could often be found in the patient lounge, glued to the screen. Eric was meticulous about applying sunscreen before hitting the courts, and a number of colleagues thought him sensitive about his skin colour, which was hardly darker than a tan. He gave one friend the impression that he was deeply offended when a policeman, writing him out a speeding ticket, assumed he was an Aborigine.

Eric was liked by many. One doctor who attended psychiatry lectures with him saw him as a gentle, sweet, unassuming guy. But he was also unpopular in some quarters at Bankstown. One colleague noticed that he seemed more than usually conscious of his place in the professional hierarchy, and keen to demarcate himself from anyone more junior. He was not known for generosity in swapping shifts to accommodate colleagues. Some of the women in the unit thought him sexist. They noticed that he paid more attention to nurses if they were good-looking.

Despite his shyness, Eric developed a reputation as a bit of a lad about town. He had a series of girlfriends, and was fussy about their appearances. He preferred young, thin women who appreciated the opportunity to go out with a handsome, charming doctor. He also chose his wardrobe carefully, and was known for preferring black and white clothes, which he thought flattering for his figure and colouring. He was slim, with a surprising tendency to worry about his weight, and friends sometimes teased him for being picky about his food. He was not slow to return meals at restaurants if they didn't meet his standards.

Some thought him a bit of a snob who placed great store on appearances, and assumed it was a relic of growing up in the privileged classes in Mauritius. But this assumption didn't fit with their impression of his parents. Colleagues who dined at the Gassy family home enjoyed the warmth, hospitality and delicious cooking. Xavier and Maud did not project any airs and graces, just an obvious pride in their eldest son.

If Eric was a touch vain and narcissistic, a tad sensitive to criticism, inclined to have his own way and also displayed some sense of personal entitlement, this was nothing out of the ordinary among young men with their sights set on a career as a medical specialist. He was much more easygoing and helpful than some of his colleagues, thought one of the psychologists working in the unit. If a patient needed to be seen urgently, you could count on Eric to help out.

His seniors found Eric less trouble than some other registrars and were confident that a bright future awaited. He would make a very competent psychiatrist, concluded one of his supervisors. Such confidence was reinforced when Eric passed the RANZCP exams at his first attempt, something that not all registrars achieve. He also achieved the distinction of having his dissertation, based on a review of the use of electroconvulsive therapy or ECT at Banks House, published in the college's journal. Not too many registrars can make such a boast.

After gaining his letters, Eric continued to work part time at the hospital for a few years, and also set up a private practice. When he learnt that a staff specialist job was available at St George Hospital, closer to his old stamping ground in the southern suburbs, it seemed a good opportunity. Pacific House, the psychiatric unit at St George, was known to be run-down, but he was told of plans for a large new facility. Eric's expectations of the new job were soon disappointed, however. It was so different from what he had enjoyed at Banks House, where he had been supported by helpful senior consultants and a pleasant, collegial working environment.

Pacific House, named in the days of unobscured views to the ocean, was an old, three-storey building entirely unsuited to the job asked of it. The ward was on the top floor, the dining room was in the basement, and there were no lifts. It was not safe or secure for patients or staff, which made it difficult to provide good care. Patients requiring involuntary admission were transferred to the old-style psychiatric facilities at Rozelle Hospital, a solid 30-minute drive away. Talk of a new building had been around for a decade, but had not shown any signs of being translated into action.

Psychiatry did not have a high profile in the hospital hierarchy, and rumours circulated frequently about plans to close the unit or move it offsite. Mental health funds were at times diverted into other services. Six months after Gassy's arrival, the psychiatrist who had been in charge of the unit for many years left in an unhappy parting of the ways. Gassy found himself reluctantly drawn into political and budgetary battles over the unit's future. He also had to shoulder greater responsibility for the daily crises that are part and parcel of the management of disturbed patients and stressed staff. Morale was poor and the unit had difficulty attracting staff. Positions often went unfilled for long periods. There were longstanding concerns about the unit's suitability for training psychiatric registrars due to the lack of appropriate supervision, and the RANZCP threatened to withdraw accreditation for the registrars' positions. This was a slap in the face for the hospital, a warning to its senior management that all was not well with Pacific House. A service that is poorly managed and provides poor supervision to junior staff is unlikely to be providing good patient care.

The upper echelons of the New South Wales Health Department raised their concerns about Pacific House in a letter to John

Campbell, the CEO of the Southern Sydney Area Health Service (SSAHS), after reviewing the facilities in 1992. The letter, signed by psychiatrist Noel Wilton on behalf of the director general, called for a comprehensive plan for psychiatric services at St George: 'The current situation is destabilising and demoralising for staff, and totally unsatisfactory.'

Where uncertainty and insecurity flourish, so too do conflict and division. It was difficult, ran the joke among some at the hospital, to tell the staff from the patients at Pacific House. When a senior nurse left under a cloud, some were not surprised when a machete and rifle ammunition were found in his filing cabinet.

After Gassy became acting director of the unit in early 1992, relations with some of the male nurses deteriorated noticeably. They felt Gassy was retreating from his responsibilities into his office and dubbed him the 'invisible man'. They were irritated that Gassy had time for his private patients with eating disorders but that they couldn't get him to come upstairs to see seriously ill patients on the ward. They were irate when Gassy responded to their requests for help, when having difficulty controlling patients on the ward, by sending secretarial staff up the stairs to say he was not available. They felt he was uncomfortable discussing clinical care issues with nurses; he believed, it seemed to them, that doctors should lay down the law without it being questioned. There were mutterings that he was lazy and disengaged. One nursing manager became so concerned about Gassy's clinical practices that he rang to report incidents to a senior psychiatrist in the New South Wales Health Department. This nurse ended up so stressed by the job that he required counselling, which he would later half-jokingly describe as 'debriefing from the visit to hell'.

When some senior nurses produced a document arguing for them to have a greater role in patient management, Gassy saw this as an attempted takeover by militants. They were taking advantage of the diminished number of psychiatrists, he thought. It seemed as if the nurses were hostile in challenging everything he did – whether diagnoses, medication, or decisions about admission or discharge of patients. He felt the nurses' anger with him was affecting patient care, in particular that it was being displaced onto patients under his care and affecting their progress. Gassy took his concerns about the nurses to his boss, the manager of the hospital division which included psychiatry. Maureen Gleeson, a Sister of Mercy nun who had worked as a nurse many years ago, had a reputation as a tough manager. But she had a soft spot for Gassy. They had shared many long conversations, and he had confided some of his family background and childhood difficulties. She knew that he took his sister to stylish restaurants, and thought that generous. She also thought him sensitive, courteous and gentle with his patients.

Gleeson asked for the nurses to withdraw and rewrite the document, describing it as unnecessarily arrogant and provocative. She arranged for a mediator in an effort to resolve some of the conflict on the unit. Psychiatrists willing to work in the public sector are valued like gold, and Gleeson didn't want to lose those she had. But she did worry that Gassy appeared out of his depth. He applied a number of times for the director's job, and was offended when it was not forthcoming.

The conflict in the unit was not only over clinical issues. Gassy's attitudes to women rankled many. He told one colleague of sitting on a selection panel and making his choice of a job applicant based on the length of her short skirt. He was known for bailing up young trainee nurses and allied health workers when they were on their own, and asking them out. Some were flattered and happy to oblige. Others felt uncomfortable and intimidated, and complained to their superiors. When an unofficial report of such behaviour reached one of the hospital's senior executives, she pulled Gassy aside quietly to tell him to put a lid on it. At the time, she didn't take the matter too seriously. She was rather susceptible to his attractive mop of dark curls herself, and thought he was just being a bit of a lad.

But Gassy went too far for a drug company sales representative who visited the hospital regularly. Familiar with the workings of psychiatric units, the saleswoman thought Gassy was lacking in clinical acumen. It was also clear to her that he was not providing the leadership which the unit desperately needed. And she thought him a sleaze. When she made appointments to update Gassy on her company's products, he closed the door behind her and steered talk to private matters or suggested moving to a cafe for a chat. He told her that he preferred thin women, and liked to weigh his girlfriends. Once he rang her at work, asking to see her socially. When she replied that she was happily married, he persisted and suggested lunch. Arriving for her next meeting with Gassy, she was shocked when he said they had to leave immediately as he had booked a launch to take them out on Sydney Harbour. He was displeased when she adamantly refused the invitation. A willowy blonde, the saleswoman was used to doctors' advances. But they had never been so blatant before. And Gassy's stroppiness in the face of rejection was unusual. He was extremely cold when she saw him next.

Others in the hospital also heard the gossip that Gassy had expensive scales for weighing his girlfriend, a thin, pale occupational therapist who was quite a bit younger than him. They lived together for a few years in the early 1990s. Towards the end of the relationship, she became concerned about some of his behaviour. When he mentioned that he would like to get a gun for self-defence, she thought it a strange thing to say.

Gassy had a habit of playing favourites. He ignored those staff members he didn't like. To others, he could be charming, kind, gentle and helpful. One of the unit's female registrars would for years after be grateful to Gassy for the support and teaching he provided. Another in Gassy's circle thought him an extremely sensitive, fragile creature. He told her of his resentment towards his father over the pressure to succeed and do medicine, and his creativity and love of music. She felt he had never been allowed to be himself.

Naomi Sommers, a friendly, attractive young woman with long, dark hair and smiling brown eyes, was one of Gassy's closest allies in the unit. She was in her early twenties when she started working there in late 1991 as a clerical assistant. A sociable type, she often organised drinks or other social events for her colleagues. She and Gassy often met over coffee or lunch. She was sympathetic, and felt some of the other staff were being nasty to him. Gassy tended to steer their conversation towards what she had been doing rather than divulging much about himself. She was surprised how little she learnt about him over the years. She knew that he liked slim women, that he didn't think he was any good with male patients because he did not feel empathy for them, and that he played guitar. She didn't know much about his relationship with his girlfriend but had the impression he was not particularly distressed when it ended.

Naomi thought Gassy socially inept, and felt comfortable chiding him when his behaviour was inappropriate. She let him know that she was embarrassed when he arrived at work with chocolates from David Jones for her but not the other administrative staff. She always knew when she had upset him. He sulked if she went home without first saying goodbye to him, or if he felt she was paying too much attention to someone else. She knew of the rumours that she and Gassy were having an affair.

Xavier and Maud regularly dropped into Pacific House for coffee, or to deliver mail or treats for Eric. It was clear to everyone that they adored him. Eric's siblings, Robert and Elizabeth, also dropped by occasionally. Eric seemed to idolise his younger brother, seeing him as hip, trendy and confident. The Gassy clan were out in handsome force when Eric held a housewarming party in his flat in Rose Bay, to which select colleagues were invited. He and his brother Robert played in a band, which entertained the gathering with a selection of middle-of-the-road songs. Some guests thought that Robert and Elizabeth seemed so much more confident and vivacious than their older brother. One colleague thought Gassy looked strangely uncomfortable behind his guitar, and assumed that the attitude seen as arrogance by many workmates was in fact shyness.

Towards the end of 1992, Gassy asked Naomi to take over all his correspondence. He didn't trust Robyn, an older woman who was the office supervisor. He thought she was conspiring against him with some of the nurses. Relations were also tense between Gassy and another member of the office staff. Robyn and her colleague felt Gassy treated them like servants, and that he had no time for any woman over a certain age. Eventually, Robyn wrote to hospital management saying she was resigning because of Gassy. He was furious when he learnt of this, and sought legal advice. The letter was withdrawn. Unbeknown to hospital management, the departures of two other staff members – a psychologist and a psychiatrist working part time at the hospital as a visiting medical officer – were at least partly due to altercations with Gassy.

Concerns about Gassy began to percolate beyond Pacific House. A human resources manager was alarmed by his behaviour on an interview panel. When it became clear that he would not get his way, he slumped in his chair and disengaged entirely from the process. Another manager, observing Gassy in various situations, came to the conclusion that he suffered the spoilt child syndrome. A local private psychiatrist thought Gassy a rather odd, vague character and unsuited to the acting director position. He wondered if Gassy was using marijuana.

When a new manager started at the hospital, she was disturbed by her first meeting with Gassy. She had come to introduce herself, and was taken aback when he asked, in a challenging way: 'Are you here to sack me?' She thought him suspicious and introverted, and made further inquiries. The general response was given with a shrug of the shoulders: he's had a difficult time, and you know how hard psychiatrists are to come by.

The steady passage of thin, young, vulnerable women into Gassy's office provoked widespread scuttlebutt. Some colleagues speculated that Gassy's interest in eating disorders was vicarious. He seemed unusually concerned about his own weight, which tended to fluctuate, and told one colleague of taking diet pills.

Psychiatrists are notoriously vulnerable to the violation of professional boundaries, and it was inevitable that sexual innuendo would rear its head. Gassy was extremely sensitive to these rumours, perhaps because he felt guilty about incidents in the past. He also knew his vulnerability – he had replied honestly when one of his St George patients had asked if he found her attractive. Yes, he told her.

6

A change agent

It is comforting to think that there is a health system to look after us. It is also a delusion of sorts. A system implies something orderly, well coordinated and efficient, which is united in a common goal or purpose, like caring for our health. Health services, on the other hand, are often fragmented, poorly coordinated and wasteful. They are as likely to be working in competition or opposition to each other as to be working together in the best interests of individual patients or the broader community.

It is far more helpful to view the health sector as a series of warring tribes and fiefdoms which fight for status, for power and, above all, for resources. It's what happens when the kitty isn't big enough to go around. In health, Paul never gets paid without Peter being robbed. For every winner in the perennial battles for funding and influence, there are also losers. The winners and losers in health reflect the winners and losers in society generally. The well-to-do tend to have better health and better access to better health care, and those who struggle at society's edges – those with the greatest health needs – have the poorest access.

In late 1993, when Margaret moved to Sydney as director of mental health for St George Hospital and the Southern Sydney Area

Health Service, she was taking over a service with a well-established reputation as a loser. St George had long struggled as the poor country cousin in the shadow of the more powerful teaching hospitals in central and eastern Sydney. It was, the New South Wales Health Minister had declared five years earlier when sacking its board of management, 'the worst teaching hospital in the state'. After years of neglect and underfunding, St George was in the midst of a major upgrade when Margaret arrived. New wards, cancer services and operating theatres were being built as part of a major redevelopment. But mental health services had little profile or clout within the St George hierarchy, and remained in the same dilapidated state as ever. They barely even rated a mention in a history of the hospital being written at the time.

This situation was not peculiar to St George. Those reformers who had so idealistically promoted mainstreaming – making mental health part of the general health sector – had underestimated the difficulties involved. It was not only the mental health empires which were resistant to the change; the mainstream was also difficult to budge – it was not used to seeing mental health as its responsibility. Those with mental illness were often seen as the difficult and despised – the 'heartsink' patients (a term coined to describe those patients who make doctors' hearts sink when they walk through the surgery door) whom nobody wanted. Nor was the mainstream properly equipped with skills or resources for the task. Emergency departments, for example, had been designed to treat the physically sick and injured, not the psychotic and suicidal. Mainstreaming also meant that mental health had to compete against general health services for dollars and influence. Faced with perennial newspaper headlines about surgical waiting lists and emergency department horror stories, hospital executives were unlikely to throw their hard-won dollars over the prominent heads of surgical and medical leaders to a psychiatric service struggling at the back of the queue. As well, public hospital mental health units often lacked strong professional leaders and advocates because of the flight of psychiatrists to the private sector.

When Margaret arrived in Sydney, it was clear just how far New South Wales had lagged behind Victoria in balancing the equation of deinstitutionalisation to ensure that when institutions were closed, funds followed patients into the community. In New South Wales, successive governments had seen deinstitutionalisation as an opportunity to flog off prime real estate to boost Treasury coffers. Nor had New South Wales found the resolve to end the era of stand-alone institutions – many would remain in operation years after Victoria closed that chapter.

Margaret's reputation arrived ahead of her, generating both anticipation and apprehension. The whispers went around: she had closed down hospitals in Victoria; she was going to shake the place up; she was the agent of economic rationalism. Mary Pryor, whose tailored dress and manner gave the impression of unflappable efficiency, had been working at the hospital for a few years as a secretary. She heard the rumours about Margaret, and thought it advisable to make some inquiries about her new boss before she arrived. She rang Lesley Hopkins in Ballarat. 'What do I need to know?' she asked. 'You will have your work cut out,' was the reply. 'She is a perfectionist, a workaholic, a great person.' In time, Mary also realised a few other things; her fearfully efficient new boss could also be a nervous flier and was absolutely hopeless with directions. Mary routinely packed Margaret off to meetings with a carefully highlighted street map to give directions. Still, the phone call would come from Margaret in her car, asking, how do I get out of here?

Margaret's presence was quickly felt. She made it clear to staff that she was not particularly interested in listening to the grievances of the past. She wanted to move forward, she had plenty of plans and buckets of energy, and little time for those who were unable or unwilling to join the ride. She was direct in telling people what she thought of them, and could be scathing if she felt they were not up to scratch or that patient care was being compromised. Shape up or ship out was the message that staff received, loud and clear. Many left. But many also arrived. Margaret worked hard to attract the fresh talent and funds needed to drive the changes she wanted. She fought for money to build a new inpatient unit, which had been an empty promise for so many years. She drove the integration of inpatient and community mental health services which historically had been separately managed and often in conflict. She set about developing consistent standards and approaches to patient care, and developing greater scrutiny and accountability of services. She had high expectations and challenged staff practices and attitudes. She wanted psychiatrists to do more than simply see patients; they were to become involved in shaping services and in providing supervision and support to other staff. It was no longer enough to be a competent clinician; they also had to influence the systems in which they worked. Registrars who complained of their demanding work conditions were famously admonished not to be 'shrinking violets'. In response, they wore hats decorated with violets to their next Christmas party. Margaret put mental health on the agenda of the hospital's powerbrokers. Successive hospital CEOs came to know that if Margaret brought a problem to their office, she also arrived with a solution and good humour. At meetings of the hospital executive, one colleague learnt to recognise when Margaret was about to set sail. She would adjust her brooch or scarf, move forward in her seat, lower her voice, and launch forth: 'Now that you have fixed the economics and the politics,' she often said, 'what about the patients?'

Inevitably, noses were put out of joint and toes were trampled. Whenever Margaret won new funds or staff for her services, it was someone else's loss. She could be impatient and blunt, and did not shy away from a difficult decision or an argument. She was always ready to argue the unpopular view forcefully and clearly. It seemed to some that you were judged as either being on her side or against her. Change pushes people beyond their comfort zone and Margaret's pace was overwhelming for some. It was like being caught up by a tidal wave, one colleague reflected – exhilarating if you could ride with it and devastating if you couldn't.

Margaret was also an outsider to New South Wales and to the invisible networks and alliances which transmit information and influence. She was used to Victoria which had a solid recent history of mental health reform. Its Premier Jeff Kennett, a radical Liberal, was steamrolling through a far-reaching restructuring of mental health, unworried by the resistance of unions or anyone else. New South Wales had been far more tentative about taking on the vested interests. In New South Wales, the rhetoric was all about the need to redistribute resources, from the traditional power bases of medicine close to the city and out to the growing population centres of western and southern Sydney. The reality was different – much of the focus of the New South Wales health bureaucracy, Margaret learnt, was on keeping health out of the headlines and avoiding public controversy at all costs. This was only reinforced by the 1995 election of Premier Bob Carr, a former journalist and master of media management who ran a conservative Labor Government. Margaret was creating waves with her persistence in pointing out that mental health services in southern Sydney received far less funding, per head of population, than neighbouring services in central and eastern Sydney. To get the changes she wanted meant challenging powerful professional interests in central and eastern Sydney which were well connected to the New South Wales Government. She wanted to take funds from the Prince Henry and Prince of Wales hospitals, in the Premier's electorate, and from the service in central Sydney run by Marie Bashir, who went on to become Governor of New South Wales. In the words of one observer, she was trying to take the toys from the biggest kids in the sandpit. Also in her sights was St Vincent's Hospital, run by the Sisters of Charity. Picking a fight with the nuns was bound to end in tears.

Margaret's long working hours were famous, but she made time to support and mentor those colleagues in whom she saw potential. She was not a motherly or empathetic figure. Not many people thought of approaching her with personal problems. But she was a nurturer of talent. She encouraged and pushed her protégés. At Christmas and other times, she dispensed quirky gifts and cards, carefully chosen for the individual recipient. Many of those who crossed her path came to look back on it as an important turning point in their lives and careers. Many remained working in public sector mental health services who otherwise might have opted for an easier life elsewhere. This was a boon for Margaret; after lobbing the grenade of change, she relied on loyal lieutenants to help mop up in her wake.

Margaret also offered formal supervision in management to many colleagues, meeting regularly with them, not to tell them how to run their services but to challenge their thinking and habits. You will get more value out of me, she told them, if you tell me about your perceptions of the system where you are working, your skills and deficiencies in managing the system, and your strategies for getting the outcomes you want. She advised them to draw a 'family tree' of their organisation to help identify who they needed to influence to achieve their desired results. She advised never staying more than five years in one position, and suggested when they were ready to move on to bigger, more demanding jobs. When one young psychiatrist manager first began supervision with Margaret, he found it frustrating because she was not doling out advice. He realised it was up to him to work out what he should learn from his mistakes. Many times, Margaret cautioned him that going into management meant his medical colleagues would desert him and see him as a traitor who had gone to the dark side. She also warned him that he would find doctors the most difficult professional group to manage. They don't like being told what to do, she said, it is an attitude instilled in them from their earliest days at medical school. Margaret was also the force behind regular meetings of a peer review group for managers of mental health services. At these meetings, she could be stimulating, challenging and dominating. But never boring.

On Margaret's office wall were photographs of loyal Bodie, as well as a series of framed black-and-white photographs of sculpted nudes. She also looked up at large framed colour photographs of her beautiful gardens in Ballarat; one for each season. When she moved to Sydney, Don stayed at Ballarat for the next few years, tending his plants. He wanted to see how the Sydney job panned out before uprooting. But he regularly came to visit, and to stock up Margaret's fridge, bake gluten-free bread, and organise her flat near the hospital. Margaret also made the long trip to Ballarat many weekends. Her father Joseph was diagnosed with bowel cancer about the time she moved to Sydney and died during her first year in New South Wales. She visited Jean often, and spent hours on the phone counselling her.

Margaret's unconventional domestic arrangements aroused much speculation. Some hospital gossips held that she was a lesbian with a marriage of convenience. Close colleagues knew better. They saw just how much Margaret enjoyed her reunions with Don. He made sure she was rested, nurtured and fit for another week's battle. She returned to work on Monday mornings describing weekends of bed, champagne and baths, and giving the impression of a woman who revelled in her sexuality. Indeed, she was frank in discussing her sex life with her mother. Jean knew that her daughter was well loved. With Don in Ballarat, Margaret was free to devote long hours to work during the week. But he kept tabs on her by phone. If she was still at work at 10 pm, he rang with instructions that it was time to knock the day on the head. 'I will ring you at home in ten minutes,' he told her.

Life in Sydney, the self-centred capital of Australian materialism and consumerism, was not all work. It was a shopper's paradise, and Margaret was like a kid let loose in the proverbial lolly shop. 'What do you think of this?' she asked a colleague one day with a twinkle in her eyes as she sashayed her new suit around the room. 'It's my first Armani.' In her early years in Sydney, Margaret's partner on shopping expeditions was Beth Kotze, a child psychiatrist. They had connected at a psychiatry meeting and quickly discovered much in common, in addition to a shared interest in health management and a sense of not quite fitting in with the conservative medical culture. They both loved crime novels, escapist movies and Saturdays devoted to exercising the plastic. They spent a fortune on the fashion hunt from Mosman to Double Bay, and also tracked down bargains at the cheaper end of town. Margaret's wardrobe began to evolve. She continued to favour conservative styles but the colours became brighter, more outrageous. Always she matched her outfits with scarves, brooches and other accessories. Margaret sought the advice of a colours consultant on more than one occasion, learning what colours suited her. She was not backwards about sharing what she learnt. That colour is all wrong for you, was the unsolicited advice given to many.

After a particularly gruelling period at work, Margaret took Mary Pryor and a few others on a shopping expedition to the Queen Victoria Building in the city, choosing outfits for them to parade in. They felt under some pressure to spend up. Margaret was meticulous about her clothes, arranging them neatly and methodically in her wardrobe. She once told Beth Kotze of spending an entire evening moving all the buttons on every shirt sleeve so they better fitted her small wrists.

Margaret also shared a passion for retail therapy and murder mysteries with Reta Creegan, a fellow executive at the SSAHS with the tough exterior common to many nurses who move up the management ladder. Reta's first impression of Margaret, when collecting her from the airport for the job interview, was of a woman 'who spends a quid'. Reta approved. She thought women in senior management positions should dress appropriately. Reta, who went on to become a New South Wales Telstra Businesswoman of the Year, was a straight shooter with a voice to suit a smoky jazz club, and her growl had left many an adversary weak at the knees. She and Margaret had their share of disagreements at work but grew into firm friends and allies. Margaret often dropped round to Reta's cute little terrace home to share a Thai takeaway, a bottle of red, and tactics for managing difficult situations and personalities at work. Another of Margaret's social rituals was Saturday afternoon at the opera with Lesley Barclay, a professor of midwifery who started at St George not long before her. They had a season ticket and went to Saturday matinees, after discovering they were too exhausted to stay awake on Friday nights. After the show, they ate at one of the restaurants overlooking Circular Quay as the sun came down on the water, delighting in the opportunity to try new and exotic dishes. If Don was in town, he sometimes joined them. Don and Margaret's closeness was obvious to Lesley. She thought that having a base where Margaret was uncritically adored and accepted gave her courage and strength for her difficult job.

The ritual of weekend reunions continued even after Don moved to New South Wales, setting up house at Shellharbour, a small working-class town on the coast about 90 minutes' drive south of Sydney and an easy train ride away. They found the town almost by accident one day, and then realised they could have a house there with sea views for a reasonable price. Don didn't want to move into Margaret's unit in Sydney because he needed a garden and a workshop to occupy his energies. Also he couldn't see the point of living in Sydney, when Margaret was away travelling so much.

On weekends at Shellharbour they went for long walks along the beach, or scrambled up and down rough bush tracks in the nearby escarpment. Some Friday nights Don tucked Margaret into bed with a hot-water bottle and left her to rest. She re-emerged at lunchtime the next day, fresh and ready to go again.

When Margaret was having a particularly difficult week, Don caught the train to Sydney and stocked her pantry. He often checked in with Mary Pryor about how things were running. 'Is she giving you a hard time?' he'd joke. 'I keep telling her to back off. I don't know how you put up with her sometimes.' Margaret loved to take staff for coffee, lunches and gossips, but Don knew that she also drove them hard. Sometimes Mary felt that no matter how productively they worked, the bar was always being raised. At times, she watched Margaret drive herself into the ground. Mary could always tell when Margaret was sleep-deprived – she needed a solid eight hours – or overdue for the regular vitamin B injection which helped manage the effects of coeliac disease. She'd become irritable, and staff would tiptoe around on eggshells. 'Oh, all right,' was Margaret's grumbling reply when Mary suggested it must be time for her shots. Not many people were allowed to see Margaret's vulnerability. Leaders could not afford to show weakness, she believed. Some thought that the immaculate, brightly coloured power suits were part of her armour for battle.

Don knew that Margaret was not nearly so tough as many thought. Any spider or beetle which found its way into their house was safe. Margaret would carefully ferry it back outside. She had a soft spot for animals and for people who couldn't help themselves, Don thought to himself.

Margaret had not been at St George long when she became aware of the cloud hovering around Eric Gassy. Some nurses had raised their concerns soon after her arrival. They felt she had seen the problem as an annoying professional turf issue, and thought her reluctant to take it any further.

However, Margaret's antennae were on alert. Hostilities between medical and nursing staff were not unusual, but this seemed different.

Nor was it at all unusual for doctors to strenuously resist change or to be suspicious and resentful of new managers, seeing them as threats. But Gassy clearly had other issues; there was something more behind his unhappiness with the changes she was making. Margaret observed his interactions with others and she listened to the talk that was going around. But she did not add to it herself. She kept her own thoughts and concerns close to her chest, although she made some discreet inquiries around town of colleagues who knew something of Gassy's history.

Margaret often discussed the frustrations and difficulties of her job with John Campbell, her CEO at the Southern Sydney Area Health Service, a former military man who had masterminded her recruitment from Victoria. Campbell saw Margaret as a kindred spirit, someone with a sense of adventure who didn't mind tilting at windmills, and who shared his view that patients' needs had been somewhat peripheral in the operation of health services. He liked Margaret's enthusiasm and her bluntness. You want to hear the story as it is, not dressed up, he thought. She also gave him advance notice when she was about to pick a fight. She thought it through, didn't just fly off the handle. But in all the times that Margaret dropped by Campbell's office for a chat, she didn't mention any concerns about Gassy.

Margaret frequently talked to Don about work; he knew who was giving her grief and who were her allies. But Don heard no word of Gassy; he didn't know that Margaret had determined she needed to take action about her troubled and troubling colleague. The catalyst was Gassy's decision to take prolonged sick leave in mid 1994, citing 'burnout'. A psychiatric colleague named Dr Ali had provided a sick certificate.

On 13 July 1994, Margaret wrote a short formal note to the Medical Board of New South Wales. 'As I mentioned in my telephone conversation,' she began, 'I am writing to express my concern that a staff member of my division Dr Eric Gassy has had a prolonged period of sick leave commencing 30th May 1994 and is not anticipating being back at work before 11th September 1994. In view of the fact that psychiatric reasons are cited for the certificate I would like to be assured that Dr Gassy will be fit to resume [a] full range of psychiatric duties when he returns to work in September. If the medical board can become involved to the point of providing independent assessment and/or specifying the range of duties – I would be most grateful. Dr Gassy has provided certificates from Dr Ali. Dr Gassy says he is not receiving treatment from Dr Ali – but Dr Ali assures me he is treating Dr Gassy. Thank you for your advice on this matter.'

Margaret went to some lengths to protect Gassy's confidentiality. Even Mary Pryor did not know the details as Margaret handled all the correspondence about Gassy to the Medical Board herself.

In April 1995, Margaret's offsider, Greg Aldridge, drove her to a Medical Board hearing about Eric Gassy. Aldridge was close to Margaret and they enjoyed many a gossip and laugh together. He had known Gassy for years and was itching to know what was going on, but on this occasion Margaret would not be drawn. She told very few colleagues about her dealings with Gassy. Perhaps she was simply exercising strict professional discretion.

Or perhaps there was just so much else to think about. Gassy was one blip on Margaret's crowded radar. Did she realise that Gassy's situation was exactly the opposite? He could think of little else other than the new director; thoughts of her and questions about her dominated his days and nights.

'What a bunch of bloody wankers,' Margaret muttered under her breath. 'What a load of crap.' She was attending a meeting of Sydney psychiatrists where various speakers were bemoaning their woeful lot. Nothing annoyed Margaret more than psychiatrists presenting as victims. They should be providing leadership and helping to reform and guide services rather than whingeing about what a hard life they had, she believed. The system could not afford for the psychiatrist to be merely a well-liked member of the team, she argued. Her mutterings caught the ear, at different meetings, of several young psychiatrists who became drawn to her vision and passion for public psychiatry. The noise and action that Margaret was generating in southern Sydney – which had never been a mecca for mental health before – began to draw attention. Margaret was developing a coterie of like-minded enthusiasts for change. They were psychologists, psychiatrists, nurses, policy experts and researchers.

Prominent in the group were Andrew Wilson and Matthew Cullen, two fit, forceful and ambitious young entrepreneurs who had become friends while training in psychiatry in the eastern suburbs. Cullen and Wilson had thought hard about how health services could be better delivered and managed, and were setting up a health call centre business, High Performance Health Care (later taken over by the multinational group McKesson), when they went to work for Margaret. They joked about being refugees from the Prince of Wales system, which they saw as old-fashioned and resistant to change. The east, on the other hand, saw them as defectors who had sold out to the enemy. Wilson and Cullen liked Margaret's energy and directness. She challenged them to think about how health systems work, and how to achieve change, and to improve quality of care. Margaret was not a micromanager; so long as they were heading in the right direction, they enjoyed great freedom to develop their ideas. It was Andrew Wilson who suggested Margaret get in touch with his friend Ian Hickie, a brilliant psychiatrist then on a Harkness Fellowship to the United States.

Hickie was a protégé of Gordon Parker, an iconic figure in Australian psychiatry. Professor of Psychiatry at the Prince of Wales Hospital, Parker was also well known, among other things, as a poker enthusiast and for writing for the *Oz* magazine and the popular television series, *The Mavis Bramston Show*, in the 1960s. Margaret had been told, even before arriving in Sydney, that Parker and his eastern empire would be one of the major obstacles on her road to change. A renowned academic held in high regard by many, including himself, Parker could be charming, witty and erudite. He could also be arrogant, intimidating and intolerant of lesser mortals, and was variously regarded with fear, loathing, admiration and respect. Parker and Tobin were well-matched adversaries, some thought. To Margaret and her cohorts, however, Parker exemplified the traditional approach to psychiatry. He ran a centre-of-excellence, hospital-based empire which was focused on specialist research and professional interests. It was the antithesis of her managerial approach to providing services based on the population's needs, with a strong emphasis on community services rather than institutions. Parker, it seemed to observers, saw Margaret as an annoying, meddling bureaucrat, and a woman of no academic standing. Worse, she was no longer even a clinician. She had stopped seeing patients in order to devote herself to management and administration. Margaret challenged not only Parker's authority and way of working, but also his influence and resources. Their battles fed legends, and Margaret spent long hours discussing tactics and strategy with her troops. She never went to a meeting without doing as much research and preparation as possible. She was anxious to succeed.

Hickie, whose research interests ranged from neurobiology to community education, was Parker's golden-haired boy. Hickie was destined for great things, Parker told various colleagues in the days before the younger man began to stretch his wings. By the time of his Harkness Fellowship, Hickie knew that he would not be made in the likeness of his mentor. He was ready to broaden his horizons, move in new directions. In the US, he met academics who encouraged him to think beyond the traditional academic currency that measures merit in academic publications, and to consider how he could contribute to public debate and policy.

Margaret impressed Hickie from their first meeting, when she talked about wanting to implement the National Mental Health Strategy, which was pushing a major overhaul of how services were delivered. Hickie thought that, unlike many he had encountered, she seemed to want more than just to talk about change, she was going to do it. Parker was horrified when he heard of Hickie's plan to transfer from Prince Henry Hospital to St George Hospital, and tried to block the move. Margaret won that battle. For those in the Parker camp, Hickie's move was seen as a low act of treachery. Relations between Parker and Hickie never recovered, and several years later their professional and personal falling out would hit the front pages of the *Sydney Morning Herald* under a headline about 'duelling professors'.

Margaret was upfront with Hickie about what she expected. She would be the boss and run the service but wanted to learn from him about research. 'I don't want you to be one of those bullshit academic appointments,' she said. Part of the deal was that as well as academic work, he would do regular clinical sessions at Peakhurst Community Health Centre, a struggling service in a disadvantaged area. Margaret was tickled that she had this bigwig academic, just back from a prestigious international gig, working out in the backblocks. 'I don't know very many people of his status and calibre who would do that,' she later reflected. 'Others might have tried to find excuses, but Ian made a commitment to me that he would do this and he did it. That says something about him, that he is really willing to demonstrate his concern for how mental health services are delivered.'

In many ways, Margaret and Hickie were an unlikely pairing. She was the working-class girl made good, a hard-nosed administrator with an MBA. He was the cerebral researcher born into privilege and a prominent medical family. But they both hailed from big Catholic families, and were unafraid of boisterous discussion. Hickie explained the influence of their backgrounds like this: 'Traditional English discourse is everyone telling their personal stories in turn whereas the Irish Catholic thing is everyone yelling at each other at the same time, filling in each others' sentences and having one shared narrative.' He and Margaret were high-energy enthusiasts with similar values. One of the reasons Hickie chose psychiatry as his specialty was because he thought psychiatrists were interesting people with a broad perspective on life and social issues. They seemed less preoccupied with the materialistic concerns that seemed to occupy other doctors, what Hickie liked to call the Australian Medical Association-related issues.

Hickie thought that he and Margaret also shared a history of having been too serious too young. Many of Margaret's colleagues were stunned to discover that she did not make her first overseas trip until her forties were well under way. A strong professional partnership and friendship quickly developed between Margaret and her new recruit. Hickie's family became used to Margaret turning up for dinner with a bottle of red in hand. His kids groaned when she arrived. Margaret did not pretend an interest in children, and her arrival meant their father would be locked in boring work talk all night. There was no distinction between Margaret's social and work personas, Hickie once joked. Socially, she still talked about work.

Margaret would later reflect that meeting Hickie was a pivotal point of her life, helping her to develop new skills and confidence in research and evaluation. 'He really changed my life,' she told a journalist preparing a magazine profile of Hickie. Told that Hickie had described her as one of his mentors, she replied that he likewise was one of her mentors. She said this in 2001, after Hickie had shot to prominence as the founding CEO of beyondblue, the national initiative led by Jeff Kennett to combat depression. Many rivalries and territorial disputes lurked behind New South Wales's refusal to sign up to beyondblue. Instead it funded the Black Dog Institute, run by Gordon Parker. For some observers, the tussle between the black dog and blue heeler was symbolic of the estrangement of the powerful father and the prodigal son.

In all her many discussions with Hickie, Margaret raised the difficulties with Gassy only once or twice. On top of everything else she had to deal with after her arrival in Sydney, there was this problem, she said. She was critical that action had not been taken earlier. It was typical of psychiatry not to have dealt with a hard issue, she complained.

Not long after Hickie started at St George as Director of Academic Psychiatry in early 1995, a bombshell was dropped. The Southern and Eastern Sydney Area Health Services would merge. Some saw it as a New South Wales Health Department strategy for ensuring the transfer of resources from the Prince of Wales, Prince Henry and St Vincent's hospitals in the east to St George and Sutherland hospitals in the south. Others thought it a tactic to shut up the whingers in the south. They could no longer complain to head office that they were underfunded but would have to fight their battles internally. The merger was an enforced, miserable marriage of warring, self-righteous regimes and clashing cultures. 'It was like trying to combine the Jewish Synagogue and the Roman Catholic Church,' thought one senior player. The east, traumatised by the closure of Prince Henry

Hospital, already felt under siege. They might be better off than the south, but still they felt poorly done by. Years of cutbacks had taken a toll on morale and services. New South Wales's spending on mental health was so low they felt it was unfair to argue that they were well funded just because they were better funded than others in New South Wales. Many in the east looked back with nostalgia on the good old days when professional life was more comfortable and less challenged – even if the wards were a disgrace. They looked down on the southern services with some disdain as backwards and parochial, while the south bad-mouthed the east as elitists who just wanted to protect their turf and bread and butter. The more the southern services were developed, the fewer patients from the south would be referred to doctors and services in the east. Nor was the eastern front united – the professorial top dogs at St Vincent's and Prince of Wales – Gavin Andrews and Gordon Parker – were antagonists of long standing. As one observer put it, the south-eastern sector was carved into four feudal fiefdoms based around hospital empires rather than a sensible analysis of what might best serve the communities of south-eastern Sydney. This applied to the area's health services in general, and to mental health in particular.

Margaret was delighted to win the job of director of mental health for the new service. Some others saw it as a poisoned chalice, but she was excited by the challenge. Her stage was expanded. She planned to create an integrated area-wide service where efficiencies could be gained from cooperation rather than the Balkanised model of four competing services. It's not rocket science, she was fond of saying. She prepared briefing papers for the new area board arguing her case for redistribution of money. The east was one of the state's highest funded mental health services and the south was one of the lowest, she pointed out. She lobbied, she politicked, she went to meeting after meeting promoting her mantra of 'equitable resource allocation'. Afterwards she debriefed with colleagues over a coffee or a drink. Often they were in stitches at her wicked, sometimes defamatory descriptions of who did what to whom and what the various players were wearing. More seriously, she sometimes worried that she had been too aggressive with the people she called 'dinosaurs'.

In the eyes of many, Margaret became identified as the agent of evil change. With limited resources, she had driven the southern services to change and now the east was also under pressure. The attitude in the east, Margaret's supporters liked to joke, was that the storm troopers were at the gates of the bastion of civilisation, and that Tobin was going to send in the tanks. How dare she? About a year after the merger, Charles Doutney took over from Gordon Parker as director of mental health for the eastern part of the sector. He had his own share of disagreements with Margaret, arguing that taking funds from the east would destroy services that had taken decades to build, with no guarantee that services of equal calibre would be created in the south. You will end up with losers all round, he warned. Overall, however, Doutney supported Margaret's general plans to push funds into community services and to modernise management. He felt some sympathy for Margaret. Medical gossip can be savage, and he thought she was being unfairly undermined in the talk around town. It's the job that's the bitch, not the person, he thought.

Gavin Andrews, professor of psychiatry at St Vincent's Hospital and one of the agent provocateurs of Australian psychiatry, enjoyed a constructive engagement with Margaret, despite their differences of opinion on many issues. When St Vincent's was left without a director of psychiatric services, Margaret pressed him to take on the job as an interim measure while she hunted for a permanent appointee. Andrews had previously promised himself, after working in the back wards of Victorian institutions in the late 1950s and early 1960s, to never again be involved in treating people who were deprived of their liberty. The job would mean doing this. 'It wasn't going to give me any more money, power or happiness. It was just going to give me a pain in the butt,' he thought. But he agreed reluctantly to take it on, and discovered that his new boss was a sensible, capable administrator.

Andrews, a mischievous type himself, also enjoyed Margaret's sense of fun. What he most liked, he thought, was that she wanted a system that delivered health care rather than a system focused on protecting the Health Department and minister. In following years, however, St Vincent's would groan with discontent at the pace of change. The ABC broadcaster Norman Swan was asked to facilitate a workshop aimed at lancing the boil of malcontent among staff. Swan, an experienced and accomplished hand at such events, was impressed by Tobin on the day. She fronted a roomful of hostile, fearful staff to explain the whys and wherefores of the changes she wanted. She told it straight, and was direct but respectful in batting back the bristling responses. Swan thought she did a good job of reducing the heat without being defensive, arrogant or compromising her message. By the end of the session, he felt that she had earned a grudging respect.

For all her reputation for toughness, some felt that Margaret did not wield the baseball bat firmly enough. John Campbell urged her to go in harder in trying to win extra funds for the south. Ian Hickie and others told her she was doing too little to break up the feudal fiefdoms and the resistance. The system remained dysfunctional, they told her. The St Vincent's crowd still can't find beds for their patients at Prince of Wales and vice versa. Staff who moved from one hospital to another were seen as defectors or, as happened with some of Margaret's colleagues who moved to the east, as spies and plants. In the end, Margaret won some battles but lost the war. While many in the east blamed Margaret for their reduction in inpatient bed numbers, she did not have great success in her push for redistribution of resources from central or eastern Sydney, although she did manage to ensure that most new funding to the area was directed south. She did not have the budgetary or operational control to achieve what she wanted. More importantly, she did not have the political backing. John Campbell, her mentor and great supporter, was not appointed CEO after the merger despite acting in the position for many months, and she did not have the same relationship with his successors.

As well, Margaret's relations with the Centre for Mental Health, a policy unit in the New South Wales Health Department, had not been as productive since Beverley Raphael was appointed director in 1996. Margaret had put out feelers for the job herself but had not received enough encouragement to formally put her hat in the ring. Raphael and Margaret never gelled and were, in many ways, a study in contrasts. Raphael, who was then in her sixties, was a professor internationally renowned for her work in trauma and grief counselling, a gifted intellectual and well connected politically, like her good friend Marie Bashir. It was not Raphael's style to make uncomfortable waves for her political masters, at least not in a public way. And she was not known for her management or administration skills, a deficiency which drove Margaret to distraction. Margaret was less than tactful in suggesting that Raphael have management training. Raphael thought Margaret could be difficult but also appreciated the challenges she presented. Margaret often had good ideas for change, Raphael thought. While Raphael projected the image of a compassionate, wise elder, Margaret was more inclined to offer tough love. She wouldn't waste time on hand-holding when she could be rolling up her sleeves to fix problems.

Margaret made no secret of her criticisms of Raphael or of her disdain for the politicisation of the bureaucracy. She irritated Raphael by reciting how well Victoria had done in mental health reform by comparison with New South Wales. Nor did Margaret make any secret of her view that she was far better qualified and equipped for Beverley's job than the incumbent. Margaret was delighted when she heard of a Machiavellian plan within the department to engineer a job for Raphael in Canberra as a way of opening up the New South Wales position. But the scheme came to naught. On more than one occasion, Margaret directly asked Raphael when she would be vacating the post. One reason she wanted the job was that it meant a seat at the table of the National Mental Health Working Group, representing federal and state governments, and the chance to influence policy nationally. The animosity between the pair was well known – the joke around town was that New South Wales wasn't big enough for them both – and didn't help Margaret's ambitions for her service.

Margaret often discussed work matters with her mother, but didn't dwell on her grumblings about Raphael. She knew that her mother thought a great deal of Raphael. Jean was now working as a social worker specialising in grief counselling at the Peter MacCallum Cancer Centre in Melbourne. Some years earlier, after three decades spent raising children, sewing, knitting, cooking and cleaning, Jean had enrolled at university, at the age of 49, and studied social work. Her eldest daughter pushed and encouraged her all the way. 'Don't be so ridiculous,' was Margaret's standard response whenever her mother wavered in her new-found direction. Raphael's book *The Anatomy of Bereavement* was Jean's bible when teaching social work students. Raphael was the guru, as far as Jean was concerned. It had also helped her, belatedly, to better understand the impact of Gerard's death and the family's difficulty in dealing with their grief.

Margaret did have the ear of the Health Department's head honcho, however. Mick Reid, the director general, was well connected in Labor circles, and in other lives had worked in arts and crafts on Aboriginal communities and running beef properties. Reid invited Margaret onto his kitchen cabinet, an unofficial group of senior doctors and advisors who met regularly to offer him advice. He had a great affection and admiration for Margaret. In his job, he often had to deal with grey people who lacked soul. But he did not put Margaret in that category. She had a light in her face and a passion in her belly, and he enjoyed the burnt oranges and other vivid colours that she wore. Reid noticed that Margaret enjoyed the company of men, and found her attractive himself. Their bond developed a few years after Margaret arrived in New South Wales, not long after Mick's son Joshua killed himself at the age of 21. Joshua had been school captain with a bright future ahead, before the clouds of schizophrenia emerged. Reid always felt grateful for the help that Margaret had offered at a difficult time. He also became a more active advocate for mental health, knowing how low it sat in the pecking order of politicians and bureaucrats, and how stigmatised it was, even within the health sector.

In 1998, Margaret was quick to put up her hand to join the first intake of the Health Leaders Network, an innovative program set up by Australian and New Zealand governments to develop the skills of senior health bureaucrats and managers. About a dozen people attended several sessions spanning 35 days over the course of the year. They visited various parts of the country and went on study tours to China and Hong Kong. Bob Wells, a Canberra man with a quiet demeanour and a sharp eye, was soon struck by Margaret's dominance in the group. She was always the first to express a view, and was never tentative about it. Nor did she leave much space for other opinions. Wells groaned quietly to himself at the prospect of spending many long days in her company. But his opinion softened as he came to know Margaret better. She was always up for some friendly banter on bus trips, a drink at the pub at the end of the day, and was quick to organise the group into dinners and shopping expeditions. As the group came to know each other better, Margaret faced some uncomfortable questions about her challenging behaviour. She seemed to take the feedback on board and gave no sign of taking offence.

At one infamous session, Margaret reduced a colleague to tears. She was unrepentant. You have to be tough to do a tough job, was her view. During the course Margaret struck a close bond with Moira McKinnon, a public health physician from Western Australia. McKinnon, who would in years to come find herself in the thick of preparations for the terrifying scenario of an avian influenza pandemic, was a quiet presence and a low-key dresser whose favourite shoes were a pair of R.M. Williams boots. It soon became obvious to some of the group that Margaret was on a mission to remake McKinnon. She took her shopping and, during a visit to New Zealand, arranged for McKinnon to have her colours done, which made them late for the group's flight to Rotorua. When the two women rushed on board, McKinnon was sporting a new look, complete with make-up. Margaret then proceeded to commandeer appropriately coloured items of clothing from the others for her friend to borrow for the rest of the trip. This incident would stick in the minds of many of the group, but it was not what most struck McKinnon about Margaret. She noticed more how Margaret thrived on long conversations about how best to improve the health of the general population, not only patients. Unlike many doctors, Margaret did not take a narrow view that medical services held all the answers to a community's wellbeing. Health was so much more than that. McKinnon felt she and Margaret had connected because they both enjoyed thinking outside of the square.

During the group's visit to China, Margaret joined Kieran Gleeson, a lanky, affable chap from New South Wales, at a karaoke bar. Gleeson quite fancied his talents with a tune and happily launched into a Frank Sinatra impersonation. The Chinese audience was delighted, clapping and cheering madly. When Gleeson joined

Margaret again at the bar, she greeted him with a big grin: 'Kieran, that was fucking hopeless.' He was very amused by her comment. A lot of people might think something like that, but never say it. That's where Margaret was different, he thought. He enjoyed sparring with Margaret and her quick humour, but also thought that you couldn't afford to suffer from a lack of self-esteem around her.

The leadership course was a welcome distraction for Margaret at a time when she felt she had done as much as she could in New South Wales, given all the constraints. The top job was not available and Raphael had made it abundantly clear that it would not be free anytime soon. Margaret sought out John Campbell to ask for advice on career directions. She wondered whether to move out of mental health into general health management. She also talked to Mick Reid of her ambitions. She did some consultancy work outside New South Wales, and threw herself into activities with the three professional colleges with which she was involved, the RANZCP, the Royal Australian College of Medical Administrators and Australian College of Health Service Executives. She also ran skills development workshops for senior managers in New Zealand health services.

As the twentieth century drew to a close, Mary Pryor could see that her boss was becoming restless. It was only a matter of time until she moved on, Mary thought.

In April 2000, Margaret bumped into one of her old colleagues from medical school, John Gallichio, at a Royal Australian College of Medical Administrators meeting at Bondi. He was now the medical director at Geelong Hospital, Victoria, and doing a practice run of the oral exams for admission to the college. Margaret was one of the two examiners at his trial exam, and put him through quite a gruelling session. It was more onerous than he might have expected given their previous connection. 'That was a bit tough, Margaret,' he complained afterwards, only half joking. 'Oh well,' she replied, 'you've got to be able to cope.'

The encounter left an impression on him. Margaret had toughened up markedly since he had first known her all those years ago.

7

Gassy's world

There is nothing perhaps so generally consoling to a man as a well-established grievance; a feeling of having been injured, on which his mind can brood from hour to hour, allowing him to plead his own cause in his own court, within his own heart – and always to plead it successfully.
Anthony Trollope

His face rarely betrayed him. On the surface, Gassy was as unlined and unworried as ever. There were no creases between his brows to hint of inner turmoil. But his mind would not rest. As 1994 gathered pace, Gassy found that his thoughts returned again and again to the same disturbing questions.

He knew that many of the nurses at Pacific House hated him and were out to get him. More than once he had caught them talking about him. He was sure they had been breaking into his office to steal his journals, tampering with the office equipment and moving his files around. He knew the whispers that he was having inappropriate relationships with patients. He had seen the knowing smiles when his eating disorder patients arrived for their appointments. He had stopped closing his door during consultations, despite the cost to patient privacy.

But now it seemed that even colleagues who once had been on his side were shifting allegiances. He had been for many friendly lunches and coffees with David Burke, the psychiatrist working with the elderly. There had been the usual share of disagreements over work matters, but relations had remained respectful.

Burke had changed since Tobin's arrival, Gassy thought. Burke had begun to act strangely towards him. Could Burke be in cahoots with Tobin? Could they be working together to get rid of him? Gassy decided to confront Burke directly, and to observe his reaction closely. Burke's denials were not at all reassuring. They just didn't ring true.

Gassy had no doubt that Greg Aldridge, who had been his tennis partner, friend and colleague at Bankstown, had already lined up behind Tobin. The ambitious Aldridge was brown-nosing his way up the ladder, Gassy thought. He no longer held any doubts about where Tobin stood. Work had become more demanding than ever since her arrival. Instead of relieving his load, Tobin was adding to it. She was asking questions, asking more of staff, and increasing their administrative burden. Gassy had been so worried about where all this was leading that he had tendered his resignation within months of her arrival. But when he later withdrew it, he realised that she would not let it go at that.

Tobin would scapegoat him for the problems in the unit, this was clear. Some patients had recently killed themselves and he feared that he would be left to carry the can. He was particularly worried about the Chinese woman who had spent months in the unit, isolated by her lack of English. She had been admitted after killing her son as instructed by the ghost of her father. On the long-awaited day of her discharge from hospital, she had thrown herself under a train. Would he be blamed? Was it his fault?

Many evenings Gassy ran the bath in his flat in Rose Bay, in Sydney's well-to-do eastern suburbs, hoping the warm water would loosen his knots. He was also fretting about his apartment. He had replaced the carpet because of its strange smell. But still the smell lingered. Another thing to worry about. He wondered whether he should have the cement floor drilled out to see if that would eliminate the odour.

As Gassy relaxed in the bath, he puzzled over what to do, how to protect himself at work. He wondered if Naomi Sommers knew what was going on. She was well connected with the hospital networks. She had always taken his side when others in the unit were trying to make his life difficult. But recently he had seen her talking and laughing with the others and looking in his direction. He thought she was talking about him, though she denied this when asked.

'Are they out to get me?' he asked Naomi more than once. 'Have you been asked to help them?' Then he would abruptly switch the conversation, with the line that Naomi had heard many times before: 'Don't let's talk about work, let's talk about you.' Inwardly, though, Gassy was not entirely sure what to make of Naomi's denials. He had trusted her in the past. Their relationship had always been very close.

When Tobin announced that he could no longer see his private patients at the hospital, he saw this as an overt declaration of his fears. She was out to get rid of him. There was no room, amid all the questions circling through his thoughts, to recognise that this was no different to what Tobin would also tell others at the hospital. She didn't want anyone's private patients seen there.

Around March 1994, Gassy employed Naomi to help establish his private practice in rooms near the hospital, where he took a long-term lease. After finishing her day's work at Pacific House, Naomi went to Gassy's new rooms, setting up filing systems and his office. Gassy was determined to keep seeing his private patients. 'She can't stop me,' he declared.

Gassy became convinced that Tobin and her cronies were monitoring him closely, and arranged for a private investigator to check his room for bugs. He discussed his fears about the bug with Anne (whose real name cannot be used for legal reasons), a young woman he had treated regularly over the past eighteen months or so. Anne had spent some months as an inpatient at the unit, and was well acquainted with the staff and the unit's politics. Boundaries had become blurred. The tenor of her consultations with Gassy was often personal, rather than professional. Gassy told Anne of his work difficulties. It was inevitable, given the dynamics of the unit, that there would be gossip about Gassy and his attractive, intelligent patient.

When Tobin first arrived, Gassy told Anne of his hopes the new director would be an ally in his struggles with the nursing staff. But lately she had noticed a shift in his attitude. Their consultations, usually scheduled as the last appointment in Gassy's day, now regularly overran their allocated 50 minutes. More and more, she noticed, they were absorbed by Gassy's ruminations about Tobin and his worries about his position at the hospital. Anne laughed when Gassy told of his fears about being bugged. She was taken aback when he walked her to her car after their appointment one evening. He was worried Tobin might intercept and speak to her. Anne was also surprised at one appointment when Gassy asked why she was carrying such a big bag. He thought she was taping their consultation for Tobin, and asked Anne to empty out her bag and reveal its contents.

When Gassy announced he was going on leave, Naomi wasn't overly surprised. He hadn't had many holidays in all his years at St George for fear that he might return to find the unit closed. Naomi thought a holiday would help. Gassy had lost some weight recently, and seemed stressed, which she thought unusual for him. He had been uncharacteristically angry when they met over coffee recently. 'No-one treats me like this and gets away with it,' he said.

Naomi didn't read too much into that statement. She thought it just another symptom of the social awkwardness that had made her feel somewhat protective of Gassy in the past. She didn't realise that Gassy planned on taking sick leave rather than a holiday.

In late May, Gassy went to see an old friend and colleague, Dr Osman Ali. They had flatted together for about a year while they were both working at Bankstown Hospital. Gassy realised many colleagues would disapprove of him consulting a friend; it was not the done thing. But he was confident of getting the medical certificate that he sought. Also, he knew just how quickly gossip spreads in medical circles, and felt he could trust Ali to be discreet.

Inevitably, however, news slipped out about the consultation, whether through the formal channels of the Medical Board's procedures, or the informal channels of professional whispers. Some psychiatrists who knew Gassy saw it as a worrying sign. Ali was not well respected; indeed, a few years later he would be struck off the medical register.

Gassy told Ali that he was exhausted and irritable, had trouble concentrating and lacked motivation. He also mentioned his tennis elbow and ongoing problems with asthma, and described the conflicts in the unit and his overburdening with work. He complained that the hospital administration was not supportive of psychiatry and that vacant positions in the unit were not being filled. He mentioned that Tobin was talking about him to nursing staff, criticising him and undermining his authority. He also said that his father, Xavier, had developed depression after suffering a subarachnoid haemorrhage, and was now having psychiatric treatment.

Ali thought Gassy had become depressed in response to work stresses, and gave his old friend a medical certificate covering from 30 May to 10 July. It said Gassy was suffering from 'burnout'.

Gassy continued to wonder about whom he could and couldn't trust. Naomi was still parking in the garage at his private rooms, as they had agreed. One day he left a note on her windscreen. Naomi couldn't believe what she read – your services will no longer be required. Furious, she rang for an explanation. They had been mates for a long time, and she expected better than this impersonal dismissal. Gassy was a stranger on the line, repeating coldly that her services were no longer needed. In a subsequent, more conciliatory phone call he said she could continue to park at his rooms.

About a month later, Naomi was puzzled when her key would not open the garage door as usual. She rang Gassy to alert him to the problem, and was stunned when he replied: 'I've changed the locks.'

'Why?' she demanded angrily. He implied that she was betraying him. He had feared for some time that she was supplying his enemies with information. As far as Naomi was concerned, that was the end of their friendship.

On 4 July 1994, Gassy returned to see Ali for a second time. He reported that he was feeling better and that it had helped to have some time away from work, playing tennis and catching up with friends. Again he mentioned his concerns about Tobin. 'She is making me look like an idiot,' he said.

Gassy learnt soon afterwards of Tobin's letter to the Medical Board requesting an evaluation of his fitness to practise. When he rang Tobin to arrange his return to work, he was told that this was contingent on his agreeing to see a psychiatrist nominated by the hospital. He was not happy with any of the names suggested, and made his own arrangements to see someone of his own choosing.

On 26 July, Gassy travelled to Sydney's northern suburbs for the first of several consultations with Dr Jill Floyd. She was not a fully fledged psychiatrist; she had passed the first stage of her college exams several years previously but not yet completed the second stage of the process. A softly-spoken woman of unremarkable appearance and a timid, sometimes scatty manner, Floyd was then working part time out of one of Sydney's best-known private psychiatric clinics, the Ellard practice. She struggled at times to combine the responsibilities of family and work. Floyd had impressed Gassy when they were in a tutorial group as registrars together. He trusted and admired her skills as an empathetic psychotherapist.

When Gassy took a seat in Floyd's rooms, she asked why he had brought himself there. She took copious notes and listened closely to his responses, observing his mood, his behaviour and how he related to her. Floyd recognised an all-too-familiar story as Gassy described the unpleasant politics, the interdisciplinary rivalries and recent patient suicides at St George. She had endured her own difficulties working in the public system and knew how destructive it could be. She knew of the damaging political alliances which could form, and the collusion that could develop in psychiatric units between deeply disturbed patients and unhappy nursing staff.

As Gassy spoke, Floyd gained an impression of a frightened, vulnerable colleague who had been unsupported in a toxic work environment. She thought him sensitive to rejection and to the opinion of others. She saw no evidence of serious psychiatric problems, and felt her role was to provide a listening ear and support. Gassy told of his concern that Tobin had a conflict of interest because she wore two hats, as director of the St George unit as well as of mental health for the Southern Sydney Area Health Service. He thought this meant she might not be held accountable for the St George unit's poor outcomes.

When he told Floyd of reporting a male nurse for having a sexual relationship with a patient, she thought it courageous. It was, she reflected, a very dangerous thing to do in a dysfunctional unit. When Gassy told of the rumours that he was sexually interested in patients and that a cartoon had been put up on the unit's notice board to this effect, she wondered whether he was being scapegoated. Gassy also told of his difficulty sleeping and his close but conflicted relationship with his family. His friends, his ex-girlfriend and his love for music were his major supports, he said.

At his next consultation, on 9 August, Gassy told Floyd he was feeling okay and planned to return to work soon. But he was concerned Tobin would pressure him to resign.

The next day, Gassy rang the deputy registrar at the Medical Board, Penny Johnston. Tobin had asked that he not return to work early, and he queried this with Johnston. She suggested he talk to his medical defence organisation and explained the process that was under way with the Impaired Registrants Panel (IRP). His registration as a doctor was not at risk, she said. He simply was being asked to cooperate with the IRP, a non-disciplinary process which strives to support doctors with drug, alcohol or mental health problems, and to keep them practising safely.

Gassy told Johnston he would continue seeing private patients but agreed not to return to public sector work. However, he rang back a few hours later saying he felt this was inconsistent and that he wanted to return to the hospital immediately. He was prepared even to do non-clinical work.

Shortly afterwards, Gassy received a letter advising that the Medical Board had arranged for him to see Dr John Woodforde, one of psychiatry's respected elders, a man known for his compassion and clinical acumen. 'You can trust Dr Woodforde,' Floyd told Gassy at their next consultation. He had been one of her supervisors at the Ellard practice. 'He is a really good man.'

Gassy also told Floyd at that consultation of how a recent conversation with Tobin had left him demoralised. He feared his position would be terminated and that she would give him poor references. He also was concerned about his reputation with GPs who referred patients to him. Floyd wrote in her notes that 'an issue of justice' seemed to be at stake. She noted that Gassy had taken appropriate steps to lift his spirits after speaking with Tobin. He had applied cognitive techniques, dined with his cousin Gilbert, watched a video and played guitar. She also noted that Gassy was trying to lose weight after recently gaining some extra kilograms.

A week later, on 23 August, Gassy told Floyd of a brief meeting with Tobin where he had agreed to confine himself to non-clinical, administrative duties until the IRP hearing. Again, he returned to his concerns about Tobin. He had been so busy since her arrival that he had had no time to cover his back or protect himself, he said, and he could not be as empathetic as he wanted with patients. He described Tobin as a powerful administrator and wondered if others at the hospital were frightened of aligning themselves with him. He felt there was little support from colleagues.

In late August, Gassy arrived punctually for his first appointment with Woodforde, a gently-spoken man who, on first meeting, gives the impression of a kindly grandfather. Gassy told Woodforde of his family background. His mother did not like him, he said, and he believed this was because his conception was unplanned and he had been delivered by caesarean section. However, a supportive family network had compensated for the lack of motherly bonding. He was close to his father.

Woodforde observed that Gassy was neatly dressed, all in black. Gassy spoke freely of his difficulties, returning repeatedly to the innuendoes and rumours about him. He described finding a cartoon about 'TheRapist', a pun on 'therapist', on a notice board close to his office. He also told how a colleague had one morning interrupted staff in conversation to announce that the Mauritian ambassador was a child molester. Both incidents were intentional slights upon himself, Gassy felt.

Gassy was distressed and repetitive as he described these incidents, sometimes seeming to ignore Woodforde's questions. Several times the older man had to ask his younger colleague to address the question put to him. Reluctantly, Gassy disclosed that about ten years earlier, he had become involved with the adult daughter of a patient. He believed this could be construed as misconduct, and that the innuendoes now circulating about him were somehow connected

100

with that matter. Gassy was guarded and suspicious when Woodforde asked for the name of the therapist he was seeing. He feared that if he gave Floyd's name, efforts might be made to influence her.

Towards the end of the consultation, Woodforde suggested to Gassy that his grip on reality was tenuous, and that he was probably deluded. Gassy thought it a ridiculous idea, and rejected it immediately.

In his report to the Medical Board, Woodforde wrote:

Dr Gassy has undoubtedly had a great deal to cope with in his professional life during the past four years. He has felt that there are expectations upon him as the most successful member of the family to continue to achieve success. Furthermore, he has had a broken relationship shortly before he went on sick leave. That may have been either an additional contributory factor or another consequence of his deteriorating emotional adjustment.

Woodforde concluded that Gassy had a psychotic delusional disorder, and required medication. He well knew, however, that most people with the fixed, false beliefs that characterise a delusional disorder never receive the medication that might help because the disorder's other defining characteristic is lack of insight. Almost by definition, people who are deluded are convinced they are not.

People with delusions can be convinced that someone is in love with them or that they have a parasite infestation or a rare illness. The most intransigent delusions tend to be those where the person is convinced they are being persecuted. Woodforde thought Gassy's delusional beliefs were both persecutory and accusatory. 'At the present time it is not possible to say if or when Dr Gassy will be fit to resume the practice of medicine,' he wrote. 'This will largely depend on whether he is prepared to follow the advice of the Medical Board.'

For Woodforde, making such a diagnosis was like piecing together a jigsaw. Each piece could appear one way when viewed separately but when combined with the other pieces, it contributed to quite a different picture. It was not that any one part of Gassy's story sounded the alarm; it was the overall picture that was worrying.

The IRP was scheduled to meet a few days after Woodforde delivered his report. On 30 August, Gassy rang the Medical Board, agitated and wanting a copy of Woodforde's report couriered to him as soon as possible. Sheryn Payne, head of professional conduct and health, told Gassy the gist of Woodforde's conclusions and suggested he arrange for his psychotherapist to attend the IRP.

But Gassy was not prepared to provide his doctor's name or to have her attend the IRP, Payne wrote in a file note of their conversation. He was confident that he could prove to the IRP himself that he was not delusional. Payne also expressed her concern that Gassy was continuing to see private patients, which she felt inappropriate in the circumstances. He was not prepared to stop seeing them, he told her.

Gassy also attended Floyd's rooms on the day he spoke with Payne. Floyd was stunned to learn of Woodforde's diagnosis. She admired Woodforde as a man of integrity, but was convinced that in this case, he had got it wrong. She thought he didn't fully appreciate the difficult context in which Gassy was working and that there was a real basis to his concerns. She had never seen any sign of Gassy 'switching' into delusional mode – there were no obvious physical or emotional changes when he spoke of the people who had given him grief at work.

On 2 September, the IRP met to consider Gassy's case. Of the two doctors on the panel, it was Dr Peter Arnold whom Gassy noticed. Arnold, a prominent GP who had been active in Australian Medical Association politics, seemed to be the driving force, Gassy thought.

Over a couple of hours, the panel heard various people give evidence, and considered Woodforde's report. Tobin told them she could see no change in Gassy and was as concerned as before. As a psychiatrist, she felt she could not ask him to return to clinical work in such a stressful situation. At least one observer thought Gassy articulate and professional in arguing his case. He explained that several of the incidents that Woodforde had thought were delusions had in fact occurred. Gassy was confident that Woodforde's report would not be accepted, its conclusions were just too ludicrous.

However, the IRP accepted Woodforde's finding, and imposed conditions on Gassy's registration. He was to consult a board-approved psychiatrist of his own choice, and to see Woodforde again for a further review. He was not to see patients while having treatment.

It was a terrible shock. Gassy was angry, frustrated and disbelieving. He was reluctant to accept the IRP conditions but felt sure Woodforde would change his mind after seeing him again.

At their final consultation, in his private rooms, Gassy told his patient Anne he could no longer keep seeing her. 'She has done it, she has finally won,' he said. Anne knew he was referring to Tobin.

A few weeks after the IRP hearing, Gassy rang Sheryn Payne again, asking her to explain the Medical Board process. He wanted to know if Tobin's involvement would continue, and if she could appeal the decision. He thought Tobin was trying to get him deregistered through her contacts in the Health Department. Payne explained that Tobin would have no further part in the proceedings and reassured Gassy that the process now under way aimed to help him get better and back to work, it was not about trying to deregister him.

Back in Floyd's rooms, Gassy accused Tobin of lying at the recent hearing. She told the panel she was concerned about his health and didn't want him to come back early from sick leave, he said, when her real concern was whether he would fulfil her needs in the workplace. Tobin was just pretending to be caring and compassionate, he felt. Floyd pondered these comments, and concluded they were a reflection of Gassy having a somewhat obsessive compulsive personality. He was someone who was very ethical and really believed in doing things the right way, she thought. He was a stickler for honesty.

Gassy also told Floyd that Tobin had asked him some very personal questions about his sleeping habits, and appeared to know of things he had previously discussed with his girlfriend. Gassy was disappointed when Floyd rejected his request for twice weekly appointments. He wanted to discuss some longstanding issues that he had meant to address for years, but had procrastinated and never got around to doing this. Floyd told Gassy that she was often frustrated and irritated by the unresolvable conflict between her work and family commitments. Gassy thought this plausible but wondered whether she was just being diplomatic, that perhaps she found their sessions demanding and that seeing him twice weekly was too much.

He felt embarrassed to have asked for something she wasn't prepared to give.

At one of their last sessions Gassy told Floyd that he had begun seeing Dr Jonathan Phillips, a psychiatrist experienced in examining medical colleagues. A small, debonair man who projects a large presence, Phillips had previously, like Woodforde, been a partner in the Ellard practice. Gassy had met Phillips as a medical student visiting the Ellard practice, and more recently knew that Phillips had seen his father.

Gassy went to Phillips's rooms in the heart of Sydney's specialist precinct, Macquarie Street, on at least three occasions, with their first meeting three days after the IRP hearing. Again he ran through his troubles at St George, mentioning that he felt unsupported and unacknowledged by Tobin.

Phillips's first impressions were that Gassy was excessively anxious and preoccupied with what others thought about him, and with what he believed might have been recent clinical errors.

Gassy spoke of his difficulties with concentration and motivation at work, and said he had been waking up early, feeling rotten. He was self-pitying and experiencing feelings of helplessness, hopelessness and guilt. As chair of the RANZCP training committee, Phillips was well aware of the St George history. He felt that Gassy, when acting director of the unit, had been caught in the crossfire of a political battle between the Eastern and Central Sydney Area Health Services over the unit's future.

He was sympathetic to Gassy, whom he thought had been thrown out of his depth into an extremely stressful work situation. Phillips respected Tobin as a tough, efficient administrator, and thought she had probably had to make some very tough decisions which could have impacted on Gassy. Phillips thought it unusual that Gassy didn't want to reveal the name of the registrar he was seeing for psycho-therapy. At one consultation, Gassy expressed concern that Phillips might not take a 'neutral stance'. There was a potential conflict of interest, he felt, as Phillips often did work for the Medical Board.

Phillips noted that Gassy was tending to interpret events in a paranoid fashion. He concluded that Gassy had a depressive disorder accompanied by paranoid thinking but doubted that he had been frankly delusional. Phillips did not prescribe medication, but focused on talking therapy and believed Gassy was showing signs of significant improvement. However, he did wonder whether the apparent resolution of Gassy's paranoia was because he had sufficient insight to keep some things to himself.

On 17 October, Phillips wrote a report urging the Medical Board to reconsider Gassy's case: 'Dr Gassy is a relatively junior psychiatrist who was almost certainly placed in a situation of intolerable emotional stress when he was expected to take high level clinical and administrative responsibility at St George Hospital, particularly in 1993 and the earlier months of this year.'

Phillips said he considered Gassy fit to continue practising medicine with some reservation, including that he was at risk of further psychiatric disturbance. Conscious of Gassy's concerns about St George, Phillips tried to arrange a supervised position for him at another hospital. Gassy was satisfied with the outcome. He had the favourable report that he wanted and could see no point in returning to Phillips. He said he was not coming back when Phillips's secretary rang to arrange a further appointment.

On 18 November, Gassy again made the trek to Woodforde's rooms, arriving on time for his appointment. It had been arranged by the New South Wales Medical Board following the IRP's stipulation that Gassy see Woodforde again for a further review. Gassy revealed that he had been organising his finances, had put his unit up for sale and had moved back to his parents' home at sleepy Oyster Bay in the southern suburbs. He was also trying to sublet his private rooms and was making arrangements to transfer his patients to other care. He was going to resign from St George as it was not in his best interests to work there again. This would also 'put Dr Tobin out of the picture' so she would not have the chance to express any opinion regarding his future employment at any Medical Board meetings.

Gassy also told Woodforde he had stopped seeing Floyd because he had sensed a change in her. He thought she had been told things about him, and that she did not like him. This was confirmed by the fact that she had not contacted him after he had cancelled further appointments with her. As well, Gassy told Woodforde, he had stopped seeing Phillips because he didn't trust him.

He also described the sleeping problem that he had suffered intermittently over many years. It was caused by difficulty breathing, which he thought due to an allergy problem, perhaps caused by an insecticide. It was like asthma, but not relieved by asthma treatment and arose in some situations but not others. He had, for example, been able to sleep in a hotel and the home of a friend but not with his girlfriend. He also said that he had been drinking more than usual lately.

Woodforde thought Gassy cooperative. He seemed flat, although he smiled appropriately a few times during their conversation. Woodforde worried about what he heard. He thought Gassy's comments about Floyd were more than simply a sign of low self-esteem, but revealed irrational suspicion and mistrust. It was also concerning that Gassy was not currently receiving any treatment despite clearly having many psychological problems. Woodforde concluded that Gassy was probably still delusional.

A few days later, Gassy formally handed his resignation to St George. Apart from not wanting to work with Tobin again, he was embarrassed by Woodforde's diagnosis and feared facing staff who might be wondering whether he was psychotic.

Gassy received a copy of Woodforde's second report on 24 November, the eve of the Medical Board's review of his case. He was flabbergasted. He felt that Woodforde was clinging to his original diagnosis on even more tenuous grounds than in his original report. Gassy asked if the review could be postponed to give him time to gather other opinions to counter the report. When this was not forthcoming, he decided not to attend the review. Clearly there was no point – it would not make any difference to the outcome, which seemed predetermined.

In making that decision, Gassy activated the Medical Board's disciplinary process. By failing to attend further appointments with Phillips and by failing to attend the review, he had contravened the IRP conditions, and his case now would be referred to the Professional Standards Committee.

As 1994 drew to a close, Gassy spent many hours contemplating the events of the year, puzzling about why things had unfolded as they had. It seemed obvious there had been a miscarriage of justice. The process had been patently unfair. Woodforde's report had been uncritically accepted. The IRP had refused to contact Floyd and had ignored Ali's opinion. Phillips was not asked for his opinion before the IRP hearing. The board said it did not ask for details from the treating psychiatrist because it wanted to protect the therapeutic relationship. But Gassy was sceptical. The bias was clear to him and surely it must be clear to others as well.

He calculated that Woodforde had seen him for no more than 90 minutes in total whereas Ali, Floyd and Phillips – who had seen him for more than twenty hours in total – assessed him to be free of psychosis. Gassy continued to ponder Tobin's role in the proceedings. He wrote on a yellow Post-it note, attached to his copy of her letter to the Medical Board: 'There must have been more info/allegations from MT to the Medical Board than this letter?'

He prepared a report, dated 29 January 1995, and titled: 'Summary of events leading to my appearance before the Impaired Registrants Panel'. Woodforde's interview style was rigid and his manner brusque, Gassy wrote. 'It impeded rather than facilitated communication. He interpreted his occasional failure to get exactly what information he wanted, in the sequence he wanted, to a problem with me rather than being a consequence of the manner in which he conducted the interview and the limited time he had made available for the interview.'

Gassy wrote that Woodforde's report contained 'a number of misrepresentations and arbitrary interpretations'. He disputed the conclusion that his resigning from St George was evidence of 'impaired judgement'.

'I resigned from St George for two main reasons,' Gassy wrote. 'I felt that my relationship with Dr Tobin had been irreparably damaged following her complaint to the Board, attempting to prevent me from returning to the unit when I was cleared to return to work before my scheduled appointment with Dr Woodforde, and finally refusing to allow me to return to work even when I offered to pay for whatever level of supervision the panel considered necessary pending my review.'

He suggested that Tobin was responsible in some way for Woodforde's report:

> It would seem likely that Dr Tobin would have communicated
> with the New South Wales Medical Board more extensively than
> has been disclosed by the Board . . . If this is indeed the case, the
> informal or undisclosed communication from Dr Tobin could
> account for the bias in Dr Woodforde's report.
>
> The sequence of events commencing with and following from
> Dr Tobin's complaint I believe represents the mishandling by the
> New South Wales Medical Board of an inappropriate complaint by
> a colleague. I hope that this will be of concern to the profession.

Gassy arranged for several copies of his report to be bound,
together with internal St George staff memos and other supporting
attachments, and sent them to a number of colleagues, including the
most senior psychiatrist in the New South Wales Health Department.
The document also included a copy of a patient's complaint about
him cancelling an appointment at the last moment. Gassy thought the
Medical Board's handling of that complaint was yet another example
of it being unduly harsh on him.

He also arranged for his former patient Anne to write a letter, 'to
whom it may concern', stating that she was aware of rumours about
Gassy taking a sexual interest in patients. This would help prove that
he was not delusional, Gassy felt. He was worried there would be
gossip and speculation about him, but was sure that circulating these
documents would prove the falsity of Woodforde's diagnosis.

Woodforde was alarmed when reports filtered back about Gassy's
strategy. He suggested to the Medical Board that he should resign
from the case. He hoped the board would choose someone else to
give any further reports on Gassy. Woodforde had become fearful of
any further dealings with Gassy.

When Bill Andrews, a psychiatrist who had helped train Gassy at
Bankstown, received a copy of the documents, he also became concerned. He had been friendly with Gassy – except on the tennis court
where they had met in serious, intense competition. When he made

inquiries at St George, he realised there was some basis to the issues Gassy had raised with Woodforde, and decided to relay his findings to the Professional Standards Committee (PSC).

Floyd also prepared a report for the PSC. 'It seemed to me that Dr Gassy was recovering from what appeared in retrospect to have been a major depressive illness which occurred in the context of a troubled work role and environment as well as the breakdown of a personal relationship,' she wrote.

During interviews he denied any psychotic symptoms and I did not find any in evidence. Regarding the question as to whether Dr Gassy was delusional and therefore unfit for practice, I can only say that some of the work conflicts and politics he described appeared to undermine his professional and personal integrity to the point where he became increasingly vigilant and was unsure of who he could trust.

As an example I cite some antipathy from certain nursing staff, which worsened after he warned an inpatient about the impropriety of a sexual relationship that had developed with one of the nurses who had then been asked to leave. I can't help but wonder whether his political inexperience, professional isolation and a certain personality sensitivity to not being accepted, combined to give this impression of psychosis.

On 10 April 1995, the PSC met for about five hours to hear evidence about Gassy's failure to comply with the IRP conditions. The committee strives to find the fine balance between keeping doctors working wherever possible and protecting the public. The committee that day comprised two doctors and a lay member but Gassy noticed that it was the psychiatrist member, Kay Wilhelm, who asked most of the difficult questions.

Wilhelm had heard of the upheavals at St George since Tobin's arrival, and felt sympathy for Gassy. It would have been a tumultuous workplace, she thought.

The PSC considered Anne's letter, the internal St George documents provided by Gassy, the contradictory psychiatric reports, and heard Andrews speak of the man he knew as a colleague and friend. Andrews said he thought Gassy had not received a reasonable hearing from the IRP and that it was not unreasonable in the circumstances that 'he should be depressed and expressing paranoid ideas'. He also said that Gassy had become fatalistic about the processes initiated by Tobin's letter.

During the five hours or so of the hearing, committee members observed Gassy closely as he presented evidence and questioned witnesses. He conducted himself appropriately and showed no signs of being psychotic or paranoid. In their deliberations, the committee tried to disentangle the relationship between Gassy's stressful work situation and his recent troubles. Was his reaction any more than a normal response to stress?

In the end, the committee decided that Gassy had been transiently psychotic after a period of intense work-related stress but found no evidence of paranoid thinking or psychotic thought processes during the hearing. It also found him guilty of 'unsatisfactory professional conduct' in breaching his undertakings to the IRP. It considered him competent to practise medicine so long as he met certain conditions, including seeing a board-nominated psychiatrist and working in a position with some support and professional supervision.

The decks were cleared for Gassy to resume the work that, despite all his recent troubles, remained so important to him. There was even the offer of a position at Orange, a genteel old town in the heart of the vineyards and fertile farmland of central western New South Wales. The Medical Board gave the nod to his taking the job.

But still Gassy worried. He felt the PSC had merely rubber-stamped Woodforde's report. And, after his experience with Woodforde, he was not at all sure about seeing another board-nominated psychiatrist. What if he was again found to be delusional? Eventually, he decided against resuming practice. The risk of another board psychiatrist and another false diagnosis was just not worth it. It would terminate his career. On 7 July 1995, Gassy wrote to the Medical Board: 'I have elected not to practise in NSW indefinitely as a result of the conditions imposed on my registration by the PSC.'

A regular correspondence ensued between Gassy and the Medical Board. The board repeatedly made psychiatric appointments for him but Gassy could see no reason why he should attend as he wasn't practising. Some observers thought Gassy was committing 'professional suicide' but so far as he could see, he wasn't breaching the PSC conditions because he wasn't practising. Over many weeks and months, he puzzled over the board's pursuit of him. It just wasn't normal, he felt. There had to be some more sinister explanation.

Other concerns also preoccupied Gassy. In October 1994, he had developed fevers, rash and an extreme malaise, suggestive of a viral infection. He was sicker than he had ever felt before, unable even to drag himself out of bed for some days. This occurred about a month after a casual sexual encounter with a woman. Not long afterwards, some AIDS-related literature arrived in the mail. He saw a connection between the two events and the deterioration in his health. He was so short of breath he could no longer run for the ball on the tennis court, and also had conjunctivitis in both eyes which persisted for months.

In February 1996, Gassy obtained a referral from a respiratory physician to see Dr Tom Gottlieb, a specialist in microbiology and infectious diseases at Concord Hospital. Gottlieb remembered that they had been in medical school together but did not feel it appropriate to mention this. Gassy told Gottlieb that he was treating himself for AIDS. He was sure he had a rare form of pneumonia, known as PCP, which is common in those with severely compromised immune systems, including AIDS patients. He also believed he had oral thrush.

Gottlieb had ordered various blood tests before the consultation, and reassured Gassy that his immune system was normal, and that he did not have HIV. He recommended Gassy stop taking the medication he had self-prescribed, and seek psychiatric help. Gassy was civil but not receptive.

In his letter back to the referring physician, Gottlieb said he doubted Gassy would follow his advice to see a psychiatrist. He thought Gassy seriously unwell and that he should not be seeing patients. Later he rang David Burke at St George about his concerns.

Gottlieb then would have no reason to think of Gassy again for many years.

Gassy was by this stage casting around for alternative employment. A few months after seeing Gottlieb, he fronted up for a training course for security guards at the Roden Training Centre in Condell Park in Sydney's south-west.

The five-day VIP Protection course included instructions on how to escape under fire, prepare for the visits of dignitaries, and to protect clients. Gassy also learnt about counter-surveillance, controlling fear when carrying out an assignment and how to escape danger zones. As well, there were lessons in combat psychology – how to prepare for encounters when on assignment.

He also learnt, in the clinical language employed by Zoran Planinic, the heavyset firearms instructor who ran the course, that Glock pistols and Speer Gold Dot ammunition were appropriate for 'antipersonnel use'. Planinic noticed Gassy because he thought it unusual for a doctor to be attending his course. He seemed a loner, someone who kept to himself, Planinic thought.

In August 1996, Gassy bought a Glock 19 pistol from Roden Security, followed in September by the purchase of a smaller model, a Glock 26.

Meanwhile, he was becoming increasingly irritated by Medical Board requests to attend various appointments with psychiatrists. He had decided against appearing at a Medical Board review earlier in the year because he had lost all confidence in its processes. On 9 September, Gassy wrote to the Medical Board:

As I have not practised since May '94, and am not contemplating resuming practice in the foreseeable future, I find it difficult to understand the basis for the Board's expressed 'concern' for my health. I would be happy to reassure the Board if the details of the 'concern' were to be outlined to me. However, this does not include attending an unnecessary psychiatric assessment!

He added in big, bold type: 'I do not wish my name removed from the medical register. I understand that the Board has the power to refer the matter to the Medical Tribunal which can have me deregistered if it considers this appropriate.'

The letter, some observers later thought, had practically dared the board to refer the matter to the tribunal.

Gassy did not mention to the board that he also had serious worries about his health. He was desperate to obtain AIDS drugs but was not able to prescribe these for himself. He continued to be troubled by the PCP infection, a fungal infection in his mouth and diarrhoea.

Six days before Christmas, he consulted Dr Stephen Adelstein, a clinical immunologist at the Royal Prince Alfred Hospital. They had worked together at St George a few years earlier but had not known each other well. Adelstein had been tipped off in the referral letter. He knew that Gassy's X-ray and CT scan were normal, and that blood tests showed no evidence of HIV.

Adelstein thought Gassy's anaemia, sensitivity to sunlight, and diarrhoea could be side effects from the unusually high doses of antibiotics he was self-prescribing. The anaemia could have been causing his breathlessness, and the oral thrush could have been caused by his asthma treatment. But Adelstein also considered another possibility; perhaps these symptoms were signalling an auto-immune disorder, systemic lupus erythematosus. He suggested that Gassy have further blood tests, to investigate this possibility. Gassy was courteous but clearly disbelieving when Adelstein explained his conclusions. He didn't have the tests suggested.

Adelstein dismissed Gassy in his mind as a hypochondriac and barely gave the unusual consultation a thought for another six years.

In early 1997, the processes of the Medical Board began to gather momentum. It arranged for Gassy's case to come before the New South Wales Medical Tribunal, which would decide whether he was fit to remain on the medical register. Affidavits were organised and witnesses contacted. Gassy was confident of a favourable hearing. The tribunal was an independent legal authority and could not be manipulated by the henchmen of the Medical Board, he thought. Some weeks before the tribunal hearing, he flew to New York to buy HIV medication.

In June 1997, the tribunal, presided over by a District Court judge and comprising two doctors and a solicitor, sat for three days. It heard three complaints against Gassy: that he was guilty of unsatisfactory conduct and/or professional misconduct for contravening the IRP and PSC conditions; that he was not competent to practise medicine; and that he suffered from impairment, a psychiatric condition.

Gassy told the tribunal of his personal and professional history. He had spent the past three years pursuing alternative interests such as reading, socialising, playing music, and various sports. He showed a diagram he had made to illustrate the cartoon about 'TheRapist' which had given such offence. He explained that he thought David Burke's comment about the Mauritian ambassador had been a deliberate slur on Mauritians or Gassy himself.

Burke, however, told the tribunal that he had no recollection of making such a comment. 'In the last few months before Dr Gassy left work I had the feeling that he felt that he was under a lot of pressure and I was concerned as to the effect that that was having on him in that in a general sense our level of communication and interaction was decreased compared to how it had been in earlier times,' Burke said.

Gassy also explained that he had circulated the documents attacking Woodforde's report in order to quash the rumours about him. But one tribunal member thought this an unusual tactic, saying: 'The problem you sought to cure, the rumours, speculation and talk about your alleged psychiatric condition, you had in fact begun yourself by telling others of the contents of Dr Woodforde's report.'

Gassy acknowledged that his claim in the document that three psychiatrists had disagreed with Woodforde's opinion was not correct, as Floyd was not a fully fledged psychiatrist when she saw him.

Judge Harry Bell questioned Gassy closely about why he had not attended two appointments the board had made for him with a Dr Fisher in 1996. 'Is there some war you are running against the statutory authorities or what is it?' asked the judge. 'I just can't understand why you would say, for example, "I will not attend Dr Fisher, even though I know absolutely nothing about him. He might be the most sympathetic man to me in the whole of Australia but because the Board has said I had to see him therefore I won't see him."'

Gassy replied that the judge was putting a 'persecutory slant' on his actions. He said: 'I was unwilling to face the risk, no matter how small that might be, of being labelled delusional again . . . There is a stigma attached to being psychotic . . . if people believed I was psychotic, I probably would have great trouble obtaining employment for a start, and people would always wonder about whether you are well or not.'

The judge was not satisfied: 'There is often a very good feeling when you stop bashing your head against the wall, has that occurred to you . . . have you heard that expression?'

Gassy was also questioned over the apparent difficulties with his legal representation. He had briefed about five different solicitors for his case, he said, but terminated the services of four of them. The tribunal heard that after engaging the solicitor Leigh Johnson, Gassy attended a conference with her in a barrister's room. Johnson's firm subsequently wrote to the Health Care Complaints Commission in January 1996, complaining that Gassy had attended the conference with two thugs.

Gassy was asked to explain this allegation. 'They didn't exist,' he told the tribunal. It was a false allegation made up by Johnson's firm, he said.

Gassy told the tribunal that he hoped to return to practise. He missed the intellectual stimulation and the social interaction. He would be prepared to comply with certain conditions, but would not see a board-nominated psychiatrist for assessment or treatment. Under pressure during further questioning and realising that he might be facing his last chance, Gassy reluctantly agreed that he would see a board-nominated psychiatrist as long as it was a professor or an associate professor at the University of Sydney.

As Phillips sat in the court room, hearing the evidence, he began, somewhat uncomfortably, to question his earlier clinical judgement about Gassy. He was also interested to learn that it was Floyd whose name Gassy hadn't wanted to reveal to him previously. Phillips knew Floyd, as she had been a registrar in the training program which fell under his responsibility at the Ellard practice.

Phillips told the tribunal that he was beginning to wonder whether 'I might have not given sufficient weight to the possibility that Dr Gassy was then suffering from some form of paranoid or psychotic disturbance'. He now believed that Gassy was unfit to practise.

So Phillips was changing his tune to sing along with Woodforde, Gassy thought bitterly. Gassy was also outraged that Woodforde, who also had not seen him since 1994, still considered him delusional. This conclusion was based, at least partly, on Woodforde's view that delusional disorder is a chronic condition which is unlikely to resolve without treatment.

Woodforde had also signed an affidavit stating that he believed there was a risk of Gassy becoming violent and that 'he also had an unwarranted suspicion of medical practitioners'.

It might seem extraordinary that Phillips and Woodforde could give such opinions without having seen Gassy in three years, the tribunal members noted in their final decision. 'But that they have been asked to do so is in large part the result of the respondent's intransigence.'

The tribunal members mulled over the conflicting evidence before them. They felt the incidents involving the comment about the Mauritian ambassador and 'TheRapist' cartoon were not conclusive evidence of delusion. 'It may be correct to say Dr Gassy was defensive perhaps even paranoid,' Judge Bell wrote in the tribunal decision.

Dr Woodforde is a very experienced psychiatrist and we would hesitate to say he was mistaken but the onus rests with the complainant to establish the diagnosis to our satisfaction.

It is common ground that at the material times the respondent was undergoing tremendous strains as a result of changed work conditions and lack of support from people from whom he expected it. We felt that Dr Phillips' original doubts as to the diagnosis that he was delusional were doubts which he properly entertained.

Notwithstanding the fact that we are not prepared to adopt the whole of Dr Woodforde's opinion, it is obvious that the respondent's judgement has been astray. Examples of the respondent's eccentricity abound in the evidence before the Tribunal. To state to this Tribunal that he would rather face deregistration than appear before a Board-nominated psychiatrist who was not personally satisfactory to him is an illustration of lack of judgement.

To summarise our findings we have doubts as to whether the respondent was truly delusional at the time of his appearance before the IRP though we are not prepared to find affirmatively that Dr Woodforde was mistaken. We do not think that the examples given are sufficient to permit us to accept his diagnosis with the necessary degree of confidence . . . We are not satisfied that he is or ever has been totally unfit to practise. We do strongly suspect that he is and has for some years been an impaired practitioner . . .

We have anxiously considered whether any order other than deregistration would suffice but have decided in the negative. This decision is not motivated by any desire to punish him for his defiance of the Board. We have reached it with considerable regret, as being the only way in which the public can be properly protected.

Judge Bell wrote that Gassy could apply for reinstatement in six months, if he provided appropriate evidence of his condition. If this happened, the judge hoped the Medical Board would be cooperative. 'That is to say, notwithstanding our disapproval of his attempt to exercise a right of veto over the Board's choice of psychiatrist, we would hope that the Board will give consideration to his wishes; the fact that he has been somewhat high handed would not justify a retaliatory response.'

On 1 August 1997, Jean Eric Gassy was formally struck off the New South Wales register of medical practitioners. When the board wrote asking for the return of his certificate of registration, Gassy replied that it could not be found. Due to an administrative slip-up, Gassy retained his Fellowship of the RANZCP, which meant that he continued to receive college publications, enabling him to keep up with the news and movements of his former colleagues.

In the three years leading up to Gassy's deregistration, there had been so many opportunities for the events triggered by Margaret Tobin's letter to the Medical Board to have led elsewhere. But Gassy

could see only the inevitability of it all. His worst fears had eventu-
ated. His enemies had won.

Around the time of the tribunal hearing, Gassy saw Robert Strand,
an old friend who shared his love of music. He told Strand about his
problems with HIV, and that a woman was giving him trouble and
influencing the outcomes of the deregistration process. He had been
betrayed by someone, Gassy said. Strand was surprised, not just by
what he heard, but also by what he saw. He had always thought Gassy
a laid-back, calm character. Now he seemed somewhat distant and
preoccupied. He also seemed to be carrying a lot of anger. Strand
thought the focus was 'a woman high up'.

Gassy continued to live in the flat underneath his parent's brick
home. It was, on the surface at least, a quiet life in a quiet street shaded
by majestic gums and angophoras. He had few phone calls and little
contact with friends, apart from his cousin Gilbert. He helped out his
divorced sister, Elizabeth, who lived just a few minutes' drive away. He
looked after her two children when she was busy with her job at
Qantas and in school holidays. And he enrolled in a Thai language
course at the University of Sydney, where he was pleased to score a
high distinction in one unit.

Medical concerns continued to occupy much of his time. Between
June and August 1997, Gassy several times made the hike to North
Sydney to see a GP, Dr Caroline Mah, about HIV and other medical
problems. In 1997, he began treating himself with antiretroviral drugs,
buying the medication from the US over the internet and also direct
from pharmaceutical companies in Australia. As well, he saw a neurol-
ogist about the tingling in his toes and fingers, and also saw another
respiratory physician – she was at least the third such specialist he had
seen – about his persistent shortness of breath.

In late 1997, Gassy found work with All Business Security
Services, a company based at Rozelle. He worked as a security guard
at the Sydney Central Plaza, a new shopping centre in the city, and
then at Coles supermarket at Broadway. Several former hospital colleagues were surprised to spot him in the security guard uniform.
They didn't stop for a chat. It was too awkward. It must also have
been humiliating for Gassy. Some years later, he would tell a court

room that the public perception of bodyguards was of 'marginal people with dubious integrity prone to physical assaults on anyone who intrudes into the zone of exclusion around the principal'.

Initially, Gassy worked full time in security but then was allowed flexible hours to accommodate his studies. In 1998, while working part time as a security guard, he began a TAFE course in information technology. Again, he was pleased with his high grades. It was impossible for someone who was so smart to be considered delusional, he thought, with some satisfaction.

Gassy had been on leave and was no longer on the roster when he resigned from the security company in July 1999. Illness also forced him to give away the IT course, and occupied much – but not all – of his thoughts and worries in the next few years. He also worried about how to fund his HIV medication, which was fast depleting his savings from the sale of his Rose Bay unit. After paying off the mortgage, he had been left with $150,000. He did not pay his parents rent but needed about $2,000 a month to buy HIV drugs.

In 2000, Gassy applied for a credit card and a line of credit with Citibank. On the applications, he described himself as a medical practitioner with an average annual income between $70,000 and $90,000.

On fifteen occasions between June 2001 and May 2002, Gassy made the short drive from his parents' home to see Dr Craig Nelson, a GP. Nelson, a tall, square-jawed man with more than a passing resemblance to Clark Kent, didn't know Gassy had been a psychiatrist. He saw before him a security guard with puzzling symptoms.

Gassy brought a letter from a haematologist stating that his haemoglobin levels were extremely low. He complained of losing 10 kilograms over a six-week period.

Yet another HIV test was ordered, but still Gassy was not reassured. He was sure that the dark lesion on his foot was an AIDS-related tumour, Kaposi's sarcoma. Nelson thought it was more likely to be an infection from an ingrown toenail.

After several weeks of diarrhoea in late 2001, Gassy became concerned for his life expectancy and also worried that recent troubles with his vision signalled the onset of AIDS-related retinitis that would send him blind. In April 2002, he asked Nelson for a referral to an eye specialist. Nelson received a report back from the specialist saying Gassy did not have retinitis.

Gassy didn't return for the results.

In July 2002, he joined a gun club in south-west Sydney, which he attended about once a month. In early September, he emailed the office of the Greens Senator, Kerry Nettle, offering to do volunteer work. 'I am able to assist with office administration and/or database management/data entry on an on-call basis or for a few hours each week,' he wrote. 'My resume is attached.'

On Tuesday, 1 October 2002, Gassy made the long drive out to the Australian Customs Service in western Sydney to collect a spare slide for his Glock 26 pistol, which he had imported from the US. Nine months earlier, in January, he had imported a new slide, firing pin and parts for his other pistol.

Violet Palmer, at the Customs Service, had offered for Gassy to collect the package from an office closer to his home. But Gassy wanted to collect it from her in person; he had spoken to Palmer several times by phone as there had been so many delays with the processing of his order. When Gassy arrived, Palmer observed a man who was casually dressed in jeans and had long dark hair and a scraggy beard. Once the paperwork was completed, she handed over the package. He unwrapped it and inspected the slide closely. It's like a work of art, he said.

Palmer went back into her office to finalise the paperwork on the job. About half an hour later she went to her supervisor's office. Through the mirrored glass wall, she could see the waiting room. How strange, she thought. Gassy was still standing there, admiring his Glock slide.

The image stuck in her mind for a long time afterwards. It was disturbing.

On Wednesday, 9 October, Gassy received a reply to his email offering his services to Senator Nettle's office. His help was wanted with a mail-out.

But the timing was bad for Gassy, who had other things on his mind. I won't be available until late next week, he told the senator's office.

8

The Adelaide mafia

Adelaide, it has to be said, is not quite what it seems. On the surface, it is a pretty, friendly place, with wide, easy streets and a civilised appreciation for the finer things of life – the arts, good food and wine. Coffee, in all its confusing manifestations, is sold on almost every city corner. For many, the bustling Central Market, spruiking fresh produce and mouth-watering delicacies, symbolises much about the city's linkage of traditions past with a pleasant present.

Adelaide is also a place of carefully demarcated social divisions where good manners and proper behaviour are properly appreciated. The English tend to feel more at home here than in any other Australian city, and not only because of the well-tended rose gardens. Locals have a habit of asking even mature adults what school and university they attended, and also want to know what their parents did, what suburb they live in, and what wine they drink.

The image that Adelaide likes to promote is of a lively intellectual centre which boasts numerous cultural festivals and a quality lifestyle. Its promoters are not so fond of acknowledging that Adelaide is ageing, conservative, and struggling to maintain its economic base and population of about a million. The bright lights of the east coast have long lured away much of its youthful talent. Newcomers to town, especially those moving in circles of power and influence, tend to stand out. 'I am still an outsider,' says one senior media figure who moved to Adelaide in the 1970s. The vast deserts and distances which separate this city from others seem somehow symbolic.

Locals take a long view of history and have a good memory for grudges. To get on in Adelaide, the saying goes, be careful not to upset someone at work as you likely will have to mingle with them on the dinner party circuit. In other places, there might be six degrees of separation between two strangers. In Adelaide, people meeting for the first time are almost certain to be linked by someone who slept with someone who had a feud with someone who was related to someone else. Newcomers inevitably are disadvantaged when trying to negotiate the entrenched networks of alliance and enmity.

Adelaide is suspicious of change, although the legacy of Don Dunstan stands fresh and proud in the minds of many. Never mind that almost half a lifetime has passed since his adventurous government of the 1960s and 70s. Locals also have an incongruous pride in their city's underbelly. Visitors invariably are assaulted by grisly recitations of Adelaide's history of brutal murders. Any local worth their salt can recite, chapter and verse, the history of the Truro, the Snowtown, and the Family murders as well as the latest theory about what really happened to the missing Beaumont children.★ Never mind that some

---

★*Source*: The Crime Library <http://www.crimelibrary.com/index.html>
1966: The three Beaumont children are abducted from Glenelg Beach.
1971: Ten members of the Bartholomew family are shot to death by a man at Hope Forest.
1972: Homosexual Adelaide University Law lecturer Dr George Duncan is thrown into the Torrens River and drowns.
1973: Schoolgirl Joanne Ratcliffe, eleven, and Kirsty Gordon, four, disappear from Adelaide Oval while attending a football match and are never seen again.
1976–77: Seven women aged fifteen to 26 go missing in and around Adelaide over a 51-day period from Christmas 1976. Their skeletal remains are discovered in the Truro district in the Adelaide foothills several years later in what becomes known as the Truro Murders.
1979–83: In what would become known as the Family Murders, five men are abducted, drugged, held captive, sexually assaulted, hideously mutilated and murdered.
1984: Sexual sadist Bevan Von Einem is tried for the horrific torture and murder of a fifteen-year-old youth. Later, Von Einem is charged with numerous other horrendous crimes relating to the Family Murders.

(continues opposite)

of these cases date back more than 40 years, or that Adelaide is safer than many other cities, or that many accounts of South Australia begin by noting that it did not begin as a convict colony. While local politicians know the populist appeal of tough law-and-order rhetoric, the 'City of Churches' takes a perverse pleasure in its reputation as the 'City of Corpses'. It makes us seem more interesting, explains one local. But the more interesting view, which is also more widely preferred, is that Adelaide tries so hard to repress its dark side that it tends to surface violently.

Perhaps this is all just pop psychology. But perhaps it helps explain why in recent decades, South Australia has achieved another kind of notoriety. Among those in the field, it is widely known as the basket case of mental health. Since the development of a national mental health policy in the early 1990s, most states have made some progress towards pushing resources from institutions to mainstream and community-based care. South Australia has made only tentative steps in that direction. It spends more on mental health and has more psychiatric beds per capita than the national average. Jokes are made about Adelaide having a private psychiatrist on every street corner. In fact, Adelaide's wealthy suburbs boast a higher rate of psychiatrists per head of population than just about anywhere else in Australia. And yet its citizens have poor access to modern mental health care. They are more likely to end up in hospital for mental health problems because prevention and support services in the community are underdeveloped. This is partly because most of the state's public mental health dollars have remained locked up in an old-style asylum, Glenside Hospital, where sprawling, unkempt grounds are littered with rotting buildings, many of which look and smell of their origins in the nineteenth century.

In South Australia, we like to keep the mentally ill behind high walls, says one senior journalist – and the higher the better. She is only half jesting. In a few short decades, the state has been transformed from

---

1994: A letter bomb kills Sergeant Geoff Bowen at the Adelaide offices of the National Crime Authority.
1999: Eight bodies are found in barrels in a bank vault in rural Snowtown, which leads police to the discovery of another two bodies buried in Adelaide.

one of the country's leaders in mental health to a chain-dragger. 'All I know is that South Australia has gone from being the best place to have a mental illness to the worst,' says the well-coiffured Judy Hardy, a prominent local figure whose husband is a member of the well-known Hardy wine family. She has worked as a psychiatric nurse, a mental health bureaucrat, a consultant to state and federal governments, and also has two children who have struggled with mental health problems. Hardy was a teenager called Judy Smallacombe when she started work at Glenside in the 1960s. Most of the patients had been there for so long that they knew how the place worked better than anyone else. On her first day on the job, a patient conducted her orientation tour.

The grand Gothic buildings of Parkside Asylum, as the place was initially known, officially opened in 1870. The first patients transferred there from the Adelaide Lunatic Asylum on North Terrace, near the city centre, were chosen because they were healthy enough to be put to work. Of the first 50 men admitted to Parkside, ten stayed for more than 30 years before dying there. The last of the original patients died in 1915 at 79. He had lived at Parkside for 45 years, after previously spending five years at the other asylum. In other words, 50 of his 79 years had been spent in what was then called asylum but might today be considered custody.

Within a decade of its opening, stone walls were erected around Parkside. Some had a 'ha ha', or a trench about six feet (1.8 metres) deep, running along their bottom. This made it difficult for inmates to scale walls which appeared to be only six feet above ground level. The story goes that they were called ha ha walls because when patients were first allowed into the airing court or exercise yard, they saw the low wall and hoped for an early escape. When they came closer and noticed the moat, this inspired dejection, prompting another patient to mutter 'ha ha'. But the walls around Parkside were not only for containing the inmates. They also kept out trespassers who had a habit of helping themselves to the olives, almonds, oranges, flowers and other produce grown on the grounds, which at one stage covered 134 acres (54.3 hectares). In the late 1800s, more than 2,000 mulberry trees were planted for raising silkworms. Their introduction was described as being 'for the enjoyment and interest' of patients. The men also had billiards for entertainment, while the women sewed. For many decades, the main therapy on offer at Parkside was fresh air and productive work. Chewing tobacco was also dispensed. Little distinction was drawn between patients who had a mental illness, intellectual disability or some other problem, such as syphilis or alcoholism. The imposing clock tower played an important part in governing the community's routines. It chimed every hour, signalling when it was time to rise, to eat, to work and to go to bed. Despite the picturesque surrounds, Parkside was not all rustic idyll. In 1895, a patient battered to death an attendant, as psychiatric nurses were then called, using a spade from the vegetable garden.

In the first half of the twentieth century, Parkside was at the forefront of medical innovation. In the 1930s, patients were injected with drugs – insulin and cardiazol – to trigger seizures as part of their therapy. Some were also injected with malarial blood, followed by doses of quinine and arsenic, as treatment for syphilis (the neurological complications of syphilis were the cause of many admissions to asylums). In 1927, the Nobel prize had been awarded to the Austrian psychiatrist who pioneered this treatment. The resultant fever was thought to arrest the infection causing syphilis, but was also potentially dangerous. In August 1941, Parkside recorded the first use of electroconvulsive therapy (ECT) in Australia. The doctor who administered it helped to make the equipment himself, modelled on the device first used by Italian researchers a few years earlier. History was made once more, in 1945, when the first Australian leucotomy, an operation on the brain, was performed. Nine months later, the 30-year-old patient was discharged after five years in hospital. A report at the time said she subsequently married, had children and was able to cope with outside life. It did not mention whether she suffered the side effects, such as marked cognitive and personality changes, which were common with this surgery. The development of new drugs during the 1950s cut the average length of stay dramatically, from twenty years or more to several weeks. New treatments also reduced the use of shackles, which had been used to tie patients to their beds, or their hands to their waists. They did not eliminate the use of bicycle helmets for many years, however. Epileptics wore these during waking hours, to protect themselves from injury during seizures. As happened at Lakeside in Ballarat and other asylums elsewhere, the opening up of locked wards and the end of segregation of male and female patients and staff marked the beginnings of the end of old-style institutional care.

But for Glenside, as the place was renamed in 1967, the end was painfully slow in coming. Closure was threatened many times since first being discussed in parliament in the 1920s. When the South Australian Government went broke in the early 1990s, it was widely expected that Glenside would close. But instead Hillcrest Hospital, which many regarded as the more progressive institution, got the chop. It was shut to save money rather than to push funds into community care. Then Health Minister Dean Brown announced in 1998 that Glenside would close. But he quickly reneged in the face of a public outcry. The long history of uncertainty was damaging. Buildings and facilities withered under the neglect of successive governments, as did staff development and training, and standards of patient care. Many Glenside nurses had spent most of their careers there and were set in their old-fashioned custodial ways. Notions such as patients' rights and dignity or quality of care held little sway. Nurses who worked at Glenside as late as the 1980s saw patients being herded naked down corridors to showers as if they were cattle. They saw that patients were frightened of some staff, suggesting there was some basis to the rumours about abuse. Long staff lunches at nearby pubs were accepted practice, and there were legendary stories about wild staff parties in deserted wards. Some night staff were known for coming on duty, doing a head count, and then locking the wards while they went to the pub or the movies. Cannabis was easily available on the hospital grounds; good customers were found among both staff and patients. This was just the way it was. Those who expressed concern about poor practices or abuses were ostracised or faced retribution and intimidation. In 1997, an Adelaide magistrate who was hearing allegations that a nurse had assaulted a patient, said a culture of fear at Glenside discouraged reporting of mistreatment of patients. The local newspaper reported that the magistrate believed in the existence of a Glenside mafia.

Throughout the 1990s, many efforts were made to kick-start change in South Australia's mental health services. An endless series of reviews, reports and restructures were undertaken, but with little impact. There was a revolving door for people attempting to lead reform; they were either sacked or moved or quit in disgust. Cynicism was the inevitable result. There was no motivation for those working in the system to change their ways. They had heard all the spoutings about reform so many times before. And seen it come to nothing so many times before. Towards the end of the 1990s, when people looked back, trying to make sense of something that didn't make sense – why South Australia had failed so spectacularly when other states had made some progress – many blamed the lack of a bipartisan approach to mental health, as well as two key events.

The first occurred in December 1992, when Dr Nandadevi Chandraratnam, better known as Dr Chandra, was stabbed to death by a patient at Hillcrest Hospital. Dr Chandra was not a psychiatrist but had chosen to devote her career to working with the mentally ill. A gentle, vivacious woman in her forties who loved colourful saris and gold jewellery, she was popular with colleagues and patients alike. David Tzeegankoff, a paranoid schizophrenic, later told a jury that he thought she was a vampire and that he had heard voices telling him to kill her. Her murder led to widespread media reporting about the dangerousness of psychiatric patients. By contrast, there was little public focus on the harms that patients were suffering as a result of deficiencies in their care. The murder was seen by many as yet another reason to oppose deinstitutionalisation, and devastated the already low morale of mental health staff. The *Advertiser* newspaper reported that in the ten months before the murder, eighteen psychiatrists had resigned from the public sector.

One of the key players in the other seminal event – a bloody-minded strike at Glenside – was Barbara Wieland, who had started there as director of nursing in 1987. She was appointed after staff had blacklisted her predecessor, refusing to attend meetings and making her job untenable. By 1992, Wieland was director of mental health nursing for South Australia and back in the thick of tussles at Glenside. She and the mental health executive team in head office were attempting to introduce a new roster. Nurses at Glenside had long enjoyed a 'two on, two off' roster. It meant they worked thirteen days out of 28, rather than the nineteen days they would work on an eight-hour roster. For many, it enabled them to hold second jobs. Nor were the twelve-hour shifts unduly onerous. Wieland knew of the research showing that staff working a twelve-hour shift paced themselves so that they did no more work than if on an eight-hour shift. On more than one occasion, nurses had been found having a quiet snooze on shift. As had occurred in many other such institutions, there was a sense of aggrieved entitlement among some staff; they were working with society's dregs and so were perfectly justified in making what they could of the situation for themselves.

Wieland believed the eight-hour roster was essential for improving patient care and enabling integration of hospital and community services. She was determined to push it through, and was not surprised when staff went on strike in July 1996 in protest. That was to be expected, given the traditional militancy of the heavily unionised Glenside. But Wieland was horrified to discover that no skeleton staff were left to ensure patient safety. The nurses had locked the wards and walked. Patients who were considered a threat to themselves or to others were left without supervision. Wieland and others who volunteered to run the wards were also horrified to discover that keys to some of the drug storage units had mysteriously disappeared, making it almost impossible to ensure patients received their medication. The striking nurses set up a picket line outside the hospital and harassed staff who came to volunteer their services. Some volunteers found their cars vandalised. The picket line refused to let an ambulance through which was carrying a patient needing treatment. During the night, the hospital's fire alarms were mysteriously activated and volunteers had to evacuate patients. There was no fire. The next day when Wieland put out a plea through the media for help, anonymous callers jammed the telephone lines, making it difficult for volunteers to get through.

The strike left an ugly aftertaste. Wieland was devastated that her own colleagues could be so callous, and thought it a miracle that no lives were lost. It was impossible to imagine that striking surgical nurses would deliberately conceal IV fluids to compromise patient care, she thought. Wieland lost the battle for eight-hour rosters. For many in the state's health system, the strike only reinforced their distaste for the mental health sector. Just as a few bad apples will always spoil the barrel, the many well-meaning staff at Glenside were tarred by the actions of a minority. The strike also reinforced the reputation and the power of the Glenside mafia. Few politicians or bureaucrats would prove brave enough to pick another such fight.

On Monday, 31 July 2000, Margaret Tobin took even more care than usual in choosing what to wear. She settled upon a dark tailored jacket, with a formal collared shirt to wear under it. The severity of the outfit was interrupted by the large metallic lizard which climbed up her left lapel. A photographer and journalist from the *Advertiser* came to record her first day in the new job, and next day the paper published a large photo under the headline 'Mental health care critic now the boss'. Margaret stood in front of the glass panels of the CitiCentre Building, with a grin stretching her mouth and cheeks, revealing her teeth and crinkling her eyes.

She beamed with confidence despite having every reason to look apprehensive. Margaret had a good idea of just how difficult it would be to haul the state's mental health services out of the dark ages. Earlier in the year, she had spent many long hours talking to those who worked in or who used the services. While still based in Sydney, she had worked on an external review of South Australian mental health alongside her friend, Peter Brennan. Brennan, a health administrator and former cardiologist, was now a Mr Fix-It consultant for the health sector. He and Margaret had met through their shared mentor, John Campbell. After their meetings in Adelaide, Margaret and Brennan debriefed over many a glass of red wine, entertaining each other with acerbic descriptions of the personalities and the politics they had encountered. Brennan also tried, fruitlessly, to coax his colleague in the subtleties of the bureaucracy and the importance of being suitably deferential to ministers. Margaret had a dangerous habit of saying what she thought, and Brennan noticed that she seemed to positively enjoy baiting ministers.

At first, Brennan was alarmed when they met with the minister, Dean Brown, to make a private presentation of their review's findings. Without waiting for polite chitchat, Margaret launched into telling Brown in no uncertain terms about what was wrong, and what needed to be done to fix it. Brennan thought her brashness might be off-putting, but Brown, a former premier, hadn't minded at all. A tall man with a firm jaw and a strong physical presence, Brown found Margaret's bluntness refreshing. She didn't waste your time, he thought appreciatively.

The State Government accepted the findings of the review, which argued that after nearly a decade of reports and disregarded recommendations, it was time for action. The review directly challenged those in the sector who believed they were doing a good job but just needed more beds and money. It said that South Australian mental health services were not underfunded, relative to the rest of Australia, but were poorly managed, provided inconsistent, dated care, and lacked leadership. It also challenged general hospitals to accept that mental health was their core business, and could no longer be relegated to institutions such as Glenside. The review recommended that a director of mental health services be appointed to provide leadership and drive improvements in the quality and safety of care. Failure to act, the review warned, would 'guarantee another decade of disillusionment'.

Not long after completing the review, Margaret was asked whether she would be interested in the new position it had recommended. Although many thought the job a poisoned chalice, they also pointed out that it would give her a seat at the National Mental Health Working Group, and the chance to influence national policy. Harvey Whiteford, a professor of psychiatry at the University of Queensland who had been a consultant to the World Bank, headed mental health in the federal department, and helped to engineer the national mental health policy, encouraged Margaret to take the job. It was one of the country's toughest mental health administration jobs, he thought. A number of influential psychiatrists, nurses and other vested interests in South Australia had become extremely skilled and powerful at defeating reform attempts. The previous conciliatory approaches had failed, and someone was needed who was prepared to take them on, even if that meant bashing heads. Margaret was the right woman for the job, in his opinion.

An important consideration for Margaret, in deciding whether to take the position, was knowing that she would have the backing of Dean Brown and his department head, Christine Charles. Some observers had taken bets that sparks would fly between Margaret and Christine Charles – they were powerful, ambitious women of strong wills and opinions. Instead, they forged a firm professional alliance. They also became close friends, perhaps drawn together by the similarities in their backgrounds.

Charles, a small woman with soft brown hair and a quiet speaking voice, grew up as the oldest girl among twelve children in Melbourne's western suburbs. Like Margaret, she had been the good Catholic girl at school – until she became pregnant in her final year, scuttling plans to do medicine. She was sixteen when her first baby was born. In later years she was grateful to the nun who scolded her for being an appalling role model and destroying her life. It made her so angry that she finished high school by correspondence, and later became a community health worker, leftist activist, public housing advocate and academic. This was followed by a meteoric rise through the state bureaucracy where she worked closely with the Liberal premiers Dean Brown and John Olsen.

Charles was not in the habit of letting colleagues come close. But with Margaret she felt safe to relax her guard. They shared an intimacy which reminded Charles of schoolgirl friendships. It provided each woman with a space away from the demands of work and home. They talked of the loneliness and difficulties of being senior women who were challenging the status quo and who were not part of the old boys' networks. They spoke about how strange it was that people who didn't even know them held such strong negative opinions about them. Perhaps it was better, they joked, to be damned as a tough bitch than to be damned as ineffective. They also spoke about the influence of their childhoods. You get sharp elbows when you grow up in an environment where you have to find your own space, Charles said. Margaret felt she had never stopped being the big sister in her family and intimated that she sometimes found it difficult to meet the expectations that role carried. She also talked about her close relationship with Jean. She was not sure if her mum knew what her job really entailed. She never wanted to let her mum down, and sometimes felt guilty about not having enough time for Jean.

A few months after they started working together, Charles confided in Margaret about her own disturbing experiences with local mental health services. Her son Jon had started to go off the rails a few years previously. In his last years in high school, his behaviour had become erratic and he had seemed a bit depressed and stressed. Until then he had been a top student. The feedback from school was that he had developed an attitude problem and at first the family thought it just a difficult teenage phase. When they realised he was suffering paranoia and hallucinations, they looked for another explanation. After a frustrating ride on the medical merry-go-round, Jon finally was given a diagnosis: schizophrenia. When he was admitted to Glenside, Charles was horrified by the institutional environment and the attitudes to patients and their families. If you treat people with no respect over a long period of time, it destroys their humanity, she observed. Glenside offered Jon very little in the way of real therapy and, if anything, exacerbated his problems, Charles thought.

Margaret offered a sympathetic ear. If someone in her family was seriously unwell, she would rather send them interstate than to Glenside, Margaret told Charles. When told of the family's difficulties in finding a private psychiatrist willing to engage with Jon's care, Margaret's reply was caustic. You do know that private psychiatry is about the deeply unhappy rather than the deeply unwell, she said.

The two women had their moments, however. Charles was livid when Margaret, realising that Jon was seriously unwell at home and not receiving adequate care, arranged for a psychiatrist to get in touch with the family. Charles initially saw this as an intrusion. She was furious in her fear that Jon would end up back at Glenside or harmed in a confrontation with police. Later, however, she was grateful when that contact led to a long-term therapeutic relationship for her son.

When Jon first became sick, Charles was reluctant to pull rank with the services caring for him. She didn't think it appropriate to wear her professional hat when attempting to negotiate the health system. That changed dramatically when, during one distressing admission to Glenside, staff refused to let her or her husband, a GP, see Jon. Furious, Charles pulled all the professional strings at her disposal to be allowed to see her son. Some time later, Charles was sickened to find an anonymous note on her desk, related to her department's plans for reform at Glenside. You need to know that people are talking about using your visits to your son to stage a demonstration, it said. The note struck Charles like a kick in the guts. For years afterwards she wondered whether its author was trying to be helpful or threatening. Either way, it only intensified her support for Margaret's plans to shake up the system.

At first, Don groaned when Margaret dropped the news about Adelaide. It didn't seem so long since he had kissed goodbye to his beautiful gardens at Ballarat. He was now settled into his new life at Shellharbour, and the thought of another move didn't fill him with joy. But Margaret said that she had a big job ahead of her, and would need his support. That was all Don needed to hear. Once more, he packed up and organised the logistics, and then drove himself and Bodie to Adelaide, some months after Margaret had started in the new job. Margaret and Don had made out their wills before the move, establishing in them a $15,000 bursary so that if anything ever happened to them, Bodie would be okay. The money was to be used to send Bodie back to his breeder in Victoria, and to ensure he remained well looked after.

Don and Margaret's new home, a modest brick place, was in the northern suburb of Tranmere. They had seen the house for sale, looked over the fence, liked what they saw, and made an offer before even having a chance to look inside. Don was soon hard at work. The sweat poured as he dug up the gravel in the garden during a stinking Adelaide summer, in preparation for the installation of native trees and bushes, camellias and roses. Fragrant shrubs and creepers were carefully placed alongside the entrance path and outside Margaret's office window. The idea, as Don often explained to visitors, was that sweet scents would welcome Margaret when she arrived home exhausted after a long day. Less often told was the story about the time Don wanted to get Margaret's attention as she worked in her home office. They had been shopping for plants and he wanted her advice on the planting outside her study window, but Margaret was distracted by work. So he decided to make a joke of it, stripping off and standing stark naked outside her window, until she looked up.

Margaret and Don soon settled into the rhythms of Adelaide. Wherever possible, they walked on their weekend outings, to the markets, the movies, the cafes. What a strange pair, thought one society hostess when Margaret and Don arrived for lunch, on foot and carrying their backpacks. She thought Margaret a difficult guest to place in dinner party seating: all she wanted to do was talk about work. Others also found the couple awkward in some social situations. They were both socially inept, thought one observer. But Margaret enjoyed the easy lifestyle and didn't miss the tortures of Sydney traffic. What a great place to live, she said to Don one day. Yeah, well don't relax too much, he quipped back, it's the land of the smiling assassins. He knew about the resistance she was facing from many local psychiatrists.

Margaret certainly provoked plenty of antagonism. Many had been stung by the Brennan review's criticisms, and Margaret wasted no time in making waves. Real change could only be achieved by pushing people out of their comfort zones, she thought, and better to have people angry and active rather than apathetic. Some locals resented her bringing in people from interstate to conduct reviews or to take jobs. Word quickly spread about one meeting she held with senior mental health service staff. Years later peoples' memories of the expletives used would vary but her general message was along the lines: *you're a bunch of fucking nitwits and it's about time to get your acts together.* Polite Adelaide was scandalised. Some at the meeting were shocked and retreated from further engagement. Others were outraged and furious. Margaret Tobin was typical of those bullies from New South Wales, muttered some. In following months, many phones rang hot with the latest Margaret Tobin story. *You won't believe what she has done now . . .*

One of Margaret's priorities was to improve the safety of mental health patients by reducing the chances of harm associated with their care. A revolution had begun in the mainstream health system over the previous decade. Researchers had produced damning evidence that many people in Australia and other countries were being harmed by their health care, as a result of problems such as side effects or misapplication of medicines, infections acquired in hospitals, and breakdowns in communication and other systems of care. Much of the harm was judged to be potentially preventable, and governments had invested millions of dollars in trying to make health care safer. But safety had been seen largely as the preserve of hospitals' surgical and medical units – mental health and community care had once more been left behind.

Margaret was determined to change that. Complaints from patients and their families would no longer be casually dismissed. Services would be made accountable for the care they provided and the mistakes they made. Every complaint or critical incident such as a patient's suicide was an opportunity for learning about problems with the system and how improvements might be made, Margaret instructed. She had no qualms about treading on powerful toes when she wasn't happy with a service's response to problems with patient care. This is not good enough, she fumed, not worried if it was a hospital CEO she was upsetting. Margaret was outraged when she discovered that a standard response was usually sent when patients and their families wrote letters of complaint to the department or minister. What a fucking useless system, she raged to one colleague. She insisted that every complaint be fully investigated so that a detailed individual response could be made as quickly as possible. She wanted to see every reply personally, and her staff soon learnt she wouldn't settle for anything less than their best.

Another priority was to fix the organisational mess that was Glenside. Different wards on the sprawling campus were 'owned' by different hospitals and services, making overall governance a nightmare. There was little consistency in how patients were assessed and treated across the campus. The main player at Glenside was the Royal Adelaide Hospital, also known in health circles as The Mighty RAH, or God on North Terrace, or one of the most powerful forces in South Australian health politics. Margaret was soon at loggerheads with the RAH's CEO, Kaye Challinger, a tough, respected manager with a nursing background. Challinger thought it her job to run Glenside. And so did Margaret. Mary Malone, the manager of Glenside, found herself the meat in the sandwich between Challinger, who was her direct boss, and Margaret, who also wanted to boss her.

Margaret took key people on tours of Glenside to garner support for her campaign for change. One of the department's executives, Jim Davidson, was horrified by what Margaret showed him as they spent three hours or so inspecting the wards. Davidson had visited Glenside twenty years before, and was shocked by how little had changed in the interim. He found the place dehumanising, and saw the effect of institutionalisation on patients, who wandered around purposelessly, looking drugged to the eyeballs. It looked more like a jail than a health service, he thought. Margaret also took Davidson to the building where patients were treated after being brought to Adelaide from the Baxter immigration detention centre near Port Augusta. She was horrified they were kept under an armed guard in an open ward. Many of them had been sent mad by the inhumanity of their incarceration behind razor wire at Baxter.

Margaret was on a mission to make mental health a priority, not just for the government, the department and those running general hospitals, but also for the community generally. When she heard that Flinders Medical Centre planned to put its new mental health unit at the back of the hospital site, she was quick to force a rethink. This isn't mainstreaming mental health, she told the hospital CEO. The plans were changed. Margaret cultivated a strong presence and used it to effect in meetings with the police, media, business leaders, churches, prisons, judiciary, unions and welfare groups to gather support and understanding for her vision for mental health. Psychiatrists were not impressed when she spoke bluntly at one meeting of the profession's failure to provide leadership. She also challenged them to change the way they practised – it made far more sense, she argued, for psychiatrists to act like other medical specialists, as consultants rather than primary care clinicians. That way, patients in crisis mightn't have to wait weeks or months for an assessment, and GPs might actually get some of the backup they needed. The state's psychiatrists later had their revenge in a stinging letter of attack. By Margaret's side in many a confrontation was her 2IC, Mike Melino, who was both friend and ally. They shared similar backgrounds as the children of Catholic migrant parents – Melino was born in Italy, moved to Australia as a toddler and was one of six. His father had worked on farms. He had worked in the South Australian health system since the early 1970s, and was a valuable source of historical information.

When she first arrived, Margaret had Melino drive her to meetings. Some months later, he told her it was time to fly solo and gave instructions for how to find Flinders Medical Centre in the city's south. Half an hour later, she rang, hopelessly lost and late for her meeting. One of Melino's main roles was to play good cop to Margaret's bad cop. She could be impatient and intimidating, and didn't tolerate fools or wafflers. Melino often found himself smoothing ruffled feathers in her wake. She also didn't like 'carpets', he noticed. People did much better with Margaret if they didn't let her walk all over them, but were prepared to debate a point. You should back off a bit, he told Margaret a number of times. We rely on these people to run our services, we have to engage them. Margaret was floored when Melino told her, six months after her arrival, that the directors of mental health services were 'shit scared' of her. She was genuinely puzzled that people confused her, the person, with her professional role as a change agent. Melino had no trouble making the distinction. He saw the funny side of Margaret, the woman who roared with laughter at Dilbert cartoons about the absurdities of management. He also laughed at her. She could get so excitable in meetings that he sometimes had to contain his laughter. Once she was so wound up she swiped his water bottle and drank from it without realising her mistake. When he told her afterwards, she cracked up laughing.

I haven't got a maternal bone in my body, Margaret told Melino when he asked why she didn't have kids. It was clear to Melino that work was his boss's grand passion. He couldn't believe her capacity; she put in twelve- to sixteen-hour days, often six days a week. David

Hughes, a trainee psychiatrist in Sydney, also had reason to be impressed by Margaret's capacity for work. He had thought her a tough, unsympathetic boss when he was training at St George and Sutherland hospitals and battling long hours and exhaustion. He revised his opinion after sending his dissertation, on training for adult psychiatrists, to her for comment. He was amazed when it arrived back in his email intray the very next day, with extensive detailed suggestions for improvement. Not many other people in her position would have made such an effort, he felt.

Margaret was also notoriously demanding of her staff. A procession of executive assistants passed through her office, sometimes reduced to tears by the admonishments – you stupid girl, get a brain, what in God's name is this? Andrej Knez, an ambitious, flamboyant young man who had previously worked for a government minister, wasn't particularly impressed when he first met Margaret after applying to work as her assistant. During the interview, he'd been annoyed when she kept interrupting him, and he wasn't sure whether he wanted to work for her. But he changed his mind when he saw that she had nude photographs by Herb Ritts on her wall. There must be more to this woman than first meets the eye, he decided.

Knez soon found himself on a roller-coaster, working eleven-hour days as he struggled to keep pace with his new boss. You work harder than a minister, he moaned to her. Sometimes he rang Mary Pryor in Sydney to share a laugh and a whinge about his workload. He was allowed to take holidays only when Margaret was away, and learnt never to go into her office without being fully prepared for whatever question she might throw at him. Margaret had him in tears on at least one occasion. She didn't understand why people took offence at her straight talking, he decided, because she could handle a verbal bashing herself.

Margaret worked Knez like a dog, and in return won his loyalty. He gave up evenings to watch her make presentations. He wanted to learn about her and about mental health so he could look after her properly. Knez also watched how Margaret dealt with patients who were angry with their care or the world. When a man came into the office one day, yelling aggressively, Knez wanted to call a security guard or the police. But Margaret told him to bring the fellow into her office and to get him a glass of water. Knez realised that the man just wanted to have someone hear his story. Sometimes people are shouting or aggressive because no-one will listen to them, he concluded.

Knez enjoyed Margaret's enthusiasm for shopping. She showed off her new purchases, and he teased her about the latest haircut or colour. One evening, Margaret was heading out to make a presentation to the Adelaide Council. She came out of her office with a red poncho and a red beret and red scarf. She flung the scarf over her shoulder and set off as if into battle. Knez looked at a colleague who had also seen the gesture and they both burst out laughing. Margaret hadn't meant to be funny but they saw the humour in her.

Emergency departments were high on Margaret's agenda. They had not been designed, staffed or resourced to treat the mentally ill. Accidents, injuries and other acute problems were their traditional bread and butter. Throughout the 1990s, emergency staff had struggled to cope with growing numbers of patients with mental health problems. The response of many hospitals, when faced with agitated, difficult patients and a shortage of appropriately skilled staff, was to revert to a technique from the dark ages – shackles. Some hospitals even employed uniformed security guards. To be tied down, for hours or even days on end, would be humiliating and traumatising for the most stable person. For someone grappling with distress, paranoia and psychosis, it could be devastating.

Some staff in emergency departments learnt to fear Margaret. She had a habit of turning up unannounced to inspect how they were treating patients, and often was not happy about what she found. In late 2001, a public scandal erupted about the physical and chemical restraint of patients in general hospital wards and emergency departments. Restraints were also being used on country patients while being transported to Adelaide for psychiatric care. Margaret told a television reporter that the problem reflected longstanding neglect of mental health and its marginalisation by the mainstream health system. Hospital staff didn't have the skills, confidence or resources to handle patients appropriately, she said, and patients deserved better.

'I apologise to them for what I consider to be an inadequate level of care, an inappropriate response to their high levels of distress,' she said. A subsequent Ombudsman's inquiry heard evidence that shackling had increased in recent years, and that some patients had been detained by chemical and physical restraints in accident and emergency departments for up to six days. It also found there was insufficient documentation to enable proper evaluation of such incidents. Margaret had her staff working long hours to develop a series of policies and procedures for emergency departments and related settings. Hospital managers and staff were being put on notice to lift their game.

On Saturday, 9 February 2002, South Australians went to the polls. The result was a cliff-hanger and it was almost a month before the new Labor Premier, Mike Rann, was named. Margaret kept her political preferences close to her chest but many assumed her commitment to social justice would make her a Labor supporter. In private conversations, she talked of her concern about the Federal Government's detention of asylum seekers. But the change of government was not a happy result for Margaret professionally. She had spent more than eighteen months working her guts out to win the support of the previous government and finally had their backing for a restructure of Glenside. Now she had to start all over again. She found the staff in the new minister's office rude and disrespectful, and felt unsupported by the incoming government. What have I done wrong? she asked colleagues. Just grit your teeth and wait it out, they advised. It is just the public service purgatory you have to go through with an inexperienced, suspicious new government. A new government always has to show that the old one wasn't working. Margaret was blunt with her superiors about her frustrations with delays and hiccups in the bureaucratic and political machinations. 'Now we need your wisdom to unblock the constipation,' she emailed one senior department executive, her email signature coloured a bright pink.

It was not entirely unexpected when Christine Charles was given her marching orders in April 2002. Health is always a contentious political issue, and Charles was associated with the previous administration, despite personally leaning more towards the left. But the shock of the news drained the blood from Margaret's face. A staff member who saw her ashen face realised at that moment just how much Margaret's work meant to her. It was as if everything that she was passionate about might be lost. Margaret was in tears in Charles's office but back in control by the time she briefed staff later in the day.

In July 2002, Margaret received the bit of paper she had once set as a professional goal. Flinders University wrote to advise that she had been conferred the title of Professorial Fellow, a three-year appointment, in recognition of her work. That month Margaret was frank in sharing the frustration and difficulties of her job during a presentation to a group at the Health Leaders Network in Melbourne. The audience empathised when she put up an illustration of a frazzled chook, eyes bulging out of its head, with the caption: 'Stress. The confusion created when one's mind overrides the body's basic desire to choke the living shit out of some asshole who desperately needs it.'

Margaret said she was overseeing a highly complex change management process. It was like juggling multiple grenades, or trying to complete a 1,000-piece jigsaw on a 500-piece-sized table. The biggest challenge was to manage the complexity while absorbing the anxiety of politicians, bureaucrats, service directors, her staff, consumers, carers and the community. The issues included community attitudes and ignorance about mental health, the disempowerment of patients and carers, the marginalisation of mental health in the broader health system, late detection and ineffective prevention by the primary health care sector, and poor integration, skills and confidence in the specialist mental health services.

She quoted a leadership guru, Noel M. Tichy, who wrote in his book *The Leadership Engine*, that: 'Becoming a world class leader requires the ability to master revolutionary change. It requires taking on the dramatic challenge of creatively destroying and remaking organisations in order to improve them. Not just once, but repeatedly. In order for organisations to win, revolutions driven by leaders with ideas and the heart and guts to bring them alive must become a way of life.'

Margaret had struck up a friendship with a group of senior, like-minded departmental executives who met regularly for a drink at the end of the working week. They took it in turns to bring a special bottle of malt whisky, but Margaret stuck to her beloved red wine. As they debriefed and unwound, workmates saw a more relaxed side of Margaret. She regaled them with her beliefs in the power of colour, and was supremely confident in diagnosing what colours worked or didn't work for colleagues. One evening, she organised some of the group to attend a session with a colours consultant. One of the whisky drinkers, Chris McGowan, was often the butt of jokes because of his dress sense and taste in ties. Margaret, who often led the attack, must have thought the teasing went too far one evening because she rang McGowan on her way home to ask if he was all right. He was surprised to get the call. Underneath that tough, confident exterior lurked a sensitive, caring person, he thought.

On Monday, 23 September, Margaret celebrated her fiftieth birthday with a cake at the office. Unbeknown to her, the malt whisky group had been conspiring over plans for her birthday party. When Margaret arrived at the party, she did not get the joke at first. Everyone had been told to wear a bright primary colour, and had drawn their allocated colour from a hat. Even the food and drinks had been selected and arranged to suit the colour theme. Margaret was delighted when she finally twigged. She also seemed quite over-whelmed that people had made such an effort. Many of her birthday presents paid tribute to her Chinese horoscope. She was born in the year of the dragon.

Christine Charles did not make it to the party but had caught up with Margaret for dinner in late August, at an Indian restaurant near the CitiCentre Building. Margaret grinned at Charles as she took off her fur hat to reveal her recently shaven scalp. It was her 'tennis ball' haircut, she had told Don when she rang from the hairdressers to break the news about her yellow fuzz. Margaret enjoyed watching peoples' reactions to her new look, and gave Charles the impression that she had no hang-ups at all about turning 50. But overall the mood of the evening was flat. Margaret was frustrated that she didn't have the backing she needed from above, and that mental health reform was slipping off the political agenda. She felt that bad behaviour was emerging in services because people felt they could get away with it.

Charles also thought that Margaret seemed apprehensive. She was stirring up a hornet's nest and wasn't sure where it was all leading. They were turning over rocks and finding some pretty slimy stuff at Glenside, she said, including a thriving market in illicit drugs. The two women also discussed the recent threats to Des Graham, whom Margaret had recruited from interstate to drive change at Glenside. Graham had begun his career as a nurse at Broken Hill in western New South Wales, and still had the square shoulders and physique of the rugby league footballer he once was. When the first death threat arrived in his mail at work, he wasn't overly worried. He'd expected to be operating in a hostile environment. But by the time he had opened several such missives and received two threatening phone calls, Graham had become more concerned, notifying police and telling his wife to travel home by different routes. One note had threatened him with being barbecued; another had told him to 'piss off and leave us alone', with a few more expletives added.

Margaret hadn't been shocked by the threats. She was a member of the panel which interviewed Des Graham for the job in the first place. At the end of his interview, she had spoken at length about what a difficult job he was taking on. Previous experiences else-where suggested there would be threats, if not actual incidents, of violence.

Margaret and Charles also spoke of the recent firebombing. Martin Reidy, a nurse manager at Glenside, had returned home from night duty to discover that his car, sitting in the carport outside his family home, had been set alight. Many were sure it was related to changes that he was trying to make to work practices. Reidy had been acutely aware of nurses' hostility in the lead-up to the incident. Silence would settle whenever he walked into wards, and his attempts to make con-versation would be ignored. Before the firebombing, he had received a threatening letter saying his days were numbered. A few days after the arson, he received a note in the internal hospital mail expressing joy at the torching. Another nasty note followed a few days later. Reidy was extremely distressed by the firebombing, which had made his wife and family fear for their lives. He reported it to police but felt they did not take the incident seriously. Many had their suspicions about who was responsible. They had a particular nurse in mind. But nothing came of the investigations.

At the end of their evening together, Charles went home concerned for her friend, and sad that she was having such a tough time. Some of Margaret's words stuck in her mind in particular. They had been talking about how to manage when you feel under threat. At the end of the day, Charles said, all we can do is get on with our lives; you can't live behind closed doors.

Yes, replied Margaret, you just need to be sensible. If someone really wants to get you, they will.

9

Driven

In spring, the 1,400-odd kilometre drive from Sydney to Adelaide is rich with the promise of budding life. Wattles along the roadside bloom golden and sweet, canola crops wave a painfully bright yellow and fresh leaves decorate the grapevines. Even closed car windows cannot repel the heady fragrance of the white blossoms on lush orange groves.

The road winds among pert, green hills and stretches endlessly across dusty outback plains and through grey mallee scrub, sandy red soils and irrigated plantations. It is a long drive – at least sixteen hours, for the law-abiding. Signposts, from the unimaginative to the frankly ridiculous, offer light relief along the way. There is Gumly Gumly, a blip on the outskirts of Wagga Wagga, the Berry Jerry rest area, and Bullenbung Creek. At Collingullie stands a sign to The Rock. Elsewhere are postings for Maud, Hell's Gate Feedlot and a town called Sedan. The frequency of road safety billboards advertising such suggestive phrases as 'Droopy Eyes?' is yawn-inducing.

As Gassy began the journey, early in the afternoon of Saturday, 12 October 2002, he had no idea of the murderous preparations that were under way elsewhere. In countries scattered around the globe, people went about their usual routines, not realising this was to be a loved one's last day. For on the tropical holiday island of Bali in Indonesia, terrorists were making their final preparations for a massacre. Gassy had also been engaged in some careful planning since finding out about his parents' trip to Vietnam. He and and his sister Elizabeth went to the airport, on the night before he began his own trip, to wave them off on a two-week holiday. By then, he already had the car, an unremarkable small vehicle, a grey Nissan Pulsar. He withdrew $1,000 from an auto teller at Sutherland shopping centre on the Friday morning and in the afternoon picked up the car from the Avis outlet at Hurstville, about twenty minutes' drive from his parents' home.

Gassy had clocked up more than 800 kilometres by the time he pulled into the tired driveway of the Shamrock Motel at Balranald, in south-western New South Wales, on the Saturday night. The motel's owner, Denise Conway, a pretty woman whose soft features and colouring told of an Irish heritage, was tidying up from an evening in the motel's restaurant, Dee Cee's, which took its name from hers. When the bell rang, a young waitress went to see who was there. He's a strange one, she told Conway when she came back to report a man wanting a room.

Conway was wary when she went to take the stranger's details. It was late and his scruffy appearance, with long dark hair falling around his face, didn't gel with the late-model car he was driving. He was perspiring noticeably. Conway, a nurse in a previous life, thought the man was ill or needed a fix. She decided to put him in room 17, one of the older rooms with a single bed, just in case. It wouldn't matter so much if he trashed it. The man spoke with a slight accent and so softly that she had to ask him to repeat himself. Conway asked him to write his details in the registration book. David Pais handed over cash when asked to pay upfront, and gave an address later shown to be fictitious.

Next morning, the man rang at 7 am asking for a late wake-up call. Conway was surprised when he came to the office about 40 minutes later, well before the wake-up call was due. He'd had a coffee and his hair was wet, as if he had just jumped out of the shower. He was in jeans and a light-coloured T-shirt, and flicked her a little smile as he dropped his key on the counter. Later she found many long dark hairs in his bedding. She wondered if he might be an Aboriginal health worker. That would explain the car.

As Gassy made the final leg of his trip into Adelaide, the rest of Australia was reeling with shock from the bombs which had torn apart nightclubs in Kuta, one of Bali's most popular destinations. At that early stage, seven Australians had been confirmed among the scores of dead, though the toll would rise far higher. Already, the bombing was being called 'our September 11'. There was a sense that Australia itself was under attack even though the bombing had been so far away. The air force was preparing to bring planeloads of burns victims to Australia for treatment as Gassy turned his car into Lindy Lodge, a shabby motel at Woodville Park on Adelaide's north side, just a short drive from the city. The motel was once known as a haunt for drug addicts and prostitutes, and the streetwise management was not particularly trusting of clientele, requesting a deposit before connecting the phone line to the rooms. The numbers for the police and crisis care were on auto dial at reception. Again, David Paes paid cash in advance for one night and gave the same fictitious address that Denise Conway had recorded. He gave a mobile number which, it would later transpire, was only one digit different from one belonging to Eric Gassy.

On the Friday that Gassy was waving off his parents, Don flew back to Adelaide after his mother's funeral in Melbourne. She died at 86 after being told in 1968 that she had pancreatitis and two years to live. Don and Margaret's beloved Bodie had also died recently. He was euthanised after a painful illness, and Margaret had taken some compassionate leave from work to oversee his burial in the garden. It had been tough adjusting to his absence from their daily routines. Bodie could always tell when Margaret was coming home, whether from a day at the office or a conference in New Zealand, because he picked up on Don's excitement.

Don and Margaret spent Saturday doing what they loved, pottering about the shops, followed by an evening at the movies. Margaret bought several new outfits, trying on clothes for some hours under Don's supervision. He was also free with his advice to another woman in the shop, who later sent a thank-you note. Margaret thought she would have a good opportunity for airing her purchases the following weekend in Melbourne. Jean and the rest of the family had planned a gathering to celebrate Margaret's recent fiftieth, and she was also going to catch up with her good mate Di Skene. They planned to sit in the sun at Southbank and enjoy a glass of red wine over lunch. Margaret had been really touched after Bodie's death when Di sent them a key ring featuring a picture of an Airedale. When Di had moved to Melbourne for a new job earlier in the year, Margaret gave her a little gift – a 'Life's Little Helper Kit' containing a marble, for those days when you have lost yours, a bear, for those often needed hugs, a rubber band to help you stretch beyond your current limits, a heart to remind you that somebody cares, and a piece of string, to hold it all together when it seems to be falling apart. Di had been both touched and surprised by the gift; it seemed uncharacteristically girly and sentimental for Margaret.

Once news of the Bali bombing broke, Margaret kept half an eye on her emails for the rest of the weekend. On Sunday, Beverley Raphael sent all the state mental health directors a copy of the disaster response manual prepared before the Sydney Olympics, and Margaret was planning what she and her unit needed to do in the wake of Bali. There would be help-lines to organise, staff to brief. That evening, she and Don spent an hour or so walking to North Adelaide for dinner at one of their favourite restaurants. They enjoyed a few glasses of red and caught a cab home.

Margaret had much on her mind as she readied for work the next morning; a big day lay ahead. But still there was time for their farewell rituals. I must deadhead those geraniums, she said as they walked out to the car. Don knew she meant that was a job for him. Standing in their driveway, Don opened the car door, as usual, and planted a kiss after Margaret settled into her seat. As usual, he checked that her car doors were locked. He always worried that something might happen. Back in their Ballarat days, Margaret had rolled her car driving on the gravel roads to Ararat one morning. She'd done time in a wheelchair afterwards, with a cracked hip. When they moved, Don had dismissed suggestions they live in the Adelaide Hills. He would have been too worried about her taking those narrow bends in the dark or fog. Have a nice day love, were her last words as she drove off. Don had some grocery shopping to do.

Margaret was at her desk before 7.30 am, and the phone hardly stopped thereafter. A colleague from New South Wales rang, wanting her advice on how to ensure better mental health services for asylum seekers and others in immigration detention centres. She was on the phone to the minister when Mary Malone rang on another line to say that she wouldn't be in to work at Glenside today as her mother had died the previous evening. Grief was everywhere, it seemed. A staffer at the Royal Adelaide Hospital had lost a family member in the Bali bombing. In the morning newspaper the Prime Minister warned that Australia must realise it was not immune from the dangers of terrorism.

Margaret was so busy coordinating the Bali response that she couldn't sit through the regular meeting of mental health service directors which ran from 9 am to 1 pm. She popped in and out. She didn't show any sign of being stressed by the demands of the day; rather she was in her element, enjoying the challenge. It was an opportunity for mental health to assist the community, she told someone. Barbara Wieland thought the directors' meeting was one of the best they'd had. Margaret was positive about the progress that was being made and how hard people were working, and indulged in some friendly banter during one of the breaks. She jokingly reprimanded the directors for giving her offsider Rebecca Graham a hard time while Margaret was out of the room. She also mentioned to Wieland that the last few months had been the toughest of her career. Trying to bring about change in South Australia's mental health services was like breaking up concrete, she'd once said.

Wieland had recently bought some brooches, of roses and camellias made out of colourful fabrics, to give to each of the directors to wear as a friendly jest about Margaret's love of floral accessories. Maybe she would give them out for people to wear at the next meeting. She hoped Margaret would see the humour. Unbeknown to

Wieland, Margaret also had some gift-giving planned. She was famous for giving quirky cards and gifts to staff and friends. This Christmas, she planned to give every mental health director a silly award that reflected their personality.

After the directors left, Margaret finalised a press release announcing details of a hotline to help those distressed by the Bali tragedy. 'The Department of Human Services wishes to advise members of the public and people affected by this tragic event that it is a normal reaction after such an event to experience distressing images of the event, tearfulness, sleep disturbance, frustration and moodiness for a few days or a week,' it said. 'Most people benefit during this time by talking through their reactions with someone who is supportive and sympathetic. This can be a family member, your local general practitioner, or a health care worker. Only a few people experience severe distress which is ongoing after a couple of weeks. This group will benefit from discussing their reactions with an experienced mental health professional, and receiving more detailed help.' At 1.30 pm, Margaret sent the final version of the media release to the departmental officers who would oversee its distribution.

The dogs of hunger were well and truly barking by the time Margaret finally had a chance to grab some lunch. It was just before 2 pm and she had to be quick. Her assistant, Andrej Knez, couldn't join her. He was eating at his desk, finalising the paperwork for her 2.30 pm meeting. Margaret and Rebecca Graham headed to the usual haunt, the elegant Symposium cafe in Gay's Arcade just a few minutes' walk away. The cafe relied on the department for most of its business. Staff knew of Margaret's gluten intolerance, and generally kept one of the quieter tables reserved for her. Graham, an intensive care nurse turned manager, had been working with Margaret for about a year. She had decided that Margaret was both the hardest and the best boss she had ever experienced. Graham, whose soft, solicitous voice and attractive blonde bob disguised a strong spine, relished any opportunity to chat with Margaret. It was a chance to listen and learn. Nor was she slow to stand up for herself when the occasion demanded. Once when Margaret had admonished Graham about having an anxious personality, Rebecca had fired straight back: 'Not before I started working with you.' A few slow moments had passed before Margaret laughed. Another time, Graham had been so relieved when Margaret admitted that Ian Hickie, famous for a fast-moving mouth which struggled to keep pace with an even faster brain, used to exhaust her. Graham had felt some satisfaction in telling her boss: 'That is what you do to us.'

As the waitress hovered, Margaret ordered a vegetable stack and Graham a soup. Graham debriefed about the directors going 'feral' at the meeting and was surprised when Margaret revealed that she had already told them off about it. Margaret shook with laughter at her companion's surprise. Graham was delighted when talk turned to more personal matters. Usually they spoke only of work. Margaret described the beautiful suit she had bought on the weekend with Don at Norwood. You would love it, Rebecca, she said. They also talked about the influence of their mothers, both called Jean. Margaret said that her strength came from her mother. She also felt guilty when she spent money because her mother had been so frugal for so many years.

Margaret was in a fabulous mood, Graham thought. She clearly was thriving on the day's challenges. Graham hadn't finished her soup, it was too hot to gulp down, when Margaret said she had to rush back to work for a meeting. On her way, she had to stop at her office on level 8 to collect the meeting papers from Knez. Graham stayed in her seat, chuffed to have had such warm interaction with her boss. She rang her husband to tell him of the morning's doings, and decided on a rare small indulgence; she would take five minutes out to wander across the mall and buy some stockings.

At 2.31 pm, security cameras captured Margaret on film as she left the arcade. She was walking quickly, as usual. The foyer of the Citi-Centre Building had no cameras to record her return. Security in the building was lax. Anyone could walk off the street and take a lift, no questions asked. It would later transpire that the average service station had better security than the building which housed some of the state's most senior public servants.

Suzanne Heath, a clinical psychologist, was waiting for a lift as Margaret entered the foyer. Heath had worked on several projects with Margaret and was somewhat in awe of her. She felt flattered when Margaret engaged her in conversation. They continued to discuss the Bali bombings as they entered the goods lift and stood at the back. The two women were too engrossed in talk of terrorism to pay attention to the two men who followed them into the lift. Grant Francis, another bureaucrat, was on his way to a meeting. He knew of Margaret, by sight and reputation, but not well enough to say hello. Francis noticed the other man before they entered the lift. He had dark hair to his shoulders and a trimmed dark beard. His skin was a light colour for an Aborigine. Francis kept his eyes down during the fifteen or so seconds that the lift took to reach level 7, where he and Heath exited. The man stayed at the front of the lift as the doors closed.

Eight seconds later, the doors opened again. As Margaret walked out into the foyer of level 8, she was fumbling for her security pass to open the locked doors into the office areas. Atanas Nikolof, a young man working at the reception desk, heard the bell announcing the lift's arrival and looked up briefly from under his dark gelled hair to see Margaret walking towards him. He did not notice the man in the lift. The man, standing less than 4 metres behind Margaret, could clearly see the back of her head and shoulders as she turned slightly to the right.

Margaret did not see the man as he reached for the small black pistol. He pressed the trigger. Once, twice, and a third time. The fourth bullet most likely was fired as Margaret was either falling to the floor or had already fallen.

Time does not move in a straight continuous line at such terrible moments. It bends and distorts, moving quickly and slowly, backwards and forwards, all at once. Margaret must have heard the loud bangs, smelt the smoke. Elsewhere, others had heard too. They thought a computer had blown up, that furniture was being dropped, that a nail gun was being used, or that metal pipes were being banged. One man thought he heard balloons being popped. Margaret knew what the noises meant. Her screams were loud enough to be heard by colleagues on the level below.

A courier heard three bangs and a woman's screams as his lift passed level 8. He was returning to the ground floor after delivering office chairs. The courier chatted with another man about the Bali bombing when the lift reached the ground floor, and hesitated before leaving the building. He had completed a first aid course recently and wondered if anyone needed his help. He looked around but didn't see anything out of the ordinary, so headed off towards his nearby van.

Upstairs, Nikolof saw Margaret fall to the floor. It was as if she was crumbling, the way her legs gave out. He caught a glimpse of dark movement towards the lifts. He felt it was the shape of a man but could not be sure. Perhaps it was a reflection in the lift door that he saw. Nikolof didn't see whether the shadowy figure escaped by the lift or the nearby fire escape. Margaret was absorbing his attention. Several people came rushing into the foyer after recognising the sound of gunshots. They were so shocked and so focused on Margaret that more than one person thought themselves first on the scene.

Margaret recognised the striking redhead rushing to her side. 'Kae, I've been shot, I've been shot,' she cried. She had collapsed with her legs pointing towards the lifts and her head towards the security door she had been about to open. Kae Martin, a senior bureaucrat whose office adjoined Margaret's, knelt on the floor and took her hand. She immediately recognised the gravity of the situation, even before seeing the four casings on the floor. The colour of death was on Margaret's face. With 25 years' experience as a nurse, Martin didn't have to stop to think about what to do. She swung into action, unbuttoning Margaret's jacket and blouse, and cutting her bra so she could tend the wounds.

Margaret was moaning as Sally Tideman, a doctor who also worked on the floor, rushed to help. Tideman had looked up to Margaret as a mentor – there were not many female medical administrators around – and asked for her advice on career matters a number of times. Tideman could not believe what was happening. It all seemed unreal. But her medical training propelled her into doing what she could. One of Margaret's staff, André Jenkins, was also in the foyer area. He held Margaret's hand and spoke briefly to her, trying to reassure her that everything would be all right. He then went on a frustrating search for the first aid kit. The first aid officer was on a day off. Nikolof was so shaken he was having difficulty dialling the emergency number.

Margaret quickly lost consciousness. Martin began moving in tune with the rhythms of life, pushing down on Margaret's heart and blowing air into her lungs. Another senior nurse bureaucrat, Deborah Pratt, was helping with the resuscitation effort. They were interrupted by the arrival of the Channel 7 camera crew, which burst out of the lifts, filming. Martin yelled at them to get out and put up her hands to obscure the camera. It was infuriating that they were there before the ambulance.

To Martin, it felt like hours before the ambos arrived, although it was only minutes since the shooting. Police escorted Clinton Daniels, a tall, strapping ambulance officer, and his colleagues to the eighth floor. Daniels began examining Margaret as he removed the rest of her clothing with shears. He felt her neck, looking for a pulse. There was none. The ECG machine showed the rhythm of a heart that was dying.

The ambulance officers tilted Margaret's head back so they could feed plastic tubing down the back of her throat, into her trachea and lungs. A machine was now helping Margaret breathe. For at least twenty minutes, they pumped her with fluids in a desperate attempt to counteract the massive loss of blood. They had some success. Her heart started pumping again and they detected a slight pulse.

Carefully, they lifted her onto a stretcher for the short trip to Royal Adelaide Hospital. The foyer they left behind was littered with debris: remnants of bandages and packaging, a water bottle, an upturned coffee cup, a coffee filter and a telephone book. Margaret's dark skirt lay stained by her blood and punctured by a circular hole. Five circular holes marked her black jacket, and her blue shirt was cut, as were her pale slip and bra. Her ID card and handbag lay abandoned, and four cartridge shells also bore witness to the aftermath.

In her office at the Royal Adelaide, Kaye Challinger was being interviewed by a journalist from the *Advertiser*. Her hospital had emergency teams in Darwin, helping the Bali survivors. After the phone rang, Challinger immediately left her office for the emergency department, where a trauma team was primed and waiting for an ambulance to arrive.

At first Don thought Roxanne Ramsay, who just a few weeks earlier had hosted Margaret's fiftieth birthday party, was joking on the other end of the phone line. That's not funny, he said crossly before realising his mistake. Grocery bags flew across the kitchen as he grabbed the keys and bolted for the door. He drove fast and furious to the hospital, thinking of how he would help tend and mend Margaret. It probably was only a flesh wound, he thought hopefully.

Within minutes of the ambulance's arrival at the hospital, surgeons had cut through Margaret's chest walls to check for injuries to her heart. Amazingly, it was untouched. The blood loss, combined with the damage to her lungs, had sent her heartbeat haywire. Three times Margaret's body jumped as the defibrillator was activated, in an attempt to shock her heart back into rhythm. The team kept pumping in fluids and trying to stem the blood flow. But it was no use.

The four tiny projectiles had done major damage to Margaret's chest, abdomen, lungs, liver and bowel. It was amazing that each one had missed her heart and the major blood vessels, the aorta and pulmonary arteries. Her brain and head were not affected. As one doctor would later remark, it was the plumbing that was the trouble. The sudden blood loss had sent Margaret's blood pressure so dangerously low that her heart was unable to keep supplying her organs with the fuel they needed. Their only option was to shut down.

If there had been only one bullet, Margaret may have had a fighting chance of survival. But the cumulative effect of all four was invincible. Twenty-five minutes after Margaret arrived at the hospital, in the cold, clinical language of medicine, she was certified extinct.

We did everything we could, the doctors told Don, but we couldn't stop the bleeding. Margaret's life was gone before he found her body. A police officer went with Don to the tiny viewing room, where Margaret lay, covered by a sheet. Only her head was visible. 'Is this Margaret Julia Tobin?' the police officer asked Don. 'Yes, it certainly is. I wish it wasn't,' he replied.

By Don's side for the rest of the afternoon were some of Margaret's close friends, including Learne Durrington and her partner Deirdre Pearsall, both social workers by training. Automatically, they went into professional mode, encouraging Don to talk to Margaret, to say goodbye, and to tell her whatever he needed to say. As Don struggled to understand what he was seeing and hearing, they made phone calls, organised flights, and began planning ahead.

Word spread quickly throughout Adelaide and beyond. No-one knew what to make of the shooting. It scarcely seemed possible that the attack was directed at Margaret in particular. As the city streets filled with the screams of ambulance and police sirens, some wondered if Adelaide itself was under attack. Perhaps terrorists were at work. Wild rumours found wings. In Parliament House, where the doors were shut, some MPs heard that there had been shootings in several government buildings.

As public buildings all over the city were being locked down, the writer Susan Mitchell was sitting in a court room, reeling from the grisly evidence presented on the first day of the Snowtown trial. She heard how the pungent smell of rotting flesh greeted police when they opened a vault in a disused bank in Snowtown. The remains of eight bodies were decomposing in the barrels, and more would later be discovered. Sometime after 4 pm, the judge addressed the jury and the court room. 'I am afraid I have just received some extremely distressing news,' he said. 'A senior public servant has been gunned down outside her office in Hindmarsh Square. So be very careful as you leave the building.'

'We stared at each other in total disbelief,' Mitchell later wrote in her book probing Adelaide's underbelly, *All Things Bright and Beautiful: Murder in the City of Light*. 'I had heard some shocking things in this courtroom today but this was really insane. What kind of city had I come home to?'

On the afternoon of Margaret's death, some of the cream of Australian psychiatry were gathering at a Sydney hotel in preparation for examinations of trainee psychiatrists in coming days. Several heard news of a shooting on their radio or mobile as they drove into the city. One of Margaret's friends from St George heard that a woman had been shot in Adelaide. She knew it was Margaret's building because her former boss had recently been a referee for her. 'Well I hope Margaret hasn't been upsetting anyone,' she thought flippantly. Not long after the meeting began, trembling announcements were made, first that Margaret had been shot and then later that she had died. Many of the 80 or so doctors in the room were friends and colleagues of Margaret. Some left, unable to continue on. The atmosphere was thick with distress. Men and women sobbed, people hugged and consoled each other.

After the initial shock came the questions. Some thought the shooting was too well planned and coolly executed to be the work of a patient in the grip of psychosis. It was more like a professional hit or assassination. Those who knew something about Margaret's job assumed her murder was connected to the changes she was trying to bring to Glenside. She had been trying to bust a drug ring at Glenside, it was said, and the place's unsavoury history was well known.

At Glenside, senior staff acted quickly once they heard the news. If the shooting was aimed at scuttling the mental health reform process, then who else was in danger? There were 1,000 staff and more than 300 patients at Glenside to protect. Des Graham rang his wife to tell her not to go home after collecting the kids from school. He would meet them later at a friend's place. He instructed staff to secure all wards and other facilities, and called a staff meeting. Within twenty minutes, the huge rambling complex with 74 buildings scattered across 85 acres (34.4 hectares) had been shut down, with security guards stationed out the front.

While Margaret was being tended at the hospital, hundreds of terrified bureaucrats remained huddled in their CitiCentre offices, fearing the killer was still in their building. Police in the special emergency response squad, the STAR or Special Task and Rescue group, went through the CitiCentre floor by floor. Wearing helmets and combat gear, they burst onto each level, guns outstretched and screaming for people to raise their hands in the air. Don't move, they shouted. Where's your ID? Are there any people on the floor you don't recognise? Some staff broke down, overwhelmed by shock. The building was slowly evacuated, floor by floor. It was a long, tense wait, and many workers were traumatised for a long time afterwards by their treatment at the hands of the aggressive STAR force.

Rebecca Graham was walking across the mall when her mobile rang. She heard that Margaret had been shot but it didn't sink in.

André Jenkins repeated himself another three times before she understood. Her first thought was that, with Mike Melino on leave, she was
acting as Margaret's second-in-charge, and that she had to look after
her staff. Graham rang her husband. 'There's been an incident at work,'
she said. 'It's not me. You need to know I am perfectly fine but please
support me. I have to go back.' She also asked him to ring her mother.

The phone rang hot at Graham's home with friends and family
wanting to know if she was okay. Some thought it was Graham who
had been shot. Her teenage son Nathan was distraught and wouldn't
believe his father's reassurances. Graham meanwhile waited outside
the CitiCentre Building, briefing police about its layout, and
rounding up staff as they emerged. The media were harassing her,
shoving cameras in her face. She focused on keeping herself together;
she couldn't let herself think about Margaret. She had to concentrate
on the present and what needed to be done. She couldn't believe it
when she realised that her husband had brought Nathan in to see her.
'What are you doing?' she yelled. 'There's a gunman around.' Crying,
she left her husband and son to return to assisting police, who had
cordoned off the building and nearby areas. It was close to midnight
before she saw them again. Graham managed to remain on autopilot
for the next few days but then started to come undone. Her hair
began falling out and she kept returning to a vague uneasy memory
of being in the lift with Margaret earlier in the day and feeling a
threatening presence.

As the afternoon wore on, many began to reflect on whether they
had seen anything unusual that morning. Elizabeth Covington, a
long-term employee, remembered looking out her window on the
first floor overlooking Hindmarsh Square. About 1.45 pm, she had
noticed a man with an olive complexion, long hair and a beard
hanging around the bicycle stand near the entry. She was trying to
write something, and looked outside as she struggled with her com-
position. Every time she looked, he was there, as if waiting for
somebody. Covington left her desk about 2.20 pm to go to the
photocopy room. When she returned ten minutes later, he was gone.

Brian Tuffin, a public servant with the Metropolitan Fire Service,
remembered seeing an agitated man in the foyer of the CitiCentre

Building about 2.30 pm. Tuffin was strolling back to work from lunch and thought the man looked lost. Tuffin had to stop himself from asking if the man needed any help. He often had to check this impulse to offer strangers assistance. It was a habit of his nature and his training as a librarian. But on this day, he did not have time to stop, he had to get back to work. When police later took a statement about the man he had seen, Tuffin noticed it contained a couple of spelling errors.

It was not until later that afternoon that Suzanne Heath realised she had been one of the last people to speak with Margaret. Then it dawned that the killer must have been in the lift with her. She gave police a vague description of the man she remembered but later realised it was of Grant Francis. For months afterwards, she struggled with her inability to recall the fourth person. It was the least she could do for Margaret, to be a good witness. It was horrific that she couldn't remember. Heath spent hours reliving the lift ride in her mind, dredging for a memory that didn't exist. She felt inadequate, that she wasn't doing her part. Years later, she would be unable to enter a lift without making careful note of its other occupants.

Terry Anderson, the department's elegantly long and lean media officer, first learnt about the shooting when he received a phone call from a friend at the *Advertiser*. 'Are you okay?' asked the journalist. 'There's been a shooting in your building.' Anderson couldn't believe it when he discovered a few minutes later that Margaret had been shot. They had worked together on various projects, and shared a love of classical music. He liked her. She was good media talent – direct and upfront with journalists, not trying to fudge the problems in mental health. When Anderson mentioned that he was thinking of writing a book about public health, Margaret had gently admonished him. It was really mental health that warranted his attention, she suggested.

At his home in country Victoria, Brendan Kelly got up from the computer in his office to make a cup of tea. He nearly dropped the cup when he tuned in to what the radio in the kitchen was telling him. It was just incomprehensible. Not so long ago he had had some news of Margaret for the first time in years. He had been at the University of Ballarat library, doing some research on his business doctorate on executive leadership, when he saw one of her academic articles, giving contact details in Adelaide. He had smiled to himself, realising that she had done so well in her work, and that their professional lives had taken some similar direction after all.

Mary Anne Holland, who had worked alongside Margaret more than twenty years earlier when they were residents at a hospital in rural Victoria, was driving when she heard the news on the radio. She couldn't believe it. She had often thought of Margaret over the years, wondering what she was doing, and wishing they'd stayed in touch. Not long ago, she'd seen Margaret interviewed on ABC television, and had recognised her immediately. Holland, now working as an anaesthetist in Melbourne, had never before known someone who had been murdered. It was terribly unsettling. She followed news of the subsequent police investigation closely.

Terry Anderson's phone didn't stop ringing for days after the shooting. A former *Advertiser* journalist and an old hand at dealing with the media, he was shocked and angered by some of their actions in the following days. He complained to Channel 7 after footage was shown of Margaret's body in the foyer. He also complained to the *Advertiser* when he heard a reporter was trying to find out which departmental staff were located on which floors. 'That is a very dangerous game because there is a killer at large,' he fumed. He heard later that the Premier also rang the paper, warning them off.

Anderson was annoyed when a journalist rang to ask about Margaret's domestic arrangements. I understand she was gay and that her marriage was one of convenience, the journalist fished. Anderson had heard the rumours before. When he worked in Dean Brown's office a few years earlier, some colleagues had assumed Margaret was 'a member of the sisterhood'. Anderson thought such speculation was based on nothing more concrete than Margaret's short hair and no-nonsense manner. Anderson made it clear to the journalist that he thought the question intrusive. I don't know anything about her personal life, and I don't think it's relevant, he replied flatly. Nor was he impressed to learn that journalists had staked out Margaret's home, trying to corner Don.

The paper didn't print the speculation about Margaret's sexuality, but that didn't stop rumours flying around town. Adelaide is fascinated by its history of gay murders and many wondered, without having any particular grounds for doing so, whether this was another one.

An hour or so after the shooting, David Paes returned to the Lindy Lodge. He had asked the motel's owner, Martin Smith, that morning to extend his stay by another night. Now he asked Smith where he could get his beard trimmed. Smith directed him to the shopping centre over the road, and was surprised some time later to see that it had been some trim. Paes was now clean-shaven and looked quite different from the unkempt man who had checked in.

Back in Sydney, Gilbert Malepa had emailed, asking his cousin to ring him back about seeing a movie that evening. 'Been trying to reach you you [sic] by phone no success,' Malepa wrote.

Next morning, Gassy began the long drive back to Sydney. As he negotiated the traffic out of Adelaide, the national wire agency AAP reported that the murder had caused immediate repercussions in 'sedate SA'. Armed police were stationed at government buildings, and the Premier and Health Minister were under police guard. The media also reported that the day after Margaret's death, the South Australian Public Advocate, John Harley, received a phone call saying he would be 'next'. Adelaide remained on edge for some time. Days later police surrounded a hospital and began evacuating staff after receiving reports of a man carrying a weapon. The man was found and searched. He did not have a weapon, but was charged with possession of cannabis.

One of the last settlements that Gassy passed before making the spectacular drop from the Adelaide Hills into the plains beyond was the small historic mining town of Truro. For many, it is a name which immediately conjures up thoughts of murder. The Truro district became the burial ground for seven women who went missing in Adelaide in the 1970s. This time Gassy didn't break the trip, arriving back at his parents' home in the early hours of Wednesday morning. Before climbing into bed, he sat at his computer and surfed the net for the latest news about Margaret Tobin.

On Wednesday, 16 October, Gassy went to the movies with his cousin Gilbert Malepa. Gilbert noticed that Gassy was clean-shaven with short hair. Last time they had met up, about two months previously, Gassy had had a beard and hair to his collar.

On the afternoon of Thursday, 17 October, Gassy returned his hire car to the Avis outlet at Hurstville, a day earlier than arranged, and paid the bill in cash. The odometer showed that he had travelled 3,110 km.

In Adelaide, he had succeeded in doing what he had failed to accomplish months earlier in Brisbane.

10

Devastation

Margaret and her sister Helena each took some pride in thinking of themselves as chalk and cheese. As children, they shared a bedroom and the responsibilities of being the two eldest, but otherwise their paths had diverged. It was ironic then that they both ended up working in mental health but not surprising that their perspectives were diametrically opposed – Margaret was the psychiatrist administrator with a Master of Business Administration, while Helena was the psychotherapist who explored the spiritual and the unconscious.

Helena was on a plane with her sixteen-year-old daughter Tegan when the bombs exploded in Bali in October 2002. They were returning to Australia from a mother-and-daughter holiday exploring the artistic treasures of Europe. Knowing nothing of the bombing, they were puzzled by the intense security during their stopover in Dubai.

On the flight between Dubai and Singapore, Helena indulged in a Scotch. Soon afterwards she was overwhelmed by an intense sense of impending doom. A hot flush began in her toes and passed upwards over her whole body. She felt nauseous and asked for a glass of water. The glass fell from her hands. She rose for the toilet, feeling she was going to be sick. But she collapsed in the aisle before reaching the toilet. For long minutes, all was black. She couldn't ask for help because she couldn't speak. Something terrible was happening but she didn't know what. Finally Helena reached the toilet, where she sat and splashed water on her face. Minutes or hours could have passed, she had no idea how long it was before she emerged again, to find a queue waiting.

Back in her seat, the nausea continued to churn her guts. It lasted for days.

It was well past midnight when Helena and Tegan finally straggled out of customs into the waiting crowds at Melbourne airport. Anxious faces pressed towards them, asking who else was on the plane with them. How strange, Helena thought. She also was surprised to see her husband Ross and their other two children waiting for them. She had not expected this. He was just not a middle-of-the-night sort of person. Ross could hardly breathe as he pushed their trolley out of the building. Helena felt his anxiety. She thought he was going to have a heart attack, and put her arms around him.

Only then could he release the news. Your sister Margaret has been killed, he said. Helena assumed there must have been a car accident. When Ross said it was a shooting, Helena immediately thought back to the time her sister was badly beaten by a patient. She also remembered the bizarre experience on the plane. It must have been connected with Margaret's death, she thought.

Margaret's sister Bernadette was thinking about the casserole she had left in the oven when she and her husband returned home from carting a load of mulch on that Monday afternoon. They were still living on the pretty bush block which neighboured Margaret and Don's former property outside Ballarat. Many of the native trees and bushes in their garden had been planted on Don's advice.

Their teenage daughter Kellie was waiting outside. I have got the worst news, she sobbed to her mother. There is nothing you can tell me that we can't work out, Bernadette replied, thinking that Kellie must be pregnant. When Kellie said that Aunty Margaret had been shot, Bernadette couldn't fathom it. Oh yeah, right, she replied sarcastically. It's true, it's true, Kellie cried hysterically.

Bernadette's first thought was that she had to get to her mum as quickly as possible.

For the first 90 minutes after that unspeakable phone call from Adelaide, Jean sat by herself in her neat little home, atop a hill in Bacchus Marsh, a small town of tree-lined avenues which lies between Melbourne and Ballarat. She and Joseph had moved there while Margaret was still working at Ballarat. All around were reminders of Margaret; the novels and detective stories that she sent every week; the drawings of the blue wrens that she had given Jean, knowing her love for the dear little birds, and the silly green frog memorabilia that had been one of their jokes.

Jean pictured Margaret as she had seen her just weeks before. Margaret had rung after seeing a brochure about tours of the Flinders Ranges, which Jean had always wanted to explore. Why don't you ask a friend to go with you, Margaret suggested. Later she rang back to ask whether Jean would mind if she and Don went too. Jean's friend Kath Rowan was a bit shy about going on holiday with a psychiatrist but Jean had reassured her. She is not a psychiatrist to us, she is just Margaret.

Wait 'til you see my hair, Mum, Margaret had teased Jean over the phone. What colour is it this time? Jean asked. It had been purple when Margaret flew to Melbourne to be master of ceremonies at her sister Mary Catherine's wedding. I won't tell you, it will be a nice surprise, Margaret laughed. When they met for the holiday, Jean was stunned to see Margaret's shaven head. What have you done to your beautiful hair, she gasped. Margaret just grinned and wrapped her mother in her arms. Later Jean bandaged her daughter's wrist. She had slipped in the toilet at work and strained it. At the end of their holiday together, Jean waved goodbye to Margaret and Don in Port Augusta.

As she wept on that Monday afternoon, Jean kept returning to her most recent image of Margaret in Port Augusta. The same thought ran uselessly through her mind. If only I could hold her again, she'd be all right. Jean was hysterical when Patrick rang from France, alarmed by the message she had left on his answer phone. He had never known his mother to lose control like this. Get your neighbour to come over, he told her.

Some hours later, Jean and Bernadette landed in Adelaide. They were driven to the tidy brick home that Margaret had left that morning. Bernadette was upset when a police officer guarding the house asked who she was. It made her feel like a stranger. Jean had never stayed in the house before. She knew that Margaret and Don liked their space, and preferred to stay in a motel when visiting.

The hours and days that followed were a blur for all concerned. Phones rang constantly, there was a never-ending procession of people bearing meals and condolences, there were interviews with police, preparations to be made. For Don, there were also some practical matters to sort out. Margaret had always run the household finances and he had no access to ready cash. Margaret's colleagues at work ensured that was fixed up.

Jean and her children struck a quick rapport with Margaret's friends from the office, many of whom had a background in social work. They found they had more in common than they had expected, and shared stories and jokes. Margaret's brother Patrick sensed that Margaret had found a group of friends where she felt freer to express herself and to be herself. With her radical haircuts and ever-more colourful wardrobe, it seemed his sister had come a long way. In her twenties, while others of her age were experimenting and rebelling, he remembered her as serious, studious and a conservative dresser. Maybe it was just that she had reached an age and stage of life where she felt a freedom to truly be herself. She wouldn't have been the first woman to find that upon hitting 50.

Black humour helped many through those surreal days. But inevitably tensions arose as old wounds resurfaced and new ones were made. Grief has a habit of magnifying peoples' differences and divulging uncomfortable truths. Jean and Don could not help each other in their loss. Jean also found it difficult to listen to other people talk about her daughter as if they had known her all their lives. They have known her for only a few years, she thought. She has been my daughter for 50 years and she rang me every week. Days passed until Jean was given a viewing of Margaret's body. She was inconsolable. She could not find comfort in prayer or other Catholic rituals. Her faith was gone.

Many of Margaret's family and friends were upset by the unflattering photograph which was appearing in newspapers. Margaret had been caught on a bad angle, perhaps after a few drinks, with that savage new haircut. It wasn't the woman they knew. Indeed, it became apparent to Margaret's family that there was much they hadn't known.

When they had met for a coffee several weeks before Margaret's death, during one of her trips to Melbourne, Damian had teased his big sister. He thought they held a special place in their mother's affection because they were the bookends of the family, the oldest and the youngest. Their mother was always skiting about Margaret's latest success to the rest of their family, he joked with just a touch of annoyance. Even so, the siblings hadn't quite realised that she really was such a prominent figure. The former Premier of Victoria, Jeff Kennett, who worked with Margaret on the board of beyondblue, was on the other end of one of the early phone calls of condolence. I'm lost for words, he told Don. That'd be the first time mate, Don quipped back. The whisky might be helping numb his pain, but it didn't slow his mouth.

Damian, a gentle man of pale skin, dark hair, blue eyes and a dry humour, had mixed feelings about what he was learning about Margaret. It was more than the age difference of nineteen years that had separated them, and somehow it was upsetting to have strangers telling him about his own sister. On the other hand he was also lapping it up. He had a thirst to know as much as he could. He began collecting whatever information he could find from the newspapers, the internet and elsewhere. He also began to think about his own position in the world. If he fell off the perch tomorrow, what mark would he have left? He looked at Margaret's success, and decided to try to make more of his own career. If she could do it, so would he. He would just have to work harder. At their last meeting, he had told Margaret of his laziness, how he always took the easiest option. He sought her advice about his work, whether he should do some study. She asked if he was saving. I am exactly the same, she said when he replied that he spent every cent, no matter how high his earnings.

The day after Margaret's death, Damian went with Don, Jean and Bernadette to Parliament House where they sat in Premier Mike

Rann's office and listened to the condolence speeches through the speakers. 'Dr Tobin constantly advocated for the most disadvantaged and marginalised people in our community,' Mr Rann told the House. 'That can sometimes be a thankless task.' Afterwards, the family had a cup of tea with Rann before being whisked home in a government car, out of the grasp of waiting media. Margaret, who had guarded her privacy in life, had no chance of a private departure. There was to be a state funeral, and various dignitaries – including some who had been her antagonists in life – were jockeying to address it. Some observers felt Margaret was becoming a celebrity of the Rann Government. They were particularly irritated, knowing that Margaret, appointed by the previous government, had not always felt well supported by the incumbents.

On Monday, 21 October, seven days after Margaret's death, more than 1,000 people walked past a colourful wall of flowers to enter St Francis Xavier's Cathedral. It was only a few minutes' walk from the building on Wakefield Street which housed the detectives investigating the murder. Politicians and public servants joined in the Funeral Mass of Celebration and Thanksgiving, and police mingled discreetly with mourners. Don, who was watching the proceedings closely, saw some police on the building's roof. On the other side of Victoria Square lay the stately stone building of the Supreme Court of South Australia where some of the mourners would again gather, almost two years later, under very different circumstances. Ian Hickie, who delivered one of the eulogies, had also spoken at a ceremony held the previous Friday at St Patrick's Catholic Church in Kogarah, near Margaret's old stamping ground in Sydney.

At the front of the cathedral, Jonathan Phillips stood with a few others, taking stock of who had come to pay their respects. Phillips had been horrified when Margaret told him recently that she now could count a handful of supporters among the state's psychiatrists. To him, it illustrated the depth of his colleagues' antagonism to change. He noted that few local psychiatrists made an appearance in church. The majority of psychiatrists present were from New South Wales. So much bad blood had been spilt between Margaret and some of her South Australian colleagues that more than a few people had suggested police include a number of prominent Adelaide psychiatrists on their list of potential suspects.

Many of the mourners had taken note of the funeral notice asking them to wear 'something joyful and colourful to reflect Margaret's flair'. The traditional black of the crowd was flecked with reds, oranges, yellows, blues and purples. The newspaper photographers zeroed in on a colourful drawing by Rebecca Graham's five-year-old son. He wrote on it: 'Dear Margaret, I like you. You are a very good boss for my mum. From Lachlan G.'

As friends and family gathered around the shining white coffin painted with dainty pink roses, Margaret was wearing one of the suits bought on her last shopping expedition with Don. It was bright orange, and he had chosen shoes to match. The man at the funeral parlour questioned the wisdom of the metallic lizard brooch. It will just melt, he said, you know it's all going to be burnt. But Don insisted. She's got to have the whole bit, mate, she's got to have her brooch and her shoes and her suit.

Annie Paton, one of Margaret's friends from work, explained in her eulogy the significance of the symbols being placed on the coffin by friends and family. The hat, scarf and brooch were signature accessories, reflecting Margaret's attention to detail and the value that she placed on colour, texture and coordination of every outfit that she wore. 'Margaret took as much care and consideration in choosing what to wear for a day trip with her beloved Don and friends, as she did when dressing to represent the Department at national meetings,' Paton said. The CD reflected her passion for classical music, opera and ballet, while the posy of flowers spoke of the gardens that Don had created and nurtured for Margaret. Also on the coffin was the Mental Health Reform Plan, representing her leadership, dedication and passion for improving public mental health services. Friends also laid on the coffin some books and a pair of red shoes. These shoes, 'glowing like rubies', symbolised Margaret's courage, confidence and sense of purpose in moving forward, Paton said.

It was so surreal to be speaking of Margaret's love for scarves, Paton thought. Just weeks earlier, Margaret had cleaned out her wardrobe and distributed various items to friends at work. Paton, a warm, bubbly personality who had been away for weekends with Margaret and Don, was delighted with her gift. At the time she saw a token of warm friendship in the fine material of the scarves. Now it felt almost like that they had also carried some premonition.

Many of those seated on the hard wooden benches, under the diffused orange light from the stained-glass windows high above, struggled to reconcile the portrait that was being presented with the woman they knew. Everyone shows different aspects of themselves to different people, and even to the same people at different times. The ritual of funerals and wakes helps mourners fill in their gaps in understanding and knowledge. It seemed to some of those present that this was particularly necessary on this day. Many of Margaret's work colleagues knew little or nothing of her family or background. Something clicked into place when they learnt she had been the eldest of eight children. It made perfect sense. Of course she was the bossy big sister. Some were surprised to learn of her loving relationship with Don. They hadn't even realised she was married. Some felt the formal Catholic Mass didn't gel with the woman they knew – Margaret had moved so far beyond the influence of the church of her childhood. Some of those who had clashed with Margaret felt guilty or ambivalent. Eulogies have a habit of making people greater in death than in life and when the dead are sanctified, it can be discomforting or even irritating and infuriating for the living.

John Campbell, Margaret's mentor from her early days in New South Wales, was not surprised that so many people were learning of other aspects to the person they knew. Recently he had spent quite a bit of time thinking back over his dealings with his protégé and of how he had asked her, so many times, what drove her fight for better mental health services. But he had never had a satisfactory answer. Campbell, who prided himself on being an astute judge of character after years in the military, had decided that Margaret was a complex individual who was careful about what she divulged of herself to others. The only time he had seen her come close to losing control was when someone had spilt a bottle of red wine over a new cream outfit she was wearing with great pride at a work function. She was still spitting chips about it years later, he remembered. Margaret had a series of Chinese walls within herself and only she had the keys, he thought. Some of her compartments were now being opened up for public viewing, but Campbell was not sure whether people would ever really understand Margaret Tobin. It distressed him to think that she would be remembered for being murdered, rather than for what she had fought to achieve.

Jonathan Phillips became increasingly angry as he sat through the formalities, which began with Cat Stevens's song 'Morning Has Broken' and ended with Puccini's 'Nessun Dorma'. Phillips was thinking of the woman who had been his wild and wonderful dancing partner at psychiatry functions. He felt that the pasteurised, polished picture which was emerging didn't do justice to the gutsy, complex person who he knew. Margaret wore her flaws wonderfully, he thought. She deserved better than this.

Barbara Wieland was also angry. She knew it was irrational but she was furious at Margaret. She had just started to make inroads in her work, she had engaged the key players and won a greater prominence for mental health. And now she had gone. They were back to square one. Reform would never be possible now.

Karin Myhill, a psychiatrist who had worked closely with Margaret in the department, was listening carefully to the eulogies. She had been shocked by her own intense emotional response to Margaret's death. She had felt a mixture of shock, fear and profound grief. Part of this, she realised, was her own insecurity. If it was shooting season on female psychiatrists, then she was vulnerable. She already had begun looking over her shoulder and had changed some of her daily routines. As her petite frame rested uncomfortably on the hard pews, Myhill was also thinking back to earlier that year when she was struck down by a sudden debilitating neurological condition. Margaret was one of the first people to her hospital bedside, offering brisk, practical help. She seemed almost taken aback by the warmth of Myhill's response, a kiss on the cheek. Later, as Myhill struggled with a painful, protracted recovery, Margaret arranged for her to keep working from home. This had helped her psychological recovery greatly, and Myhill had been deeply touched by Margaret's concern, especially as they had been more professional colleagues than personal intimates. Myhill felt that the eulogies were telling her a lot about Margaret the bureaucrat and the reformer, but she wanted to hear more about the person. She wanted others to know that the woman some called a bully could be warm and sensitive. Margaret was deeply compassionate despite her blunt, forthright persona, Myhill thought. She had seen that Margaret could switch in a second from being the tough manager to the caring psychiatrist. She knew that Margaret could be hurt.

Myhill put a funeral notice in the paper, signed 'Karin'. 'Vale courageous sister, you dared to care, to dream and to lead. May your spirit soar even higher, your determination empower others, and your dedication hold hope for a better tomorrow,' it said. Myhill felt she had lost the most generous mentor she had ever known. Perhaps she was also so gutted because she felt in some way that Margaret was the big sister she had never had. It was so distressing because this side of their relationship had not yet had the time to develop. Myhill was also mourning what might have been.

Brendan Kelly sent a card and flowers on the day of the funeral. He had thought hard about whether to attend in person but had reluctantly decided against it. It might be too much for the family, after no contact for so many years. He also put a notice in newspapers in Adelaide and Melbourne which said simply, 'always loved, Brendan'.

As colleagues and friends mingled afterwards, many spoke quietly of their fears. The most common view was that someone in the state's health system had orchestrated the execution. The problems at Glenside – the death threats, the drug-selling, the firebombing – were on many people's minds. In Adelaide, even the taxi drivers speak about the Glenside mafia.

Privately, some people were also engaging in self-recrimination. Christine Charles, who had given one of the eulogies, blamed herself for recruiting Margaret, and for not ensuring there was better security in the building. Andrej Knez kept thinking back to something Don had told him: 'You look after her during the day and I look after her in the evening.' Knez felt he had failed both Margaret and Don. Peter Brennan was not at the funeral; he preferred to do his grieving in private. But he was also dwelling on some 'what ifs'. He wished he hadn't talked Margaret into taking her last job. He had known Don wasn't so keen on the move. The guilt lingered for months.

At the private cremation after the funeral, Jean could no longer hold in her grief. She wept as if her heart was broken. Don pulled down his dark sunglasses.

Some of Margaret's friends were bemused as the public accolades continued to pour forth in coming days and weeks. Roxanne Ramsay wanted Margaret's siblings to understand their sister was not the paragon of perfection that was being suggested. It was not helpful for them or fair to Margaret, she thought. Ramsay described the times that she had seen Margaret acknowledge her vulnerabilities and speak about her mistakes. Margaret was not always as astute as she thought. Sometimes her colours were over the top, sometimes she did not realise the effect she was having on other people. Ramsay remembered the evening her physicist daughter had enjoyed a long, intense conversation with Margaret. Ramsay had difficulty following its threads, which crossed science and philosophy. She thought that Margaret and her daughter were both so bright that it sometimes could be to their detriment. Their intolerance for sloppy arguments could be mistaken for arrogance.

Ramsay also thought of how the circle of friends who met for whiskies on Friday nights had delegated her the job of having a quiet word to Margaret about her lipstick. It was often a bit crooked. A few people had chuckled about this without being brave enough to mention it, but thought Ramsay was up to the job. Ramsay never got the chance to have that conversation.

In contrast to the public eulogising, the vitriol was released in private. Some of Margaret's friends were upset by the unkind comments and jokes. *So many people had hated her, who do you think hated her the most? I could have killed her myself at times. It just shows that she was going in the wrong direction. Served her right.* Underlying some of the comments was a distinct sense of relief – now we can relax and go back to doing things the way we like. Also lurking was the intimation that Margaret had brought her death upon herself.

The upper echelons at Flinders Medical Centre were horrified when some Glenside staff formally objected to the move to name the hospital's new mental health unit after Margaret. The objection was soundly overruled. The irony was that Margaret hated buildings being named for people. She thought a hospital's psychiatric unit should be called exactly that. Anything else was giving in to stigma, the notion that some things should be left unsaid or unnamed.

Meanwhile, Australian Nursing Federation officials were careful about how they eulogised Margaret in newsletters to members. They knew that some nurses would be furious if the tributes were too glowing.

In death, as in life, Margaret was arousing strong emotions.

11

Coincidentally

On that Monday afternoon in mid–October 2002, Michael John Edwin Standing was driving towards a job in Adelaide's northern suburbs. On the way, he planned to drop in to see his elderly mother in hospital. She had recently suffered a recurrence of cancer, twenty years after its first appearance, and he didn't think she would be around much longer.

The radio was tuned to a commercial network, and Standing hardly had to think twice after a newsflash about a murder in a government building. He turned his car around and headed back to the city.

Few obvious traces lingered of the country lad who had joined the South Australian police force almost 40 years before. Standing had developed a thick neck, impressive girth and a face which didn't give much away. No doubt some people made the mistake of under-estimating him because of his slow-moving bulk. Now a detective sergeant with the Major Crimes Investigation Branch, Mick Standing had helped solve some of the state's most high–profile murder cases.

About 40 minutes after the shooting, Standing arrived outside the CitiCentre Building to find panic and chaos. He was worried, as people streamed from the building and huddled in groups, that a sniper might be waiting to strike. Police were urging the crowds to take cover. The shooter could be anywhere.

Standing realised the significance of the crime as soon as he was given the victim's name. He had listened to Margaret Tobin on the radio and he knew of the troubled state of mental health services. There would be a long list of potential suspects, he thought. So many people had grievances with the mental health system. He knew that the victim had only recently arrived in South Australia. They would have to check out her history in New South Wales. Standing reached for a notebook and began noting down the tasks that were his immediate priority.

Everyone in the building was a potential suspect or witness. Their names would have to be recorded and interviews conducted. Footage from all security cameras in the area would need to be collected. How frustrating that there were no cameras in the building itself. Taxi drivers who had been working nearby would need to be identified and interviewed. All rubbish bins in the area would need to be checked, in case the killer had dumped his weapon. Relatives would have to be notified. The list went on and on. It was late evening before police found time to search the nearby bins.

It was also late in the day before Standing had a chance to inspect the crime scene. He caught the lift to the eighth floor in search of understanding, to get a feel for what had happened. There he chatted with one of the crime scene investigators he knew from the police pistol club. Shooting had been an important part of Standing's life for as long as he could remember. As a kid growing up on a station, he'd shot rabbits for food and foxes to protect the sheep. For many years, he'd been a pistol enthusiast, competing in national events. In more recent years, he'd turned to rifle shooting as his main hobby. Standing prided himself on his knowledge of firearms.

The crime scene told the detective plenty. He saw, from the marks on the four ammunition shells found lying on the floor, that a Glock pistol had fired them. He saw from the name on the bullet case, signifying an expensive brand, that this was no run-of-the-mill job. It also became clear to Standing that the shooter knew what he was doing. There was no sign the killer had had any trouble firing his weapon. An experienced pistol shooter had been at work. Standing guessed the killer had used his own firearm.

As Standing stood and looked at the place on the carpet where Margaret Tobin had lain dying, he saw something else. Most murderers are content to inflict one or maybe two bullets. This one had put four into the victim. Standing knew that this was no small matter. It meant the murderer was absolutely determined on his course. He was not going to risk leaving his target with any chance of life.

As he collapsed into bed late that night, Standing knew a huge job lay ahead. But he was confident. He loved reading military history. It was in his blood. His father and his grandfather had served in the two World Wars. His reading had taught him that successful military leaders were single-minded, with outstanding problem-solving skills and an ability to command and to plan, to get things done. They were also the skills a successful investigator needed, he thought.

Standing was not impressed the next day when he picked up his phone several times to take calls from various senior South Australian bureaucrats. The shooting had shocked and terrified them. They demanded, can you guarantee the safety of my staff? No, was Standing's terse response. That was not his job. He could not afford to be distracted, his team had to remain focused on finding an accomplished killer.

In the following days, police interviewed more than 600 people who had been in the CitiCentre Building at the time of the shooting. Standing's team soon had a long list of potential suspects. Margaret's husband, friends and colleagues had no difficulty thinking of people who bore her ill will, including a number of prominent Adelaide doctors. One list given to police included dozens of people associated with the mental health sector who might have felt some cause for a grudge. More than 100 suspects had to be interviewed, and their alibis investigated. Hundreds of calls to the Crime Stoppers hotline also had to be followed up.

Donald Clyde Scott came under scrutiny, even as he grappled with funeral arrangements and struggled to get a grip on household finances. At least one person advised the police to seriously consider the husband. But Standing didn't give the suggestion much credence.

The murder was more likely connected with a work-related griev-ance, he thought. Scott was just an ordinary, down-to-earth bloke struggling with the shock of an extraordinary loss. In years to come, when Standing got to know Scott better, he would think of him as the sort of person who, in other circumstances, might have become a friend.

Scott spent long hours talking with police. Their questions turned to Margaret's sexuality.

'I don't need that sort of detail,' said the police officer when Don launched into an explanation of the nitty gritty of their physical relationship.

'You asked the question so you are stuck with it,' Don batted back.

Standing soon satisfied himself that the whispers about Margaret's sexuality had no basis. He assumed that her recent dramatic haircut had fuelled the speculation. From what he could gather, the haircut symbolised nothing more than a woman who wanted to mark her fiftieth by doing something outrageous, having a makeover. It had just been her way of making a statement, he thought.

The more Standing learnt, the stronger the impression that he formed of Margaret. She was someone who trod on toes, who wanted things done her way, and who pushed people out of their comfort zones, he realised. She aroused intense feelings. It became abundantly clear to him that people either strongly liked her or strongly disliked her. Few took the middle ground.

The police held several press conferences appealing for informa-tion about the shooter. 'He is in the community at the moment,' a spokesman said. 'That person has friends, family, relatives, contacts, people who know him and know what motivates him.'

A few days after the shooting, police realised they had issued the wrong description. The first description to hit the airwaves was in fact of Grant Francis, the bureaucrat who had shared Margaret's last lift ride. No longer were police seeking a tall slim man in his early twenties. Instead, they were looking for a man of medium height, with dark, collar-length wavy hair, a slight to normal build, a dark olive complexion and a full dark beard. On Friday, 18 October, police spent several hours questioning an Aboriginal man who had made threats against mental health staff. Some of his clothing was taken for forensic testing. That day, police also staged and videotaped a re-enactment of Margaret's last minutes, with a female officer taking her part.

At a press conference, also on that Friday, police released a computer-generated identikit image of the shooter. Grant Francis, who had seen the murderer in the lift, spent a few hours helping compile it. It didn't fit perfectly with his recollection, but he thought it about 75 to 80 per cent correct. Television cameras and newspaper photographers ensured the image was widely seen around the country.

In Sydney, a nurse recognised the face immediately. It was the eyes and lips that were so distinctive, she thought. She remembered noticing Eric Gassy's boyish good looks on his first day at St George Hospital. His lips were curved and full, and he had a great mop of curly black hair and big, brown eyes with a twinkle. Over time, she had watched the twinkle dull and die away. The nurse told her husband that she thought she recognised the identikit, but she didn't ever ring the police.

A few weeks before Margaret's death, two men who had worked together as nurses at St George Hospital bumped into each other at a coffee shop in the Blue Mountains. It was the first time they had seen each other in a long while and they stopped to rehash old history. All these years later, and Eric Gassy still intrigued them. Was he mad all along and we just didn't pick it, they wondered. Was that why he held so many grievances against us?

When these men heard of Margaret's death, not long after their chance encounter, Gassy was fresh in their minds. Another nurse who had worked at Pacific House also shared their questions. Could Gassy have done it? They knew he had been working as a security guard since his deregistration and wondered if this had given him access to guns. Each of the nurses contacted South Australia police with their concerns, a little anxious about whether they were doing the right thing. After all, they had no evidence.

'Yep, that is the bastard,' one of the nurses was told. The police already had Gassy's name.

★

When sound engineer Bob Champion heard that Margaret Tobin had been shot, he thought back to the last time he had seen her. It was only six months ago, at a Royal Australian and New Zealand College of Psychiatrists congress in Brisbane. Champion knew Margaret from other college conferences. She was a powerful sort of woman who you couldn't help but notice.

Champion was watching the news at his Gold Coast home, interested to know if there had been any more news about the murder, when the identikit image came up. His phone rang soon afterwards. Champion didn't have to ask who it was. He picked up the handset and, without any preamble, said: 'Yes, that's him, isn't it?'

On the other end of the line was his business partner, Peter Summers. Their audiovisual production business, QAV, had been contracted to service the psychiatry congress in April. Champion and Summer had each recognised in the identikit the man they had seen acting suspiciously during the congress at the Brisbane Convention and Exhibition Centre on Saturday, 27 April.

On that morning, Champion, a tall man with sandy grey hair and a goatee, had nipped outside to catch some fresh air and a cigarette. It was the first day of the congress and a busy time lay ahead. He was standing on the Plaza Terrace, an outdoor area connecting the convention centre to the nearby Rydges Hotel, when a loud clatter interrupted his enjoyment of the still moment. Champion turned and saw a stranger crouching. As the man stood up, he tucked something into the back of his trousers. The stranger looked jumpy, out of place, and he stared straight back at the tall man with large glasses and a cigarette in his hand. Champion was the first to look away, unnerved. He was sure the hollow metallic sound he had just heard was a gun dropping on concrete.

Sound was Champion's thing. He'd played guitar in a rock-and-roll band and worked in a music shop before setting up this business. He prided himself on being able to recognise strange noises. Once, when there had been a loud cracking noise at his home, everyone else was perplexed, but he recognised immediately that a poster had come off a wall. His sound library had thousands and thousands of sound effects, including the noise that a gun makes on concrete. He also knew it from when he had worked on a blood and guts movie called *Street Fighter* at Movie World. He had been familiar with the sounds of guns from his earliest years, growing up on a farm in Tasmania. Yep, he was sure that he knew the noise he had just heard.

Champion was used to keeping a weather eye open at conferences. He'd worked at many such gigs over the years where there had been demonstrations and protests. But this man gave off a different vibe from those sorts of interlopers. It felt more sinister. Champion stayed where he was, watching as the man went through the glass doors into the sprawling spaces and smooth modern interiors of the convention centre. Its oversized dimensions made people look small and irrelevant. The man stopped to study the signs showing the location of various conference sessions. He was wearing a suit but didn't look comfortable in it. His hair was dark, pulled back in a ponytail, and he had a beard and an olive complexion.

Champion then went back into the building and rode the escalator down to the mezzanine level to chat with Peter Summers and some convention centre staff. 'Does anyone recognise him?' he asked as they watched the man on the escalators. 'I think he just dropped a gun outside.'

Summers, with a head of luxuriant silver-grey hair and matching beard, kept a close eye on the man over the next fifteen to twenty minutes. He followed the stranger as he moved between the building's foyer, mezzanine and plaza levels, checking out notice boards. When the man went into the toilets, Summers waited about thirty seconds and then quickly opened the door. The man was at the hand basin, facing the mirror and adjusting something around his waist area. As Summers walked in, the man turned with a surprised look, and then walked smartly back out. Summers followed soon after. By this stage, a number of security and other staff were on the lookout. One noticed that the man was carrying himself strangely; he kept his right hand in his jacket pocket and his left hand across his stomach and flat against his hip as if holding something.

Soon after, the man left the building by the doors where he had first entered. He briskly crossed the terrace where Champion's peace had earlier been disturbed. Summers and Gary Hennessey, the centre's food and beverage manager, watched the man walk down the stairs to the street where his car was conveniently parked. He must have arrived early to get such a good spot. The man unhurriedly unlocked the car, took off his jacket, put it in the car, and then drove off. At the top of the stairs, Hennessey took a small notepad out of his shirt pocket and jotted down the registration number. 183 GEO. Was the last letter an O or a Q? They couldn't be sure.

The security guards returned to their control room and entered details into their log about the man and his car. They also reviewed tape from the security cameras. These showed the man, with a notice-able bulge in the back of his jacket. The incriminating tape was put aside in case it was needed again, but somehow it later ended up being recycled back into circulation, erasing the footage.

By the time the man drove off, the rituals of the conference were well under way. People were wearing the badges and satchels of belonging, queuing for coffee and indulging in the mindless chitchat and political intrigue that inevitably marks such gatherings. The smokers, as usual, were cast outside. In meeting room 1 on the upper level, not far from the doors where the man had first entered the building, Margaret Tobin and two colleagues, Beth Kotze and Janice Wilson, were setting the scene for their day's discussions. The topic of the workshop they were conducting was 'Administration, Management, Leadership – Roles for Psychiatrists'.

After seeing the identikit image on the television, Summers contacted South Australia police. The registration number in the security log was the lead they needed. It took them to the Kings Cross branch of Budget Australia. There they discovered that at about lunchtime on Thursday, 25 April, a man called Jean Eric Gassy gave his driver's licence and contact details when hiring a car. It was a Nissan Pulsar, registration number 183 GEO. He returned it just before noon four days later, on Monday, 29 April. By then it had another 2,067 km on the clock, consistent with a return trip from Sydney to Brisbane. Gassy paid his bill, $333.12, by credit card.

Now the police knew where to start looking. They ran Gassy's name through the New South Wales Firearms Register. He owned two Glock pistols, of 9 mm calibre.

182

Soon after, Standing had word back from the detectives he had sent to do some digging at St George Hospital in Sydney. They told him of Gassy's deregistration.

So they were definitely on the right track, Standing thought. The phone call from Queensland had been a lucky break, speeding up their investigations. But he was sure they would have found Gassy, even without that tip-off.

One weekend soon after Margaret's murder, Jonathan Phillips flew to Melbourne for a meeting at the headquarters of the Royal Australian and New Zealand College of Psychiatrists. He was shocked to find a security guard at the front door and to be asked for identification. What was the world coming to when a former president of the college couldn't be trusted? When Phillips queried the arrangements, he was told that the precautions were necessary as police had a prime suspect who was close to psychiatry. There was a hint that it might be someone from New South Wales.

Phillips was unsettled. If the murder had something to do with an angry colleague from New South Wales, then there was a good chance that he might have been involved in the case through his work for the state's Medical Board. Phillips insisted on more details. He was given a name. It rang a bell but nothing more.

When Phillips arrived back in Sydney on Sunday afternoon, he went straight to his offices in Macquarie Street and rummaged through his filing cabinet. His heart sank as he read through the manila file marked 'Gassy'. It told of a young psychiatrist carrying more responsibility than he should, his conflicts with Margaret Tobin, and Phillips's diagnosis. At the time, he had thought Gassy had a depressive illness with some paranoid features and that it had been brought about at least partly by his struggles at work. My God, Phillips thought to himself, this is terrible. It got worse as he read on. He was reminded that he had later changed his diagnosis after receiving more information. Gassy had a paranoid disorder with depressive features, rather than vice versa. This was much more worrying.

★

Gassy had rented a car from Bayswater car rental at Kings Cross at 3.30 pm on Friday, 4 October 2002. It was due to be returned on 11 October but was returned on 8 October, after travelling 116 km.

On the evening of Tuesday, 8 October, he rented a car from the Sydney airport branch of Avis Australia. It was due back on 15 October but was returned at noon on 9 October to Sydney airport after travelling 20 km.

At 3 pm on Friday, 11 October, he hired a grey Nissan Pulsar, registration RSX 366, from the Hurstville branch of Avis Australia, which was about twenty minutes' drive from his parents' home. The car was returned on the afternoon of Thursday, 17 October, a day early, after travelling 3,110 km. Gassy paid the fee, $478.98, in cash upon his return.

When they discovered the records of these rentals, police speculated that Gassy had been trying to see if it was possible to get a car without giving his driver's licence. Or perhaps he was just trying to build up a record, to suggest that it was nothing unusual for him to hire a car. Gassy, however, would offer another explanation.

Oyster Bay is a leafy, established suburb which hugs the banks of the Georges River in southern Sydney. It is old-style suburbia, from an era before McMansionism. The home at 23 Georges River Crescent is a slightly shabby, double-storey, red-brick dwelling which is remarkable only for being so ordinary. Gums and angophoras line the street, and soft light streams through their branches. It is a sleepy, peaceful spot far removed from the busy, dirty rhythms of the city.

In the last days of October 2002, this home was under close surveillance by police. They followed Gassy when he left the house on Saturday, 26 October, to drive his father's car to a gun club at Bankstown. The next morning, Xavier and Maud arrived back home from their holiday in Vietnam.

On Tuesday, 29 October, police from South Australia and New South Wales met at 8 am for a briefing about the day ahead. The New South Wales police were casually dressed in jeans and shirts; the

South Australians were more formal, wearing ties and jackets. What might happen was unpredictable, they were told. The suspect was known to be armed and thought to be dangerous. The Tactical Response Group was not available to assist with the operation, and the plan was for a low-key, non-confrontational approach. The main priority of the supervising officer, New South Wales Detective Inspector Geoff Leonard, was to protect his team. The worst-case scenario which ran through his mind was that one of his officers might be shot.

After the briefing, the police drove in a convoy of unmarked cars to the small cluster of suburban shops at Oyster Bay. They stopped there to get an update from the surveillance team and to work out a battle plan. A shop selling hot meat pies also caught their attention.

Maud Gassy was running late to give a scripture lesson at a nearby school when she pulled away from her home in a small white car just before 10 am. The surveillance team radioed to alert the police at the shops, who saw an opportunity too good to miss. As Maud drove down the hill, a man wearing jeans and a dark shirt stood out on the road, waving her down. When she pulled over, Leonard explained that he and his offsider were police officers investigating Margaret Tobin's murder, that her son was a subject of their investigation, and that they wanted to search her house.

Maud collapsed into tears, and Leonard soon lost count of how many times he reassured her that they were not about to arrest her son. Would she take them back to her house? Maud was distraught. She was already late for her class. Leonard and a South Australian detective, Steve Kinsman, climbed into the car to accompany her to the school, where she made her apologies. Maud was weeping so much that she was having difficulty driving, and one of the officers eventually took the wheel. Kinsman was sure that Maud recognised the name Margaret Tobin but she would dispute this later, insisting that she had never heard the name before.

Maud was still distressed when they arrived back at Oyster Bay. She knew her husband would not be home; he was at the funeral of a good friend. When she opened the front door, Eric was on his way down the internal staircase, coming towards his mother. Maud said something in French, and he turned to go back up the stairs. A New

South Wales officer, Detective Senior Constable Matt Moss, knew he had to act quickly. The situation could quickly spin out of control if the police didn't immediately establish their dominance. Moss moved towards Gassy and touched him on the back lightly. Eric, you have to come back downstairs now, he said. Gassy obeyed immediately, showing not a hint of resistance.

Moss had been in many such situations before, and carried some scars from his time with the Tactical Response Group. In 1985, when he was 22, Moss was shot when searching the house of a man known to have a gun. He was in hospital for three months afterwards, and still carried 160 shotgun pellets in one arm. One hand suffered constant pins and needles. Moss quickly came to the conclusion that Gassy posed no immediate threat. He was polite, cooperative and matter-of-fact. It was unusual, Moss thought, that Gassy made no protestations. There was none of the usual, you have got the wrong bloke. Moss had the feeling that Gassy had almost been expecting the police to show at some stage, although perhaps not so soon.

Moss went upstairs with Maud and made her a cup of tea. He felt sorry for her; she seemed a decent lady. He had a cuppa with her, and held her hand as he explained what the search would involve. They started chatting about their children. When Moss told of seeing his two children every second weekend, Maud seemed genuinely interested. Always hug your kids, she told him.

Kinsman introduced himself to Gassy and cautioned him: 'We are going to ask you some questions but anything you do say may be given in evidence and you don't have to answer any questions.' Gassy declined when asked if he would be prepared to participate in an identification parade. Okay then, replied Kinsman, we will use photographs instead.

Leonard, a solid man with the deep voice of a radio announcer and an intent blue stare, was standing outside the house when he realised there had been a minor mistake with potentially serious consequences. The warrant gave the address as 23 St Georges River Crescent, instead of Georges River Crescent. In years to come, it would be revealed as no trivial error. Hasty arrangements were made to have the warrant amended. The search could not begin until this was organised. Leonard was annoyed, watching valuable time pass. Finally, at 12.35 pm, the warrant was executed.

Leonard thought the elderly couple seemed plenty decent. The father was a quiet, reserved chap and showed no antagonism towards the police despite his evident shock when he arrived home. But Leonard was puzzled by Gassy. What was a middle-aged man doing living at home with his parents? It was the life of a recluse, it just didn't seem normal. He thought Gassy had the colour of sickness about him. At first, Leonard kept an open mind about the case. He had learnt not to judge people on appearances. The year before this, he had been in charge of a lengthy investigation into the brutal stabbing murder of a couple and their daughter. Sef Gonzales, a well-spoken young man who had sung an emotional farewell to his parents and sister at their funeral, was later convicted. Murderers don't have one ear missing or one eye missing, Leonard was fond of saying. They can be meek and mild, someone you'd never expect.

The entrance to Gassy's one-room flat was an internal door secured by an electronic keypad. Gassy punched in the code to give the officers access to the room. Asked if he had any weapons, Gassy offered to open his gun safe. Inside were two pistols – a Glock 19 and a Glock 26 – and boxes of Speer Gold Dot ammunition. The police also seized two spare slides for the pistols, a laser sight, a device used to reload spent cartridge cases, a New South Wales firearms licence, a mobile phone, speed loaders and copper brushes used for cleaning guns. They also took a shooter's bag, a black carry bag, a private investigator's licence, some thin surgical gloves and a receipt for $100 from the Queensland Gun Exchange.

They found a video of Dr Nelson, the GP who had tried to reassure Gassy he didn't have AIDS. He had been covertly filmed leaving his surgery and climbing into his car. There was also a long stretch of footage of his home. On Gassy's desk was a photograph of a solicitor who acted for him at one stage of his deregistration proceedings. It appeared to have been taken surreptitiously. The police also found a firearms training video, a Glock assembly/disassembly video and videos taken of Gassy when on holiday in Thailand where he was often surrounded by young women. In one video, he was displaying used shooting targets in a hotel room. It appeared that he had been shooting at them in his hotel room with an air rifle. Mick Standing was particularly interested in this video when he later watched it in Adelaide; he knew that shooting air rifles was an effective way of honing skills for pistol shooting.

In the filing cabinet near Gassy's bed, the police found pistol cases with pistol parts in them, more boxes of ammunition, and a folder marked 'doctors'. In it were two pages with photos and the personal details of several doctors. On the front page was a photograph of Peter Arnold, next to a handwritten note describing his weight, hunched posture, spectacles, hearing aid, hairstyle and height. Next to Arnold's private address, there was another handwritten note, 'security system (effectiveness?)'.

Accompanying two photographs of Jonathan Phillips were his email and phone numbers. The second page carried a photograph and contact details for David Burke, who had worked with Gassy at St George, as well as an address and phone numbers for Stephen Adelstein (misspelt as Edelstein), the specialist who had refused to treat Gassy for AIDS. The second page also listed work contact details for Beth Kotze and Kay Wilhelm, who had questioned Gassy closely during the Professional Standards Committee hearing back in 1995.

When asked about the list of names, Gassy told Leonard 'they are people I am interested in'. It later became clear that this interest was ongoing rather than historic. Some of the details on the list reflected a recent knowledge. Peter Arnold was not wearing a hearing aid when he questioned Gassy at the Impaired Registrants Panel hearing in 1994. One of the photographs of Phillips was from 1999. In a recycling bin in the garage, police found a map showing Wilhelm's office at St Vincent's Hospital. She had moved out of that office in March 2002.

As soon as he saw the list of names, Moss recognised the danger. It showed a clever, capable, calculating killer who paid great attention to detail, he thought. This was no ordinary case.

The police were surprised when they opened the oven door. Inside was a small cardboard box stacked with papers. Lucky no-one turned the oven on, one officer joked to himself. The papers included correspondence relating to Gassy's deregistration, including a copy of Margaret Tobin's letter from July 1994, and a document titled 'Summary of events leading to my appearance before the Impaired Registrants Panel'. This detailed, amongst other things, Gassy's views about an 'inappropriate complaint by a colleague' to the Medical Board. The box also held copies of the reports by John Woodforde, Jonathan Phillips, Jill Floyd and Osman Ali, as well as a document titled 'Comments on Dr Woodforde's report of 30.8.94', and a copy of the Medical Tribunal's reasons for its determination of 1 August 1997. There was also a letter with a coloured drawing of a butterfly and a number of addresses.

Gassy crossed his arms but remained calm and collected as the detectives moved around his flat. He went upstairs several times to check on his parents, and looked genuinely concerned about them. He chatted with the police about travelling, playing guitar and other things. At one stage, he told Leonard that he had been in Brisbane. Gassy wanted to be as cooperative as possible because he was worried about what might happen when they found the medicines in his fridge and cupboards. He feared they might be confiscated. When indeed the police did find his supplies, Leonard asked for an explanation. It had better be good or he might have to charge Gassy for having such a large stockpile of medicines.

Leonard was shocked when Gassy explained quietly that he was treating himself for AIDS. Leonard agreed to treat the information sensitively, and didn't broadcast the news to his colleagues. A courier also delivered medication sometime that afternoon. Later, police would estimate that Gassy had spent well over $4,000 on HIV medication in the four weeks between the shooting and his arrest.

Early in the search, Gassy asked if he could leave later that afternoon to attend a doctor's appointment at Chatswood, in Sydney's northern suburbs. He left at about 3.30 pm and returned shortly after 6 pm.

Police searched Gassy's wallet carefully before he left for the appointment. They found a New South Wales firearms licence and a torn railway ticket with addresses beside three initials – PCA, JMW and JP. There was a name too, it looked like Louise Sally, followed by a question mark. The railway ticket dated back to 1996. Peter Chester Arnold had lived at the addresses next to his initials since mid 2001; John Marcus Woodforde had lived at the second address from about October 2001; and Jonathan Phillips had lived at the third address around 1999–2000.

It became clear to the detectives involved in the search that there were many faces to Gassy. In some photographs, where he had long hair and beard, he could almost not be recognised as the clean-shaven, short-haired man seen in other photographs.

Gassy's brother Robert, who arrived soon after the search began, remained present during his absence. Robert had been stroppy with the police at first, but eventually calmed down. He spoke often with his brother in French. The police couldn't read much about the content of the conversation from the brothers' body language; they both kept their cards close to their chest. Matt Moss struck up a conversation with the younger brother, asking what he did for a quid. Robert explained that he worked in the fashion, modelling and television industry. He helped cast people for television ads.

It must be terrible going to a job every day where you are surrounded by good-looking sorts, joked Moss. You'd think so, replied Robert, but some of them are really high maintenance. I'd like to have that problem, said Moss.

The police also seized two computers. Later investigations found a forged medical practitioner's certificate, in the name of Jean Eric Gassy, on the hard drive of one of them. They also showed that in June 2001, one computer had accessed a website, <www.firearms. id.com>, which details the techniques used by forensics investigators to link individual weapons to crimes. Analysis of one computer showed it was used regularly on most days until 6.30 pm on Friday, 11 October. After that it was left running but not used for another four days. The next user-initiated action on the computer occurred at 2.56 am on Wednesday, October 16, when it was shut down. It was then used again regularly in the following days, including to make a number of searches for news about Margaret Tobin's death and the police investigation. The most recent such search had occurred on Monday, 28 October, the day before the police search.

The search went slowly. The logistics were considerable. An independent officer oversaw the execution of the search warrant to ensure proper procedures were followed. Other officers operated the video camera, took photographs, and identified and secured exhibits. The video camera rolled as every piece of evidence was photographed, bagged and written up in the exhibits book. The police had to pause every 30 minutes so the video tape could be changed. They worked solidly up until a few minutes before the expiry of the warrant at 9 pm. Leonard was preparing to leave the premises when Gassy approached him in the front yard and thanked him for respecting the matter mentioned in confidence.

Several months later, another search would be conducted at Oyster Bay. On Tuesday, 11 March 2003, a search warrant was formally served on Xavier Gassy. From Gassy's flat, the police took credit cards, a calendar with April 22 and 29 circled, a Brisbane 2002 street directory, which contained photocopies of maps of the highway from Sydney to Brisbane, and some diaries and address books. They also found some ammunition in the drawer of the sink.

A few days after the initial search Leonard returned to the house and arrested Gassy. He was taken to nearby Sutherland police station, charged over the unlawful storage of his shooting gear, and granted bail on condition he report daily to the station. This also helped police keep track of his movements while they sought the evidence they needed to arrest him on a more serious charge. Even though Gassy's guns had been confiscated, many psychiatrists were extremely apprehensive about their safety. News had spread quickly about the persons of interest list.

Back in the City of Churches, Standing and his team were spending long hours ploughing through the papers and other evidence shipped back from New South Wales. Standing knew that his next challenge was to show that Gassy had been in Adelaide at the crucial time. He would need some solid evidence along those lines in order to make an arrest.

On the afternoon of Sunday, 3 November, Denise Conway was catching up on some paperwork in her office at the Shamrock Motel in Balranald. The temperature outside was starting to climb towards summer heights. The service station over the road was one of the few still offering old-fashioned driveway service. The attendant also offered a simple answer to questions about how hot it gets here in summer. Fucking hot, he was known to say.

When two men in suits walked into the motel, Conway assumed they were looking for a room. They showed their IDs and the identikit image of the shooter, and asked if she remembered any suspicious characters from mid October. Conway opened her register and ran her finger down the page. 'Oh,' she said, remembering the strange character who had booked in late on that Saturday night. For the next few hours, the police questioned her closely. They were so controlled, she didn't pick up on their excitement. They had been to more than 100 motels and this was their first decent lead.

They told her they couldn't stay at her motel that night in case it was seen to compromise the investigation. Conway was apprehensive when they put up some photographs on their computer screen. What if she couldn't recognise anyone? But when she saw the face, she knew straight away. She picked the photograph of Gassy. That was the man who had booked in to her motel as David Pais. You are now a witness, the police told her. This weighed on her mind over the next eighteen months or so.

Now Standing had a name. It was something to go on. It might help with the next job, a massive door-knocking exercise. The team planned to check every motel, caravan park, hotel and boarding house in Adelaide in search of anything which might link to Gassy or Pais. Their plan was to start in the southern suburbs and work their way north. They kicked off their search on Friday, 9 November. But they got an early mark.

On that same Friday, police issued a public appeal to Adelaide hoteliers asking for information about a Mr Pais who had been driving a Nissan and who might have stayed about the time of the murder. Martin Smith, the owner of the Lindy Lodge Motel, knew the face in the identikit. Smith contacted the police immediately; he didn't need to check his motel records first. He was sure he knew the man and in which room he had stayed. Smith had seen the man on the night he checked in, the next morning when he extended his stay, and then later that afternoon when he asked where to find a trim for his beard. Smith remembered being surprised when he next saw the man; he looked so different after his visit to the hairdresser. When interviewed by the police, Smith had no difficulty identifying a photo of Gassy. They noticed that the mobile number David Paes gave Smith was only one digit different from Gassy's own number, just as the name he gave was only one letter different from that given to Denise Conway in Balranald. The following Monday, the *Advertiser* reported that Smith's evidence had given police the breakthrough they needed to charge a Sydney man with the murder.

It was one of those glorious spring days that Sydney does so well when police returned to Oyster Bay to arrest Gassy, on Saturday, 9 November. The house had been under surveillance but they weren't sure if he was home. They climbed the stairs to the back door, uncertain of what to expect. Maud answered. I don't know where he is, she said. The officers heard a noise downstairs. They went to the door of Gassy's flat and knocked: 'It's the police, open the door.' A few moments passed before the door opened. Gassy stood there in shorts.

It all seemed so surreal, thought one police officer. This was the sleepy Sutherland Shire. The local joke held that once people moved to the Shire – as the locals called it, half in irony, half in pride – they never left. It was God's own country, after all. The officer found it difficult to believe that this attractive man, who seemed so mild-mannered and who lived so close to her own brother, was about to be charged with murder. Goodbye papa, Gassy said. Take care, my son, came the reply. It was all so low key, so unremarkable, the policewoman thought. They could have been taking him in for a driving offence.

When Gassy appeared at Sydney Central Court on Monday, 11 November, he tried to block his extradition to South Australia by claiming that he needed surgery for a possible tumour on his tongue and required constant HIV medication, which might not be available in an Adelaide prison. Steve Kinsman told the court that Gassy had hired a car three days before the murder and driven to Adelaide, giving a false name and address along the way. He said that a woman had seen Gassy with a beard and long hair in the foyer of the building on the morning of the shooting. Gassy turned around in court to wave to his family, and his sister approached the dock showing a letter of support from her children. Maud held up a cardigan to hide her face from the cameras as she and Xavier walked down the court steps afterwards.

Matt Moss was in the car which took Gassy to the airport. He decided to try a humorous approach; he was interested in the reaction of his charge. Eric, he said, it's good to work with a professional from time to time, because you have clearly paid attention to detail. It looked to Moss as though Gassy smiled at the comment and gave him a wink. We will see how it all ends up, Gassy replied.

As South Australian detectives waited with Gassy at the airport, a television reporter from Adelaide approached, camera in hand. She filmed him there, and again on the plane where he leant forwards in his seat, trying to hide his face with a shirt, and then again on the tarmac in Adelaide as he was walked to a waiting police car. Gassy was furious the police didn't stop the reporter. He made sure that he found out who she was. Kinsman also wasn't happy about the filming. He didn't want his face on television.

Mick Standing was waiting when Gassy arrived at the Adelaide City Watchhouse, a maximum security holding cell. Standing wanted to have a look. He eyeballed Gassy but didn't ask any questions; he just waited to see if the prisoner would say anything interesting. He didn't.

A week after Gassy's arrest, Marie Lajoie, a close friend of the Gassy family, was quoted in the *Sun-Herald* newspaper in Sydney. 'He was deregistered and it ruined his life,' she said. 'He took it very badly. Imagine a boy of his competency being deregistered and having no job. He was trying to put his life back on track and then nobody knows what happened.'

The newspaper said that Xavier Gassy, when approached by the reporter at his home, held his hand over his heart and said: 'I am too shattered, I cannot talk about it. The worst has been done now he has been called guilty before he has been tried.'

★

The detectives who returned to headquarters with Denise Conway's news of a man called Pais also brought security camera footage from service stations along the highway to Sydney. Members of the investigating team spent long hours straining their eyes in front of the screen. Finally, they were rewarded by footage from the Mobil station at Renmark, a well-watered pretty town on the banks of the Murray River, about three hours' drive from Adelaide.

It showed that at 10 am on Tuesday, 15 October, a man pulled up in a small, light-coloured car. He was slim apart from a modest pot belly and wore a white T-shirt, jeans, white runners and dark sunglasses. He pumped some petrol and then walked into the shop where he handed over $16 for a 600 ml bottle of water and 15.6 litres of unleaded fuel. The man then returned to his car, cleaned his windscreen, and rummaged in the boot, retrieving a plastic bag which he dropped in the rubbish bin before driving away. All up, he spent less than fifteen minutes at the service station. Perhaps he didn't notice the sign in the shop which clearly advises customers that closed-circuit surveillance cameras are in operation.

Standing recognised the man on the video immediately. He'd seen him not long before at the charge counter at the City Watchhouse.

A few weeks after retrieving the video, the police returned to Renmark and asked the service station manager, Brenton Poole, if he recognised Gassy's face. He did. Renmark is rich with many nationalities, but Poole had noticed this man because he couldn't place his ethnic background. He wasn't Aboriginal or Lebanese, but what was he? His skin colour was unusual.

On Tuesday, 19 November, police made the short drive from Renmark to the town's tip, signposted as the 'refuse dump'. The drive took them past groves of grapes and fruit trees and other symbols of productivity. At the tip, huge wedgetails, scavenging ibises and even seagulls circled the orange-red sands and rotting rubbish. Black crows rested like silhouettes on the dead trees, facing into the wind. If they turned one way, they looked on the lush deep green of citrus orchards. In the other direction lay the washed-out grey of mallee scrub.

Dozens of people – police officers, SES volunteers and other locals – gathered to help with the search. They wore protective clothing, with masks and gloves. A marquee, portable toilets and a first aid station were set up. Before they began sifting through the rubbish, there was a briefing. They were looking for anything that might be of interest; it could be parts of a Glock pistol – the bullets recovered from the victim had been fired by a Glock and the suspect was known to have Glocks registered in his name. They were also asked to search for any documents dated on or around 15 October.

All afternoon, the group toiled. It was stinking, hot and fruitless.

Next day, they enlisted the help of the kindly, gently-spoken Brenton Poole. He climbed down into a trench, looking for familiar rubbish. He recognised some large promotional signs, and then found several large plastic bags from his service station. An excavator came to remove the rubbish and the volunteers began poring through it.

An SES volunteer opened a white plastic bag. Inside was a receipt for Chris King from the Edmonstone Motel, and part of the receipt given to David Pais at the Shamrock Motel in Balranald. There was also a mini pizza box, and a medium-sized, man's collared shirt. It was a Country Road brand, heavily stained. The police video rolled as the items were laid out on the tables under the marquee for investigation.

One detective was quickly on the phone. Where is the Edmonstone Motel? he wanted to know.

The motel, an unremarkable brick facility servicing travellers of modest means, lies a short walk from the Brisbane Convention and Exhibition Centre. Early in the evening of Friday, 26 April, Chris King had booked into the motel, giving a false address at Punchbowl in Sydney's south-western suburbs. He gave his car registration details as GCO 183 and paid cash in advance for his stay in room 15.

Among the boxes and boxes of evidence gathered from the Oyster Bay home were the details of a business in Brisbane.

The Queensland Gun Exchange, with its shop front advertising 'Guns and Fishing', once would have been right at home in the seedy streets of Fortitude Valley. But these days it looks out of place amid the gentrification of its once grungy surrounds. The shops nearby now retail lifestyle rather than vice.

On the footpath in front of the shop stands a pathetic mannequin, her left arm bound together with masking tape. She wears a jet black wig, a leopardskin bra and mini skirt, and dangles handcuffs from one wrist. A fishing rod is propped in her knee-high white gumboots. She looks just as tragic as the fox, deer, boar and other animals whose stuffed heads adorn the walls of the dark interior. All manner of knives, slingshots, rifles, pistols and other instruments of violence are for sale here.

Scott Allen, the sales manager, has a shaven head, smooth, clear skin and a tightly coiled energy. He looks more rock star than gun expert. Allen had good reasons for remembering the man who came here in April 2002 to order a bare slide for a Glock pistol. The man had dark curly hair, about shoulder length, tied back in a ponytail, and was of a medium height and slim build. He had rung a number of times before coming to the shop, and Allen was surprised to see that he was reasonably well dressed. It didn't gel with the agitation that had come down the phone lines.

Allen was suspicious about the man's order. It was unusual – slides don't usually break or wear out. He asked to see a firearms licence and satisfied himself that the photo of Jean Eric Gassy was indeed the man in front of him. He recorded the number and took a $100 deposit. Gassy didn't want to pay by credit card or to collect the part from the shop, so Allen gave him the details for electronically transferring his payment into the shop's account. That stuck in his mind afterwards; it was a bit unusual. In the following weeks, Gassy rang Allen a number of times about his order. When the part finally arrived a few months later, Allen repeatedly tried to contact his customer on the mobile number he had left.

But Allen didn't hear any more about the order until Monday, 18 November. That was when police arrived at his shop, un-announced. They were following up a lead from the Oyster Bay search. Allen wasn't overly surprised. He'd thought all along that Gassy was a strange one. The police spent three hours asking him what he could remember. They were suspicious that Allen had tried to ring Gassy on his mobile just a few hours before the shooting. Allen had no difficulty identifying Gassy from the photos the police showed him. It was the fine eyebrows and the lips that he remembered.

Learne Durrington spent most of the days immediately after Margaret's death at Don's house, providing support to those immersed in the surreal world of grief. On Friday, 18 October, she went to her office to check how her staff were doing. When she saw the identikit image of the man being sought by police, it suddenly hit her. She knew the face. He had been in the lift with her on the morning of the murder. Perhaps he had been doing reconnaissance of the building.

Just after 11 am on the previous Monday, Durrington had dashed out from work for a reviver. When she returned to the building, coffee in hand, a man had followed her into the lift. He had an olive complexion and fine features, high cheekbones and wide-browed brown eyes. His hair was a very dark brown, wavy, coarse and shoulder length. It was hard to pick his age; he could be anywhere between his late teens and late twenties, she guessed. Durrington had never seen him before and struck up a conversation about the weather. Have a good day, she said as she left the lift on the seventh floor. They made fleeting eye contact. She was intrigued by his appearance and wondered about his cultural background. He was not Anglo, that was clear. He also had a distinctive voice, melodic even. He sounded well educated and there was an accent, but she couldn't pick it. She'd been watching the cricket and wondered if he was Sri Lankan.

On Monday, 11 November, Durrington went to police headquarters to view a selection of photographs. None was quite right. Her first inclination was to pick the one whose features were like those of the man she saw. But he had a ruddy colouring whereas her man had an olive complexion. She wavered between picking this man and another, who had a darker skin colour.

Eventually, she went for the latter although it still didn't feel quite right. As she left the room, a policeman asked what made her choose one photograph over another. As Durrington sat waiting for a lift back to her office, she decided that she had made a mistake, and to stick with her original decision. She asked to do the procedure again. This time she went with her first inclination. It was a photograph of Gassy.

The identification reinforced Mick Standing's hunch. He had no proof but he was sure the killer would have done some reconnaissance on the morning of the shooting. Gassy would have caught the lift to level eight and then left the building by the fire escape stairs, pleased that he would be able to make a discreet exit after the murder.

Analysis of the telephone records from the Gassy household in the days before and after the murder showed a consistent pattern of regular calls, until the morning of Saturday, 12 October. Then no more calls were made until 7.33 pm on Monday, 14 October. This eighteen-second call was to an unlisted number for a mobile phone. Gassy said he was trying to ring his cousin but dialled an incorrect number. The phone numbers differed by five digits.

The truck driver who owned the phone lived at Prestons, on the south-western fringes of Sydney. Most Monday evenings at about that time found him putting his son to bed while his wife was at netball. If he ever answered a call from the Gassy household, he would store no memory of it. He had never heard of the Gassy family until contacted by police investigating the call.

There were then no more calls from the Gassy landline – until early on the morning of Wednesday, 16 October, when a 22-second call was made to Elizabeth Gassy's mobile.

The phone at the Gassy household rang unanswered several times between the mornings of Saturday, 12 October and Wednesday, 16 October. Gilbert Malepa was trying to contact his cousin Eric but could get no reply.

12

The brief

When the pistol fired at Margaret Tobin, the movement of the trigger sent the firing pin flying forward. It struck the head of the cartridge case, containing the primer, and this caused a flash which set fire to the propellant. This burnt quickly, causing a rapid increase in pressure, and expelling the projectile. Burnt and unburned propellant also exited the muzzle, along with a small amount of smoke. Meanwhile, the recoil pushed the slide to the rear, ejecting the spent cartridge. Then the slide returned to position, pushing the next round into the chamber. Almost as quickly as the trigger was pulled, another bullet was ready to fire. It was easy to fire four times in quick succession.

In those split seconds, the gun was also leaving its signature on both the cartridge cases and the projectiles. The spiral grooves inside the barrel, which gripped the projectiles and sent them spinning through the air, left their mark. The breach or bolt face (the surface behind the back of the barrel, which supports the back of the cartridge case when it is fired), the firing pin, the extractor (which drags the spent cartridge case from the chamber after firing), and the ejector (which throws out the spent cartridge) can also leave their mark on the cartridge cases. So can the magazine, the box-like structure at the bottom of the pistol, which holds the rounds in a stack.

Some of these microscopic marks are generic – being similar for all firearms of a particular make and model – and some are specific to the individual firearm, being caused by wear, corrosion, or manufacturing variations. These mechanical fingerprints can help link firearms to crimes.

Within hours of Margaret's death, an experienced ballistics expert was at the scene of the crime. Peter Lawrence joined the police force in 1976, and belongs to an international expert group called the Association of Fire and Tool Mark Examiners. He collected four cartridge cases from level 8 at the CitiCentre Building, and then went to the hospital to collect the projectiles recovered from the victim's body. A few weeks later he received two pistols, other gun parts and ammunition seized from Gassy's flat.

The distinctive shape of the spent cases and certain identifying marks told Lawrence they had been fired by a Glock pistol. The projectiles were Speer Gold Dot 9 mm, whose advantages in antipersonnel use are well known amongst the firearms fraternity. The hollow point means there is a weakness at their front. When it strikes soft tissue, the metal on the front folds back and makes a larger diameter, ensuring the projectile stops quickly in the tissue. This helps ensure maximum injury to the target, while stopping the projectile passing cleanly through the body. Lawrence takes a philosophical view on debate about whether 9 mm bullets are the best calibre for shooting people. Everything in life is a compromise, he says, and ammunition is no exception to that rule.

Lawrence took note that the ammunition recovered from Gassy's flat included both Speer Gold Dot as well as other types more suited to target shooting. He noted that the spring on the Glock 26 pistol had been replaced with a device enabling use of a laser sighting system. This projects a red laser dot onto the target, showing where the bullet will hit, and eliminates the need to line up the sights visually. He also noted that the spare slide for the Glock 26 was missing a firing pin.

Lawrence thought it significant that the two spare slides for the

Glock pistols showed signs of being recently polished. Small grains of a grey metallic dust still clung to them, and sections were bright and shiny as if they had been rubbed by a fine abrasive paper. It was impossible to know whether either of the slides had fired the fatal shots before being polished.

Lawrence conducted various tests to determine whether either of the pistols had fired the fatal shots, including comparing the mechanical fingerprints on the projectiles fired by the two pistols with those recovered from the victim. He concluded that the barrels of both pistols could neither be ruled out nor conclusively established as having fired the fatal shots. The class characteristics – those generic marks common to all Glock pistols – were the same. But there were not enough individual characteristics to conclusively link or rule out either barrel. This was not surprising. Glock barrels are known for being smooth with very few microscopic imperfections, and are thus less likely than some other guns to leave individual marks.

It was possible that the fatal shots had been fired by either of the spare slides before the breach faces were polished, but they couldn't have been fired by any of the three firing pins Lawrence examined – those from the two pistols and the one from the spare slide for the Glock 19.

Lawrence also determined that the cartridge cases from the scene had been made with the same head stamp as some of the ammunition found in Gassy's flat. The same head stamp is generally used to manufacture about 30,000 to 50,000 rounds before being replaced due to wear and tear.

On the screen, whether big or small, it always seems straightforward. Fingerprints are found, DNA is recovered and the bad guys are apprehended. In the real world, everything is more messy and complicated.

Fingerprints, those minute random patterns which form in the first months of sloshing around in the womb, are one of the many small things which set one human being apart from another. But they are just as fragile and uncertain as life itself.

Put two people in the same room, handling the same cup and the same kettle. One may leave fingerprints; the other may not. The person who is older or who is unfit or who rarely perspires will be less likely to leave a decent print. What they ate for lunch can come into play. People who touch their heads often generally give good prints; those who are obsessive about hand-washing do not.

The quality of the print also depends on the receptacle. Smooth surfaces like glass, plastic, metal and paper are good for capturing such clues. Dusty surfaces are not. Even an ideal surface loses prints if handled regularly. The weather and time of year also have a bearing. In summer, the oils in a print do not last so long.

In the right circumstances, a fingerprint might outlive a dog. At other times, it might be lucky to survive a few minutes.

A search was made for Gassy's fingerprints in many places, including the eighth floor and lift of the CitiCentre Building, the Lindy Lodge in Adelaide, the Shamrock Motel in Balranald, and on many of the documents he was known to have handled. Apart from a couple of fingerprints on documents at Gassy's home, including the persons of interest list, none of his prints were found.

In the voir dire – the hearing before the jury trial began – Gassy told the judge that he was in the habit of wearing the surgical gloves found in his flat when handling meat. They stopped it getting under his nails: 'When we cook our meat, we cut off all the sinews and the fat.' He also wore them when checking the oil in the car, where he kept cotton gloves for when the steering wheel became too hot in the sun. 'There is absolutely nothing sinister about it,' he insisted.

Looking in a motel room for DNA, the scientific shorthand for an individual's genetic fingerprint, is something like trying to find a needle in a haystack. But at least a needle is visible, and makes its presence felt, pointedly. When investigators went to the Lindy Lodge and Shamrock motels in search of Gassy's DNA, they made an educated guess about where to put their swabs. They swabbed in the places where DNA might be left in bodily fluids like saliva, sweat and blood. They collected hairs, although these were likely to yield DNA only if there were cells around their root and they were in a growing phase.

Even if the investigators found DNA, there was no guarantee it would be of any use. It might be damaged, by ultraviolet light, cleaning agents or something else, or be insufficient for useful analysis. The analogy the investigators liked to use was that they were stabbing in the dark with their swabs. They didn't quite know if they would find anything or, if they did, whether it would be useful.

No-one was surprised that DNA was not recovered from the killer's cartridges. It doesn't have much chance of surviving the heat of a gun in action. None of the hairs recovered from either motel room were of any use; they either did not have DNA or did not have enough of it. DNA was also recovered from a sun block label, coat hanger, keys and phone hand piece at the Shamrock Motel, but there was not enough for comparison with the suspect's DNA. The same problem arose with DNA swabbed from the Lindy Lodge bathroom. Testing of the shirt recovered from the Renmark tip showed the staining was not blood, and DNA was not found on the shirt's collar or cuffs. The source of the stain was not discovered.

When a gun is fired, particles so tiny that they are measured in microns or thousandths of a millimetre are ejected from the muzzle. The particles, of lead, aluminium, barium and antimony, are from the burnt propellant.

Eleven days after the murder, on Friday, 25 October, police took swabs from a Nissan Pulsar at the Avis car rental branch at Hurstville. Tests conducted six months later revealed the presence of gunshot residue (GSR) on the front passenger's seat and in the boot. Some irregular particles on the front driver's seat also may have been GSR. The gunshot residue found contained the same elements – lead, aluminium, barium and antimony – as did Speer cartridges of the kind used in the shooting. The people who hired the car before and after Gassy told police they had not been carrying guns and had not been shooting.

Gunshot residue was also identified on a black parker jacket seized from Gassy's wardrobe.

★

So much more is revealed by our handwriting than what it says. An expert who looks through a microscope at the lines and loops and funny little squiggles on the page can tell whether someone was writing quickly or slowly, whether they wrote an 'o' in a clockwise direction, or whether they were pretending to be someone else.

When handwriting examiner Elizabeth Ockleshaw looked at samples of Eric Gassy's signature, she saw a complex specimen. There were many turning points, where the pen changed direction, and crossing lines. He clearly was a skilled writer.

She was unable to directly compare his signature with those on the paperwork from the Edmonstone, Lindy Lodge and Shamrock motels. Like must be compared with like – the signature of Eric Gassy could not be compared with the signatures of Chris King or David Pais. Instead Ockleshaw scanned Gassy's diaries, taking out examples of the letters found on the motel documents.

She looked at the proportion and size of the letters, the slope of the writing, the spacing of the words, where the pen had left the paper, and the fluency of the writing.

There were indications it was Gassy's writing on each of the motel documents. Her expert opinion was backed up by Gassy's former secretary, Naomi, who told police that she recognised the writing on the Brisbane motel slip as that of her former boss.

In early 2004, the prosecutor Peter Brebner took a fortnight just to make a preliminary read of the thousands of pages of the police brief. He knew that a tough job lay ahead. There were so many pieces to fit together in the jigsaw. The evidence was largely circumstantial and some crucial pieces were missing. We'd like some more evidence, he told Mick Standing.

Grant Francis and Suzanne Heath had been unable to identify Gassy from an array of photographs as the man in the lift. Bob Champion and the others at the Brisbane Convention Centre were also unable to identify the suspicious stranger. Margaret Tobin was not mentioned on the persons of interest list or the railway ticket. There was no incriminating DNA or fingerprint evidence. There was also the phone call made from the Gassy's home on the evening of the murder. Perhaps it had been made by Gassy's sister's children. Or perhaps he had used his computer training to arrange it through a dial-up modem. But there was no convincing evidence to support such speculation. As Gassy would later argue, the simplicity of his alibi was also its strength. Who in their right mind would set up an alibi hinging on a split-second phone call to a wrong number?

13

Ricochet

The vocabulary of those who make their money out of guns and other weapons of destruction is deliberately obtuse. The Glock pistol, for example, is favoured by military and law enforcement agencies because of its benefits in 'antipersonnel use'. Speer Gold Dot costs more than some other types of ammunition but, according to one retailer, 'delivers optimum performance and terminal penetration without over penetrating'.

It is a language which blurs and blunts the brutality of what is achieved by these expertly engineered instruments of death. When the pistol was fired that Monday afternoon, the grooves hidden in its barrel sent the bullets spinning through the air towards a defenceless woman who had no idea of what was about to strike.

The bullets drilled quickly and easily through Margaret's flesh, leaving entry wounds in the shape of a circle. One bullet passed through her upper right arm, fracturing the arm bone, before re-entering the right side of her chest. There it tore through the lower lobe of her right lung and fractured her sixth and seventh ribs before coming to rest in her chest.

Another bullet entered through the lower right side of Margaret's chest, tearing through her diaphragm and the lower lobe of her left lung. It passed between two of her back ribs and ended its journey beneath the skin on the left side of her back. Another shot entered through the top right side of her back, causing extensive damage to the right lung, and passed to the left of the chest. The bullet was found beneath the skin of her left breast.

The other shot entered the right side of Margaret's lower abdomen above the pelvis. It ripped through the loops of her small bowel, liver, stomach and a sheet of fat before coming to rest on the lower chest wall. Most likely this bullet was the last, and fired as Margaret was falling or already collapsed, according to a forensic pathologist.

Those four small bullets took the life from a woman who had made more of hers than most. The passion, the drive, the impatience, the anger, the spark – all were extinguished. The woman who would wake at 3 am, excited about an idea that had just come to her, would wake no more.

The impact of those four small bullets ricocheted around many lives. One violent death leaves many people wounded and changed in ways large and small. It made many question their lives and their priorities. What's the point of sacrificing yourself for your work? was a common response. Some questioned their own commitment to working in such a difficult and potentially dangerous field as mental health. Some changed jobs, a few moved countries. Many thought twice about disciplining recalcitrant colleagues or signing letters of dismissal. Some were galvanised into striving harder, realising, as Don was fond of saying, that life is not a dress rehearsal. Many people, and not only psychiatrists, found themselves looking uneasily over their shoulders, and worrying more about the nasty letters and phone calls that they received at work.

In Victoria, a set of twins struggled with their year 12 final exams. It was their aunt who had been shot. In Adelaide, a teenage boy didn't return to school after the shooting. He had been having a hard enough time before it but perhaps it was the anguish of that dreadful afternoon, when he was convinced it was his mother who had been shot in the CitiCentre Building, that tipped the balance. It would be months before his life regained an even keel.

On the evening of Margaret's death, André Jenkins, who had been one of the first to her wounded side, came home from work and tried to explain to his three young sons what had happened. It was something he felt he had to do, knowing that the murder would be on the television and that they would hear him talking about it. He also had to explain why he couldn't let them play some games anymore. Many months would pass before Jenkins could bear to hear the sound of guns on his kids' computer games. Years later, the bang of a car backfiring or a book dropping would leave him glued to the ceiling. By then, he would be able to laugh about his automatic overreaction to loud noise. But he couldn't stop himself from doing it.

Des Ryan, the editor of the *City Messenger* community newspaper, was knocked by Margaret's death. He remembered that she had been forthright, funny, persuasive and passionate when addressing a staff meeting of his journalists about a year earlier. 'Afterwards, we went to lunch with a few senior paper editors and over a glass of wine she was again funny and forthright – off the record, of course – about certain politicians. She was an easy woman to like,' he later wrote in his newspaper. At her urging, the paper had done a series of articles on mental health.

For some, Margaret's murder became entangled with other losses.

In Mick Standing's memory, Margaret's death would always be associated with his mother's. His mum died a fortnight after the CitiCentre shooting. Standing had been so busy with the murder investigation, working sixteen-hour days, there hadn't been much time to pause and take stock.

Vince Ponzio was seven when his father died suddenly of a heart attack at the age of 37, leaving a wife and two children. One of the rituals of Vince's adult life was to accompany his mother to his father's grave to mark the anniversary of his death, 14 October. After Margaret's murder, that date gained an added poignancy. Ponzio, a psychologist, had worked closely with Margaret at St George Hospital, playing the role of good cop to her bad cop. Her death struck hard. She had been the mentor who pushed him to explore his potential. She had also helped him through an extended period of depression. Initially, he had linked his depressed mood to the way Margaret had pushed him to meet her expectations. Ponzio was always grateful that she did not respond defensively. She stuck with him, offering kind and generous personal support throughout those difficult times.

Michelle Bradley, another of Margaret's protégées in Sydney, was terribly affected by the murder. Not long after she first went to work for Margaret, Bradley's brother-in-law died in a skiing accident at age 40. Margaret was supportive when Bradley took extended leave to help care for her sister and family. In October 2002, Bradley was staying at her parents' place while mending an ankle injured when she stepped into a mutton-bird hole on Norfolk Island. Bradley had just hobbled out of the shower when her mother came into the room saying, I have some terrible news. Her mother clipped all the newspaper stories, knowing that Margaret had been much more than just a boss to her daughter, who initially trained as a nurse. Margaret had helped Bradley's transformation into a senior health service executive. Bradley was still grieving Margaret's death several weeks later when her mother died suddenly of a stroke. Years later, Bradley was glad that she hadn't thrown out the farewell card Margaret had given her before leaving Sydney for the South Australian job. Margaret wrote, 'It was great knowing you, and I have watched your growth in courage, determination and confidence with warmth and interest. Good luck.'

For Russell Firmin, who fell into working in mental health after abandoning plans to teach drama, Margaret's death would always be mixed up with the horror of the Bali bombing. Not long after hearing news of the shooting, Firmin was at Sydney Airport, helping to greet and assess hundreds of young people who were pouring off planes with suntans, wounds and burns. Some were limping and others were in wheelchairs. One particular scene stuck in his mind: a young man talking to his teenage sister. They had been separated in Bali and had just been reunited after arriving on separate planes. The sister thought their parents were both still alive; the brother knew otherwise. For Firmin, it all seemed surreal. He had just learnt that one of his best mates was murdered, and here he was, dealing with hordes of people who had been wounded, physically and emotionally.

Firmin was Margaret's 2IC in the South Eastern Sydney Area Health Service for three years. When he started, she told him that his job was to protect her back. If Gordon Parker starts having a go at me in a meeting and it looks like I am losing, your job is to get in there and sort him out, she joked. But Firmin saw that his job was also to be straight with Margaret. He thought she needed people around her who would laugh at her, tell her when she was talking bullshit, and to deflate the mystique that was building up around her. Firmin had first met Margaret at Willsmere in the 1980s, during his second stint of working there as a psychiatric nurse. In 1997, she recruited him to the Sydney job. Over coffees and lunches and drinks, they sometimes talked of the dreadful, evil things that had happened in psychiatric institutions in the past, including assaults, thefts, murders, rapes, corruption.

Firmin never saw it himself but heard patients talk of bygone years when there had been a practice called 'dusting the ceiling', used as a punishment to quieten psychotic patients. They were thrown in the air from a blanket and caught several times. Just when they started to relax, expecting to be caught, the four attendants holding the blanket would let go. Because they were relaxed, this minimised the risk of broken bones. Another former technique, when patients were raging out of control, was to choke them unconscious with a towel. With Margaret's death, Firmin lost more than a friend. She had been a fellow traveller. They had shared a history as well as a determination to leave that past behind.

14

Taken hostage

At first, it all seems so foreign and intimidating. But familiarity develops as the various players and observers grow accustomed to each other and the routines of a court at work. In the mornings, two of the younger jurors often meet over a coffee and cigarette at a cafe only a stone's throw from the court entrance. Ms Morticia has a severe dark fringe, full lips and dramatic eyeliner, while Ms Sultry's nickname speaks for itself. Mr Foreman, who is perhaps in his fifties, has a tan, a tattoo that appears home-made and a neatly trimmed grey beard. He exudes an outdoors strength and often stands in front of the court building, smoking with concentration. It transpires, in fact, that many of those inhaling intensely in front of the Sir Samuel Way Building are not, as might be assumed, nervous defendants, but are police officers or jurors.

Others find their fix at the top of the marble staircase, near Court Room Two. There volunteers sell styrofoam coffee, with two biscuits, for the no-frills price of $1.20. The service aims to provide ready, affordable relief to those stressed by their day in court. Xavier and Maud Gassy do not join the regular customers, however. Xavier likes real coffee. But at home they drink tea, he says, because Maud cannot stand percolated coffee and he cannot stand the instant variety.

On the seats outside the court room are some of those waiting to be called as witnesses. Often they sit near people connected to the defendant or the victim although perhaps they do not realise this. The court watchers are usually in attendance as well – curious people feeding their curiosity or their retirement or their empty days with the real-life tragedies offered up by the courts. It's more real even than reality television. At different times, this case draws a retrenched public servant, a retired nurse, a university student and holidaymakers from interstate. As the days pass, two of the female court watchers take it upon themselves to offer support to the elderly Gassys.

One of the regulars to Court Room Two looks like an English country vicar. He is a tall gent in a blue blazer tightly buttoned across his erect back and expansive chest, and he lives in a stately residence which would not be out of place on a country estate. He often chats with Xavier and Maud, about their visit to the jail on the weekend, or what they have been buying and cooking from the Central Market. Sometimes they reminisce about the good old days in Mauritius and the people they still know there. But appearances can be deceiving. Many assume that Tom Young is a friend of the Gassys but in fact he is here on business, of sorts. Before retiring, Young enjoyed a long and profitable business association with Mauritius, exporting grains to the island for stock and human consumption. For the last decade or so he has been an honorary consul, whose duties include providing assistance to Mauritians who run into trouble. He found the Gassys some suitable accommodation, close to both the court and St Francis Xavier's Cathedral, where Maud goes often to pray. When Young first met the Gassys, their colouring and facial features told him they were of predominantly Creole heritage although Mrs Gassy's brown hair also suggests a French connection. A Vietnam veteran and enthusiast of military and Mauritian history, Young is impressed by Maud in particular; she is clearly well read and well educated.

Young has been keeping the Mauritian Embassy in Canberra well informed of developments in the Gassy case. There is a lot of interest from Mauritius, he says. But it is more than duty that brings Young here most mornings. He had never been inside a court before but has become fascinated. It is like living theatre, he says. At first Young came with an open mind. He knew what Xavier and Maud thought of it all. But he soon developed his own view. His watching became a waiting. He thinks Gassy is going to make a mistake that gives him away. In one of those little twists so typical of Adelaide, Young has another connection to the case. When he first came here, during the pre-trial legal argument, Peter Brebner spun around on his chair, and said: 'I know you. You were educated on Dequetteville Terrace. You rowed in the first eight. I rowed in the under sixteens in the same year.' What this means is that Young and Brebner are alumni of one of Adelaide's most toffy private boys' schools, Prince Alfred College.

Sometimes, another matter must be heard in Court Room Two before the Gassy trial can begin. One morning it is a bail application for a young chef charged with murdering his father; his mother and grandparents have put up the bail. Another day, the man in the dock hears how an elderly woman has been affected by his breaking into her home while she was there. The Sir Samuel Way Building, named for a former chief justice, is a grand old establishment but it has neither the space nor the facilities to cope with the modern world's demands. In their annual reports, the judges of the Supreme Court have repeatedly stressed the 'unsatisfactory standard' of the facilities. 'Being involved in court proceedings is a stressful experience for most people, and the facilities at the Court should be of a kind that will, as far as possible, minimise that stress. They fail to do so,' the judges say, admonishing the State Government for its failure to respond to their concerns over a number of years. The judges are working so hard, they say, that they have insufficient time for judgement writing, reading, reflection and participation in professional development programs.

Inside Court Room Two is a fluster of activity, even before the official proceedings begin. There is so much paperwork, so much administration to be attended to, it is not at all like the legal dramas on the telly. Gassy, who is representing himself, enters the dock briefly to put his papers on the bench in front of where he will sit. The bench was specially installed for his use; most defendants have no use for such a fitting. He is then escorted back through the door, to wait in a small room out of sight of the court. It is bare, apart from the stainless steel toilet and water sink, and he sits on a hard wooden bench.

When Gassy first arrives from the prison each morning, he is taken to a cell in the bowels of the building. Because he is a high-security prisoner, he doesn't have to share his space. The cell complies with the recommendations of the Royal Commission into Aboriginal Deaths in Custody. It is all smooth surfaces, without points where prisoners can hang themselves. Perspex over the bars prevents a tie or rope being lethally knotted around them. The holding cells may comply with the letter of the royal commission's recommendations, but there is no sense of life or hope in these airless, viewless, claustrophobic burrows. When they are opened for inspection during public tours, people are often surprised by the austerity. They expect, from their reading of the tabloid press, to find luxury, says one of the officials who takes the tours. Perhaps this grimness helps explain why Gassy sometimes gives the appearance of enjoying his time in court. There, at least, he has authority. The judge treats him with courtesy, he has plenty of opportunity to display his fine intellect and to enjoy some contact with the outside world. Indeed, one of the slim, fair court reporters becomes quite unsettled by Gassy's attempts to strike up a contact with her. You're a better-looking version of Helen Hunt, he says to her when he gets the chance.

Small talk fills the room as the minutes tick towards the start of the formalities. Three burly security guards, contracted to escort Gassy to and from jail, lounge untidily at the back of the room. They look far more dangerous than their charge. Sometimes the media cameras are waiting when the guards arrive with Gassy, who often hides behind dark sunglasses.

When the judge is announced, the room quietens and stands. Justice Ann Vanstone marches purposefully towards her seat, arms swinging in an almost military style. She wears a red gown to her knees, over her civilian clothes, with a broad black tie at her waist, and smart black shoes with heels. It is a judge's lot to stand above and beyond the rest of us, but the room catches occasional glimpses of the woman obscured by wig and robes. It is the little signs that give her away – the way she rubs the side of her neck when tired; the stare and slight reddening of the cheeks when she is cross; the smile of pleasure when she is found to be correct on a disputed point. Vanstone also enjoys a small joke. 'I don't know why I smile whenever I mention his name, I just do,' she says one day. She is referring to Detective Sergeant Mick Standing, who has been standing by for days, ready to give evidence when there is no other witness available to fill a gap in proceedings. Many jokes are made at Standing's expense during the trial, in fact. It is water off a duck's back to Standing. He is big enough to take it.

Vanstone has a soft, pleasing voice but it can also turn to a cutting steel. She runs a tight ship and has little tolerance for those who waste the court's time or resources. 'It is all extra expense. I feel that keenly,' she says when it looks as though a witness might have to be recalled from interstate. She also has a lovely formal way with words. 'I have a preference for the agreed facts to be drafted because they are attended by greater clarity,' she says one day. The way she says 'yes' can give it the meaning and weight of a sentence.

A few weeks into the murder trial of Jean Eric Gassy, it becomes clear that a court room has much in common with a hostage situation. A strange intimacy develops when circumstance throws a roomful of strangers close together. It is a drama with an uncertain ending, where alliances rise and fall and where strangers gain some knowledge of each other's quirks and foibles. Boundaries and roles can have moments of blurring. One morning, Don Scott holds the door open, politely, for the father of the man accused of murdering his wife. Margaret's sister Helena is pleased one lunch break when she walks past Xavier Gassy, and they exchange smiles. On a Monday morning, Xavier leans forward, smiling, and surprises the woman sitting in front of him, a journalist. Can I straighten your collar? he whispers. Maud often exchanges friendly greetings with the court staff and police; one day she plants a kiss on the cheek of the New South Wales officer who made her a cup of tea while her house was being searched back in October 2002. Another day, a bulky police-man, with the jowls of a bulldog, kneels gently beside Maud. In a previous year, he had spent many long days tracking down the evidence to nail her son but now he asks how she went at the doctor's yesterday. The doctor thought the pains in her neck might be osteoporosis. Everyone else thinks that stress must be the culprit.

At the end of a day of mind-numbing detail about Gassy's handwriting – he writes the number '6' with a 'fairly tight body and a long descending stroke' – onlookers file out of the court room moaning about how boring it has been. *Boring!* exclaims Xavier in agreement as the crowd moves past him. On another day, a witness inadvertently calls the judge 'your majesty'. Perhaps this isn't so silly; Justice Vanstone does sit under a royal coat of arms, bearing a Latin inscription meaning, in part, 'Shamed be he who thinks evil of this'. Still, the slip fetches a few chuckles in the next break. The court reporter who looks like Helen Hunt enjoys the joke but doesn't commit it to posterity. 'It didn't make it to transcript,' she says. Xavier also has a little laugh when told of the witness's faux pas. Then he adds, bitterly, *crawler.* He doesn't think much of the judge although it appears to many that she is bending over backwards to help his son. It's a kangaroo court, Xavier tells someone the day that New South Wales police give evidence about their first search of the Oyster Bay home.

Maud also reveals her anger one day. A stranger is sitting in the chair usually occupied by the judge's associate, the angelic Beth. The new woman says: 'This court is adjourned.'

''Til when?' Maud mutters, glaring angrily at the unfamiliar face. In an instant, the sweet, affectionate old woman has been transformed into someone seething with impatience. The contrast is remarkable.

Xavier is tickled by something he reads one day in Terry Lane's book, *God: The Interview*. He shows it to someone, smiling: 'Most misery and pain in the world has been caused by people who were convinced that they were doing good; most happiness has been caused by people who mind their own business because they are too modest to presume that they know what is best for anyone else.' On another day he is reading a book in court, whose title asks something like, *Why is God Silent when You Need Him the Most?* Xavier says he believes in God. But not all this, he says, gesturing to the paperback. He is making a point to read it only because a good friend gave it to him. We are just a speck in the universe, he says. How could we think God is listening when we pray?

Stevo, or Mr Tipstaff as the judge calls him, gives the appearance of being as serious as his title suggests. A tipstaff was originally the name given a staff which carried at its tip silver or some royal emblem denoting that the bearer was invested with royal authority. In the days of Dickens, the tipstaff was the man who carried people off to prison but the office has since evolved to denote a judge's 'personal and confidential attendant'. Amongst other, more onerous duties, Stevo carefully adjusts the judge's chair before she enters each morning. His dark moustache and squared bearing suggest a military background. Stevo oversees the room sternly but behind the formalities – he always buttons his suit, as if standing to attention, before calling the court to silence – lurks a larrikin. Thick, dark eyebrows dart expressively around his large forehead, which has the shine and creases of an old leather boot. The court reporters are often in chuckles at his quips. It's as useless as an ashtray on a motorbike, he says in one aside to the prosecutors, after a video tape has failed to play properly. Stevo is also a football tragic. His demeanour on a Monday morning depends on how his team, Port Adelaide, went on the weekend.

Stevo calls Barry, the sheriff's officer, Baz. The Sheriff's Office has a long, proud tradition and represents, according to a history on the court's web site, the oldest existing Anglo-Saxon legal office. Once preoccupied with collecting tax for English kings, sheriffs were responsible in the early days of European settlement of Australia for arranging the execution of prisoners sentenced to death. Some days it seems that paperwork will be the death of Barry. A trim, sprightly man, he is much happier handing out mints and smiles to the Tobin and Gassy families or clucking over the jurors than in dealing with the administration of jurors and witnesses. Barry is such an exuberant soul, he can't even be miserable quietly. When he sighs loudly during a break, this often signals disapproval at how much a witness is claiming in recompense for lost earnings. He still can't believe that a labourer put in a claim for $1,800 for one day. What really gets his goat is when someone makes an extravagant claim, and then also wants a $3 toll reimbursed. The pettiness of some people. Barry's sighs

221

inevitably are followed by a chirpy whistle or humming or perhaps a drum roll of his knuckles on the wooden benches. In the breaks, he often walks around clicking his fingers, in time with some tune in his head. Barry's wife gardens but his great passion is music; he plays trumpet in a military band.

Sheriffs used to be employed mainly from the ranks of the police and military, but these days ex-nurses are favoured for the job. 'They get so little trouble at the courts because they treat the prisoners as people,' a court official explains. Barry regularly does refresher courses in self-defence but would rather talk himself out of a tricky situation. One day Maud Gassy gives him a book of crosswords with a hand-written note on the front, 'to a very nice person'. Barry worries sometimes if his attempts to bring humour and lightness to the court room are inappropriate. He suggested one day that Jean Tobin take advantage of an unexpected day off court to explore the Barossa Valley. He felt awful when she replied, Barry, I have got other things on my mind. It is too easy, in this court room, for the living to forget the dead, and to overlook what has brought them here. Gassy wants the jury to see the photos of Margaret Tobin's torn body, as it was at post-mortem. He thinks, in some strange twist of logic, that this would be less prejudicial to his case. 'People's imagination is always worse than the reality,' he says. The judge refuses, however. She finds such photos distressing herself and sees no reason to burden the jury with the images.

Sometimes people who are really rather plain become quite beauti-ful as the passage of time reveals their internal qualities. With Gassy, the opposite occurs. His good looks recede on acquaintance. There is no spirit or spark to illuminate them; it is as if a blind has been drawn to stop people looking inside. Because Gassy has chosen to represent himself, the court room has far greater opportunity to observe him than normally would be the case. He is on his feet much of the day, asking questions of witnesses, objecting to something Brebner has said, or querying a decision by the judge. The room gains a sense of his irritations, and his supreme confidence in his own beliefs and capacity. But otherwise he is mostly inscrutable, with little showing of his interior. Gassy has clinical detachment down to a fine art. When he hands documents over the Perspex barrier to Mr Tipstaff, his face has the expression and warmth of a stone.

Gassy has a particular way of speaking. His lips wrap around syllables, enunciating so clearly that they seem to have trouble letting go of the words. His voice is mostly flat although it sometimes shows annoyance at an opposing point of view and becomes animated when discussing certain subjects, such as the finer technicalities of ballistics. Sometimes there is a glimpse of what Gassy must have been like as a little boy, in that slight whining 'everyone is against me' tone or the occasional sullen look he shoots the judge. Towards the end of the trial, Gassy makes a habit of shouldering on his jacket every time he rises to question a witness. An unguarded look is surprised on his face one day when he realises that he has forgotten to do this. On another day, he smiles at some repartee between the judge and Peter Brebner, and it changes his face completely. But there are only a few such slips of the mask. The only sign of tenderness that Gassy shows is, not when speaking with his parents, but to himself. Sitting in the dock, he often gently rubs his lips and chin with the fingers of his left hand. It may be a sign of anxiety, or deep thought, or perhaps just a habit. But it looks so tender. Some days he looks more tired than others. Sometimes a red rash, the size of a 50 cent piece, flares up behind his right ear. That, and his habit of blinking often and sipping repeatedly from his water cup are the only telltales of stress.

Before the trial even began, Gassy terminated the services of several lawyers. Among them was Mauritian-born Roger de Robillard, who flew from Sydney to represent Gassy during part of the voir dire. De Robillard, who was once jailed for contempt of court in Vanuatu and also has made headlines with various financial and tax problems, displayed an unusual approach to his brief. Not long after assuring the judge of his client's fitness to stand trial, he confided in the court that: 'My knowledge of ballistics is as vague and terrible as my knowledge of psychiatric science.' A small, elegant chap, de Robillard was not above enjoying a spot of mild flirtation with Gassy's gorgeous sister, Elizabeth. When a guard told Elizabeth one afternoon that she must have a pat-down security check before meeting her brother, de Robillard joked that he would like to be given this task. The guards laughed appreciatively, and Elizabeth smiled, taking the remark as a compliment.

Justice Vanstone was well briefed on de Robillard's chequered past, and was keen to see evidence of his right to practise. Her ire was roused when de Robillard was slow to meet her requests for documentation, and Gassy also became worried about his representative's behaviour. On the nineteenth day of the voir dire, de Robillard told the court he was withdrawing from the case as Dr Gassy was extremely concerned that de Robillard's exchanges with Justice Vanstone could be seen to be provoking the judge. 'He said he would rather take his chances and represent himself,' de Robillard said. 'I am disappointed in Dr Gassy's decision and so are his parents.'

Because Gassy is representing himself during the trial, many witnesses find themselves in the uncomfortable position of being cross-examined by someone they have cause to fear. Some are clearly petrified. On some days, it is just bizarre when Gassy is placed in a position of authority and power over the hardened detectives who worked on his arrest. One witness found the experience of being cross-examined by Gassy so traumatic that she had nightmares and difficulty sleeping for many months afterwards. She couldn't block his voice out of her head, and felt nervous about being alone at home.

For Anne, who sought psychiatric help from Gassy ten years earlier, the experience drags her away from the new life she has built into a public confrontation with the demons of her past. She took years to recover from her therapy with Gassy, where the boundaries between patient and doctor were so blurred. She asks to give evidence in camera from a nearby room so that she does not have to submit to Gassy's questions in person. The judge agrees to her request, and also suppresses the woman's name and any identifying information. At one stage, Gassy asks Anne to describe her opinion of men during the time she was in treatment. He then withdraws the question. He also suggests that Anne has been conspiring with his former secretary, Naomi Sommers, concocting a story that he thought his office at St George was bugged.

The six doctors whose personal details were included on the 'persons of interest list' are also called to the stand. When it is John Woodforde's turn, Gassy's eyes flash as he hears the reasons Woodforde diagnosed him with a delusional disorder back in 1994. The witness has the shrinking physique of the elderly, and speaks in a kindly manner although fear renders him hoarse. He does not recognise the man in front of him. Woodforde remains as polite as pie during his lengthy interrogation.

Gassy is like a dog at a bone, relentlessly pulling at the detail of Woodforde's diagnosis in an effort to destroy it. In the end, he demands: 'Is your diagnosis of delusional disorder in my case not a fabrication and does not your involvement in my deregistration constitute political abuse of psychiatry?'

Gassy disputes even the way in which Woodforde wrote his report.

Gassy: You think it is the standard approach?

Woodforde: Yes, I believe it is.

Gassy: Well, it is not . . .

Woodforde: Well, we obviously differ on that one, Dr Gassy.

A number of times the judge has to ask Gassy to stop interrupting Woodforde. It is a rare example of him losing control. For once, he cannot hide what he feels. From where she sits, the judge can clearly see Gassy's hatred for Woodforde. It is so intense it is palpable, she makes a note to herself.

The judge makes a similar observation when Jonathan Phillips is called to the stand. Phillips is pale and attired in classic medical consultant's garb: a checked suit with a neatly pressed handkerchief in his top pocket. For weeks, Phillips has been waiting anxiously for his day in court. In some strange way, his life has become so entangled in this case. Years ago, he treated both father and son, Xavier and Eric. Margaret Tobin was more than just a valued professional ally to Phillips. They were friends, and he took great delight in her quirky ways, how she was never without a book, and her over-the-top wardrobe. He enjoys a theatrical flourish himself. 'I was consulting in my office in Macquarie Street in Sydney and received a phone call to alert me to the fact that Professor Tobin was in serious and perilous health at that point in time,' he tells the court.

Phillips thinks about Margaret just about every morning as he gets out of the lift on level 8 of the CitiCentre Building. He is now doing her old job, trying to pick up the threads of mental health reform in South Australia. But after a long career in private practice in Sydney, Phillips does not have the background in public sector management, and is finding the task immensely difficult. The last year has been the most frustrating year of my life, he is fond of telling people. Sometimes he adds darkly, mental health reform may not be possible in South Australia. Phillips would not be in this job if his friend hadn't been murdered. He has told people that he fears for his own life too.

Gassy looks down, a hint of a smile on his face, as Phillips is shown the persons of interest list. It contains two photographs of him, including one where he wears the ceremonial hat of presidents of the Royal Australian and New Zealand College of Psychiatrists. It also lists two of his phone numbers and his email address. Gassy also looks down, as if to hide his emotions or at least keep them in check, when Phillips is shown the torn railway ticket with the address of an apartment where he once lived in Pyrmont, in inner Sydney. The address was not listed in the phone book.

Many witnesses seem reluctant to antagonise Gassy. A solicitor, who sat on the Medical Tribunal hearing in 1997, is almost fawning under his questioning. She smiles broadly at him and exudes charm. At one stage, the judge instructs the witness to stop deferring to Gassy when answering his questions. As the solicitor leaves the courthouse, she tells the elderly couple who accompanied her to court, her parents perhaps, that she didn't want to aggravate him.

Gassy's sister, Elizabeth, comes to the witness stand one day, determined to paint a sympathetic picture of her brother. She works for an airline in Sydney, and is pencil-slim and darkly exotic, with fine, even features. Her luxuriant long, dark hair is pulled back off her face and she is elegantly dressed in a dark jacket and skirt with an open white collared shirt. Her occasional appearances in the court room suggest that, like her brother, she prefers a wardrobe of black and white.

Elizabeth sends Gassy a brief smile before Brebner's questions start. She replies in a soft voice with a slight accent and a large measure of charm. She smiles tenderly whenever her brother Eric's name is mentioned. Elizabeth tells the court that she is the youngest child and has two older brothers. She has two teenage children herself, a girl and a boy. She has been divorced for many years and lives just a few minutes' drive from her parents' home. She saw Eric most days, and relied on him to help with the children, ferrying them to and from school and sporting commitments. She especially relied on Uncle Eric and their grandparents in school holidays when she was working.

Asked about her relationship with Eric, Elizabeth replies, 'Since I was told that he actually changed my nappies, I have always had a soft spot for him. He's been someone that I've always looked up to. He's a brother who has never been aggressive or an angry type of person. He is a gentle person. The way he has looked after my children, the manner and the patience that he has for my children, that aren't his but might as well be, I couldn't explain to you how gentle he is. As a brother he has been very, very supportive. He is someone that I can ring up anytime, anywhere and know that if he can do something for me, he will do it, regardless of what it is. He's the most beautiful brother I could ever have wanted.'

The audience hangs on her words. She is so lovely to look at, so pleasant on the ear. But something changes when Brebner shows Elizabeth a copy of a photo of a man with a beard. The court room already knows that this is Gassy, photographed some time before Margaret Tobin's murder. But Elizabeth, whose appearances in the court room have been sporadic, cannot recognise the face. 'It is quite blurred,' she tells Brebner. 'It could be a number of people.'

Pressed further, she concedes that it has a likeness to a few people that she knows. Name them, instructs Brebner.

Elizabeth considers the photo for another few minutes. 'It does look a bit like an Aboriginal Rugby player,' she says reluctantly, 'but I can't remember his name.'

It is one of those peculiar moments when the current in the air changes. The consensus at the break is that at that point Elizabeth

Gassy lost the sympathy of the jury which, until then, had been so well cultivated.

On Friday, 6 August 2004, it is day seventeen of the trial, and Gassy's old friend and colleague, Osman Ali, is called to the stand. A small man in a neat dark suit, Ali has a shaved head, a goatee, light olive skin, and bags under his eyes. He qualified in medicine in Cairo in 1978. Ali sends Gassy a small smile before describing, in a smooth, soft voice, how his former flatmate came to him for a psychiatric consultation in 1994. Ali diagnosed burnout from work–related stress. Ali mentions that he doesn't have his original notes of the consultation because he has been retired for five years. This is the only hint of explanation that the jury receives about why Ali is being called 'Mr' rather than 'Dr'. If they were regular viewers of the television show, *A Current Affair*, they might understand more.

In 1999, Ali's wife rang Grant Williams, a former detective who was then working as a producer with the show. She had arranged for a private investigator to secretly film her husband at work in his Bankstown surgery. The tapes, which she later handed to Williams to put to air, showed Ali kissing, rubbing and engaging in other sexual intimacies with a number of female patients. In some of the footage which was not broadcast, Ali was seen, as Williams describes it, 'dry rooting' patients. Apart from the sensational manner in which his misdemeanours came to light, there was otherwise nothing particularly unusual about Ali's transgression. He was not the first, or the last, psychiatrist to be struck off the medical register for sexual misconduct.

Unlike Ali, Gassy has insisted upon being addressed as Dr throughout the trial. No doubt it adds to his standing and authority – it is easy to forget he is the defendant when he also plays the part of barrister and doctor. But perhaps it is also a sign of his reluctance to surrender his medical identity. The jury knows nothing of the discussion about how Gassy should be addressed, however. So much is kept from them. Before this trial even began, the judge, Gassy and the prosecution spent 30 days in this room for the voir dire hearing, arguing about what evidence should be allowed to go to the jury. The judge did not exclude nearly as much as Gassy wanted, nor did she include all that the prosecution wanted. The jury is not told that Gassy covertly filmed Dr Craig Nelson, the GP from whom he had sought treatment for HIV. Nor do they know of the surreptitious photograph taken of a solicitor involved in Gassy's deregistration. The judge also rules against the admission of evidence suggesting Gassy forged a medical certificate, as 'that tends to imply a criminal propensity'. When a witness is called to the stand, the judge, prosecution and defence have a reasonable idea of what will be said. They have read the witness statements and know what areas are permissible for examination. The jury cannot know how much of what they hear is carefully orchestrated.

There are only occasional jolts to this ordered process. One occurs early on, when Beth Kotze is called to the stand, wearing a grey suit, a translucent complexion and short, spiky hair. It is almost a decade since she and Margaret Tobin devoted their Saturdays to retail therapy. Kotze is now doing Margaret's old job, as director of mental health for the South Eastern Sydney Area Health Service, and is irate to have wasted so much time waiting outside the court room. She is a busy woman. Kotze is surprised to see Gassy; he looks far younger than she expected. She guesses that he is in his thirties. Kotze is even more surprised when, after a few minutes of asking about her memories of the psychiatry congress in Brisbane, Gassy drops his bombshell: 'Would you agree that the victim was of a same-sex orientation?'

When the judge interrupts to ask the relevance of the question, Gassy explains that the defence case is that police haven't identified the real shooter because the victim was part of an underground lesbian world. The jury and Kotze are sent from the room while discussions are held about how to proceed. Gassy argues that the victim was a closet lesbian and that there thus must be a group of potential suspects who have not been investigated by the police. When the judge rules that Gassy may put the question, Kotze tells the jury that Margaret Tobin was heterosexual. She bases this belief on seeing Margaret's interactions with Don and other men, and on the intimacies that the two women had shared, as friends, about their marriages.

A few days later, Gassy raises the issue again. In the box is Learne Durrington, a small woman with strong brown eyes, red lipstick, cropped dark hair and a shawl draped over her shoulders. She and her partner Deirdre Pearsall were friends of Margaret. Deirdre has been Don's prop throughout the aftermath of the murder and has taken leave from work to sit with him through the trial. Deirdre started smoking again after Margaret's death and is finding the court process excruciating. She has begun to grind her teeth in her sleep.

Durrington changed jobs within the Department of Human Services after Margaret's death. She is now one of the leaders in the mental health unit and her desk is in Margaret's old office. Gassy grills Durrington about her identification of him as the man she saw in the lift that morning before Margaret's death. He then asks if Margaret was a closet lesbian. When Durrington answers with a firm 'no', Gassy responds: 'I suggest that you are protecting the victim's reputation and, in fact, you know she was a lesbian?'

'My understanding is that she was a happily married woman,' insists Durrington.

Gassy suggests that Durrington's motivation, in identifying him in court as the man she saw in the lift, is 'retribution for your personal loss and for the sisterhood's loss of its leader'.

'That is just outrageous, that is incorrect,' splutters Durrington.

Xavier and Maud often make apparent their displeasure with the judge, a witness or the prosecution. They tut under their breaths or mutter quietly to each other. During Durrington's evidence, they are more vocal than usual, ridiculing some of her statements. As Durrington walks past them to leave the court room, she is sure that Maud swears at her. Questioned about this later, Maud tells Barry she was saying prayers.

Gassy also planned to question Don Scott about his wife's sexuality but changes his mind after being told he would not be allowed to put rumours and speculation to the witness. He could only ask, was your wife heterosexual? The judge also points out that the defence usually strives to avoid the spouse being put on the stand, presumably because of the potential for provoking the jury's sympathy.

*

Above: Jean and Joseph cuddle Margaret and Helena during their early years in Australia.

Below: The Tobin family in the late 1960s. Left to right: (back) Joseph, Jean, Margaret and Helena; (front) Gerard, Patrick, Mary Catherine, Peter and Bernadette. Damian is not yet born.

Photograph courtesy of Brendan Kelly

Above: Brendan Kelly and Margaret outside St Mary's College, Melbourne University, 1974.

Below: A radiant bride: Margaret wearing the wedding dress that Jean had crocheted, 18 January 1975.

Left: Graduating from Melbourne University in December 1978.

Below: Lakeside Hospital at Ballarat was an institution trapped by its history when Margaret arrived as the new director of clinical services in May 1989. She faced a tough learning curve.

Right: Don and Margaret married quietly in the backyard of their bush property near Ballarat on 2 March 1990.

Below left: 'Eric is respected and liked in the Faculty and should do very well in the future,' read Gassy's entry in the University of Sydney's 1979 Senior Year Book.

Below right: Photograph of Jean Eric Gassy leaving the Medical Tribunal hearing in 1997, which led to his deregistration.

Photograph from Senior Year Book 1979, Faculty of Medicine, University of Sydney

Above: On 31 July 2000, her first day in the new job in South Australia, Margaret was photographed for a story published in the *Advertiser* under the headline 'Mental health care critic now the boss'.

Below: Margaret and Don enjoying a weekend visit to Mannum on the Murray River in South Australia, some months before her death.

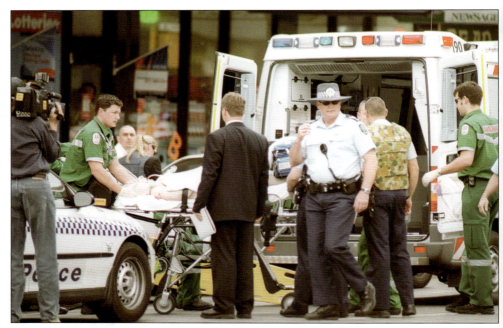

Above: Ambulance officers worked on Margaret at the scene of the shooting before the short trip to Royal Adelaide Hospital.

Below: After the shooting, police in the special emergency response squad, the STAR or Special Task and Rescue group, went through the CitiCentre building floor by floor.

Dr Peter Arnold

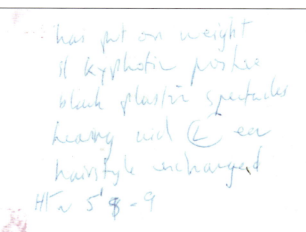

... has put on weight
il kyphotic posture
black plastic spectacles
heavy with C ear
hairstyle unchanged
HT ~ 5'8 - 9

Above: The photograph of Dr Peter Arnold which appeared on the 'persons of interest list', along with Eric Gassy's handwritten notes, found during the police search of Gassy's premises on 29 October 2002.

Middle: One of the two photographs of Dr Jonathan Phillips which appeared on the 'persons of interest list'. It was taken from a 1999 psychiatric publication and shows Phillips in the ceremonial hat worn by presidents of the Royal Australian and New Zealand College of Psychiatrists.

Bottom: Margaret's sister, husband and mother – Bernadette, Don and Jean – leave the court after Jean Eric Gassy's conviction, to face the media's microphones and questions.

Above left: Jean Eric Gassy remains impassive as he is driven back to prison after being convicted of murder, 23 September 2004.

Above right: The pathetic mannequin wearing a leopard-skin bra and handcuffs which welcomes customers to the Queensland Gun Exchange at Fortitude Valley in Brisbane. Scott Allen, the sales manager, identified Jean Eric Gassy as the man who had placed an order there in April 2002.

Below: Yatala Labour Prison in Adelaide, where Jean Eric Gassy was held until being moved to Port Augusta prison in early 2006.

A noticeable anticipation fills the court room on day 32 of the trial, Wednesday, 1 September 2004. The tension dissolves the relaxed intimacy of the previous eight weeks. The seats are packed with schoolchildren, police and family. Journalists jam in the front row against the piles of prosecution papers.

Terry Anderson has left his poky office just down the hallway to be here. Anderson took the brunt of media calls for the Department of Human Services at the time of Margaret's death and funeral, and is now the media officer for the Courts Administration Authority. He felt Margaret's death personally and has a particular interest in this case. He will be glad when it is over. He hates the American pop psychology behind the notion of 'closure' but that is what he wants. He wants it for himself and he wants it for Margaret and her family.

On this day, Gassy will take the witness stand to give evidence. The prosecution has prepared carefully for the grilling about to be inflicted. Until now, Brebner has been polite, even deferential, in most of his dealings with the defendant. Perhaps he is aware of the view of some court watchers that he recently lost another murder trial, which many had thought certain to bring a conviction, by being too tough on the accused, and too aloof from the jury.

But when Brebner rises to cross-examine Gassy, his manner is far removed from the friendly nickname which is freely used, *Brebs*. Today he is the hawk, toying with his prey. His voice is hard, and his tone is, by turns, sarcastic, needling, insinuating, incredulous. He taunts Gassy, repeatedly suggesting that his evidence is flimsy and that he is lying. A bravura of gestures accompanies Brebner's performance. He bounces on his soles, rests his hands on his hips, crosses his arms and jiggles a foot as he interrogates.

Gassy is paler than usual. He sips often from his cup, and sometimes his chin comes up slightly as he answers one of Brebner's slicing questions.

During questioning about the Brisbane incident, Brebner suddenly changes tack: 'Incidentally why do you refer to her as "the victim" all the time and not as "Dr Tobin"?'

Gassy: Because of what I have read on how to conduct a trial, it says that you shouldn't personalise the opposition.

Brebner: Do you have difficulty in personalising Dr Tobin?

Gassy: Not at all.

Brebner: You don't seem to have any difficulty in calling me 'Mr Brebner' rather than just 'Mr Prosecutor'.

Gassy: Not at all.

Brebner: Why not refer to Dr Tobin as 'Dr Tobin'?

Brebner returns, again and again, to the same phrases to underline his point. 'It is the truth of the matter,' he repeats when offering a version of events which challenges Gassy's account. He insists that Gassy is in Brisbane at the time Gassy says he is in Lakes Entrance, on the south coast of New South Wales, revisiting the scenes of an old love affair. He says that Gassy is lying when he says he doesn't recognise his handwriting on a receipt from the Edmonstone Motel.

The audience is soon transfixed. Gassy is going to be torn apart, says one observer.

Brebner plays the video tape of the first police search of Gassy's flat. Gassy's arms are crossed, and he wears runners, blue jeans and a tight, white T-shirt accentuating a modest bulge.

Brebner then plays the video tape of Gassy on the day of his arrest. He is again wearing a white T-shirt and blue jeans.

It is a powerful moment when this image is juxtaposed with those from another video tape. The security cameras at the Mobil service station at Renmark, on the highway between Sydney and Adelaide, have captured a man of Gassy's height and hair colour, wearing a white T-shirt, blue jeans and runners. The image is not clear but when seen immediately after the tapes from Gassy's home, it seems obvious who has been caught, pumping petrol and paying his bill.

More than once Brebner asks: 'That is you, isn't it, Dr Gassy?'

'No,' Gassy replies. He blinks as he looks at the jury.

As Brebner continues his questioning, the image of a man who looks very much like Gassy remains frozen on the screen.

Brebner: Did you put on a couple of kilograms in the last fortnight of October 2002?

Gassy: I don't think so.

Brebner: Because you were feeling content and happy?

Gassy: Why do you say that?

Brebner: Because you'd shot Dr Tobin.

Gassy: No, that's not true at all.

The consensus in the break is that Brebner has put on a brilliant show and that Gassy is performing poorly. Tell Brebs to stop having so much fun, a journalist instructs Brebner's junior.

The next morning Gassy looks sullen when Brebner asks about his shooting history.

Brebner: Have you ever taken aim at a human being with a loaded gun?

Gassy blinks and moves his head back slightly before he answers: No.

Brebner: Isn't it the case that you did shoot Dr Tobin, Mr Gassy?

Gassy: No.

Brebner: Isn't it the case that you were feeling a little tense when you pulled the trigger?

Gassy: I didn't pull the trigger. I wasn't there.

Gassy blinks rapidly as he replies and a muscle in his right cheek flickers.

When Brebner turns to the railway ticket, Gassy agrees that the initials PCA, JMW and JP refer to three of the doctors involved in his deregistration, Peter Arnold, John Woodforde and Jonathan Phillips. Brebner asks Gassy what was on the bottom bit that has been ripped off and suggests it was a 'a reference to someone else who was connected with your deregistration' and a 'word starting with "M"'. Brebner also asks who was the other person named on the ticket who has not been identified. The writing looks like 'Louise Sally' or 'Salby'. This name is followed by a couple of characters and an illegible word starting with 'M'.

Gassy can't recall why the ticket was torn or why he wrote that name. He can't read the word starting with 'M'. He says: 'Ever since I have had this exhibit, I have been trying to figure it out . . . Nothing seems to fit.'

Brebner then turns to Gassy's belief that his deregistration was an abuse of politics and psychiatry. Gassy says this has been his view since the Professional Standards Committee hearing in 1995.

Brebner repeatedly asks whether Gassy believes there was a conspiracy against him but it is a word Gassy does not want to touch.

It is a deliberately loaded term, he says. He agrees, however, that he was unhappy with doctors on the list who were involved in his deregistration.

Brebner turns to the three cars that Gassy hired in October 2002. Gassy says he wanted to practise vehicle surveillance as part of his plans to find work as a private investigator. His red sports car was not suitable because it was so noticeable. He says he covered only 116 km in the first car because he wasn't very good at surveillance and kept losing people. He returned the second car, a Hyundai, after one day although it had been rented for six days because he didn't like the vehicle.

Gassy is asked how he managed to travel 3,110 km doing vehicle surveillance on Sydney's roads over six days in the third car that he hired. His previous unsuccessful surveillance prompted him to make a more determined effort, he replies. Asked many times about the types of cars that he followed and the localities, Gassy's constant response is that he doesn't remember.

Brebner then asks about Gassy's activities on the day of the murder, 14 October. Gassy says that he got up at the usual time, about 7 to 7.30 am. He doesn't usually have breakfast but he had a coffee and read the papers before setting out on vehicle surveillance. He can't remember where he had lunch that day or where he went or which vehicles he tried to follow. He knocked off about 9 pm. He usually goes to bed at midnight.

There is a pause when Gassy realises what he has just said. He must have gone home before 9 pm, he adds, because he remembers making a phone call. This is a key part of his alibi, that a phone call was made from his parents' home at about 7.30 pm on the night of Margaret's murder, and that there is no-one else apart from himself who could have made it.

Brebner responds sarcastically: 'That is the one thing you remember with precision about the whole of the Monday, is it?'

'Yes,' says Gassy.

It is a fascinating and horrible spectacle to watch. At the break, someone is disappointed at Gassy's showing. 'I thought he'd be much better,' she says. 'He has had a lot of time to think of a better story.' Brebner advises Don against getting his hopes up prematurely. 'It is not how bad Gassy is,' he says. 'It's how strong my evidence is, and he didn't leave many tracks.'

Back in court, Brebner returns to niggling Gassy about the political abuse of psychiatry. Gassy agrees that he thought Woodforde, Phillips, Arnold and Wilhelm were most likely to have been behind his deregistration. But he refuses to agree it was a conspiracy, charging that Brebner is trying to use a loaded word like conspiracy to link him to delusional disorder.

Brebner bats back: 'Do you think that is my purpose, do you? . . . Are you paranoid?'

Gassy: No.

Brebner: Did you think there was a conspiracy involved? 'Yes' or 'No'?

Gassy: I think there's been a group of people who have accepted a false diagnosis of a psychiatric disorder in instituting a process that has been against my interests.

Gassy says he would rather use the term 'an unfair process' than conspiracy.

'What about a "pact" or a "scheme" or an "agreement",' suggests the judge.

Gassy: I think there is no specific word that needs to be used.

Brebner: And the last word you'd want to use is 'conspiracy'?

Gassy: I don't wish to use that word, no.

Brebner: Do you believe Margaret Tobin was part of a conspiracy to bring about your ultimate deregistration?

Gassy: No.

The next morning brings the thirty-fourth day of the trial and Gassy's third in the stand. A small crowd gathers outside the court room, waiting for another matter to finish. Brebner is complimented, you did well yesterday.

'That is not for us to judge,' he replies. 'That is for the jury to judge.' If there is a new hit list, Brebner is sure he will be on it. 'He was looking at me yesterday as if he would rather be looking at me over a Luger.'

Back in court, Gassy says it is reasonable to use the word 'collaborating' to describe the actions of doctors who were trying to have him deregistered. Asked why he maintained the persons of interest list,

Gassy repeatedly replies that it was for no particular reason, or that he can't remember, or that it just seemed like a good idea at the time.

Under further questioning, he says he felt it might be useful to have some information about the doctors involved in his deregistration.

Brebner: Did you eventually decide to exact some degree of retribution against these people?

Gassy: No, not at all.

Gassy protests to the judge when Brebner repeats the question: 'He is badgering the witness, your honour.'

Brebner returns relentlessly to questioning Gassy about why he set up the list.

Brebner: You hated these people, didn't you?

Gassy: No.

Brebner: You thought they were part of a conspiracy, didn't you?

Gassy: I thought they acted against my interests.

Brebner: You thought they were part of a conspiracy, didn't you?

Gassy: I wouldn't use that word.

Brebner: You thought they collaborated against your best interests?

Gassy: Some of them.

Brebner shows Gassy the map revealing the location of Kay Wilhelm's office at St Vincent's Hospital, which was found in the rubbish at his parents' house. Gassy says it relates to his surveillance training regarding WorkCover fraud.

Brebner: It was just a coincidence that it takes one to Dr Wilhelm's office?

Gassy: That is it.

Brebner: Pure coincidence?

Gassy: Absolutely, pure coincidence.

At this, one journalist scribbles a note to another. 'Down in flames', it says.

Some hours later, after lunch, Brebner returns again to the persons of interest list, asking if Gassy set it up to keep track of the whereabouts of those involved in his deregistration. Gassy rejects suggestions that he either did something similar with Margaret Tobin's details or kept the information in his head.

Now Gassy tells Brebner that the bottom of the railway ticket was torn because he met a girl on a train and gave her his email. She was slim, Asian, in her mid twenties and had shoulder-length hair. Her name was Hoi, he says.

Brebner: Did you ever get an email from her?

Gassy: No.

Brebner: Did you hope you would?

Gassy (with a glimmer of a smile): Obviously.

Brebner asks if the initials 'MT' were on the bottom half with Margaret's home and work address. Gassy is '100 per cent' certain they were not.

Gassy agrees that he blames Woodforde, Phillips, Wilhelm and, to a lesser extent, Peter Arnold and David Burke, for his deregistration. But he attributes no blame to Margaret Tobin.

Gassy pauses when asked how he found out about Dr Tobin's death. 'I must have been on the road when it happened,' he says. 'I must have read it in the *Sydney Morning Herald*.'

He says he also searched web sites for further information which might be of interest given that they were both psychiatrists. When Brebner picks up on this point a few minutes later – reminding Gassy that he is no longer a psychiatrist – Gassy shoots him a look of pure hatred.

He pauses before replying. 'Legally speaking, yes.'

Brebner: You resent the fact that you are no longer practising medicine, in particular psychiatry, don't you?

Gassy: I'm not happy about it.

A few minutes after this exchange, Brebner says he has no more questions for Dr Gassy. Shortly afterwards, Andree Maud Gassy limps to the witness stand. It seems somehow pathetic that one of the only witnesses Gassy can muster is his frail old mum.

Many mornings Maud greets the court staff and police with a cheery 'bonjour'. One afternoon, she places a friendly hand on the arm of Detective Sergeant Mick Standing, to wish him a good weekend. On another morning she stops to chat with a journalist. 'I like it when you smile at me,' she says. 'It cheers me up. I am very sorry for everything. It is very tiring.'

On this Friday afternoon, she cuts an even sadder figure than usual.

Her small face is heavily lined, she moves awkwardly, clasping a hand over her mouth, her arms across her chest. She smiles at her son but often has to raise tissues to her damp eyes.

Maud tells the court that she is a retired high school teacher. She retired about twenty years ago but she is never bored. She teaches scripture three times a week, she plays indoor boules, reads widely and has quite a network of friends. Very rarely did she visit her son's flat downstairs.

It is excruciating to watch as Gassy questions his mother about his appearance and health before her holiday in Vietnam in October 2002. She looks haunted, devastated. She has trouble hearing and speaks with a heavy accent, sometimes lapsing into French. She pulls her ears, jerks her bony hands. She has an old woman's involuntary facial gestures.

As Brebner takes his turn with the witness, Maud pulls her necklace through her mouth and plays with her lips with her hands. She is the perfect picture of terrible nerves. She kneads her neck with her fist as Brebner asks if she recognises photos of her son. It does not look like him, she cries out.

She says her son did not have a beard when she left for Vietnam.

Brebner: Are you absolutely certain?

Maud: Well, I cannot remember but he did not have a beard.

Brebner: Are you certain about that?

Maud: Yes.

Brebner: He did have a beard when you left for Vietnam, didn't he?

Maud: He did not have a beard.

Brebner: You have spoken to him a number of times since his arrest?

Maud: Yes.

Brebner: Has he told you on a number of occasions that he didn't have a beard when you left to go to Vietnam?

Maud: He's never – we never talk to him about that. We see him for 40 minutes. We don't have time.

Brebner: Do you think you might be wrong about him not having a beard when you went to Vietnam?

Maud (crying, wiping her eyes): I am not wrong.

Maud looks stricken when Brebner asks if her son often wore a white T-shirt. 'I don't know,' she says.

She looks like a sad little monkey, rubbing herself, as Brebner asks her to watch the video from the Renmark service station.

Brebner: That was your son, wasn't it?

Maud: I don't think so.

Brebner: Why do you think that man wasn't your son?

Maud: Because my son has got more . . . is bigger.

Brebner: Your son has put on a bit of weight since he's been arrested, hasn't he?

Maud: Just a little bit, not much.

Brebner: He's put on quite a lot, actually, hasn't he?

Maud: If that's what you think. I don't think so.

Again and again Maud denies that it is her son on the video. Her son is taller, bulkier, has wider shoulders, doesn't look like that man, has a different shape to his body. The man is wearing sunglasses. 'I very rarely see him with sunglasses,' she says.

Brebner shows the video again. Maud holds her right hand over her mouth.

Brebner: He walks like your son, doesn't he?

Maud: How does my son walk? I don't know.

Brebner: He holds his body the way your son holds his body, doesn't he?

Maud: I don't know how my son holds his body.

Brebner: He holds his head the way your son holds his head, doesn't he?

Maud: No.

Brebner: Such mannerisms as we could see, the way he waved his arms?

Maud: No.

Brebner: Why do you say it's not him?

Maud: It does not remind me of him.

Brebner: Does not remind you of your son?

Maud: No.

Brebner: Not at all?

Maud: Not at all.

Brebner: Not in the slightest?

Maud: No.

Brebner: As far as you are concerned, that man is totally dissimilar in appearance to your son's appearance, as of when you came home from Vietnam?

Maud (speaking so quietly, it is almost impossible to hear her): Yes.

Should we be impressed by her maternal devotion or irritated by her maternal blindness? Opinion is divided. One annoyed observer says that it would be fair enough to say you couldn't be sure from the tape that it was Gassy. But to say it definitely wasn't him . . .

Either way, it seems cruel of Gassy to trap his mother in such a dilemma. She looks utterly destroyed as she hobbles out of the room.

The next morning, Gassy says he has changed plans. He will not call his father to give evidence.

15

Difficult circumstances

One Friday morning finds Jean Tobin sitting at a table outside the cafe popular with those who frequent the nearby courts. Ten minutes earlier, as she walked out of the court building, Peter Brebner asked how she was faring.

'Very angry,' she replied, eyes flashing. There had been yet another delay, and she was furious that the whole process seemed to be bending over backwards to accommodate Gassy. Four days earlier, on the Monday, the judge had adjourned the case until today to give Gassy extra time to prepare his summing-up. Then today Gassy had complained he needed more time, and asked for the case to be adjourned until the following Wednesday. The judge allowed an adjournment until the Tuesday.

'Look at it this way,' says Brebner, somewhat tactlessly. 'It gives me some more time to get organised.' This inspires little cheer in Margaret's siblings, Damian and Helena, who have flown from Melbourne to hear the prosecution summing-up, which was due to start today.

Jean's eyes flash again as Maud hobbles past the cafe to make a call at a public phone booth. 'Her family has won again,' Jean says as a parade for athletes returned from the Athens Olympics occupies the street.

But memories of 50-odd years ago soon intervene, giving Jean temporary distraction from her anger. She recounts the story of visiting Ireland halfway through her first pregnancy. It was her first visit to Tipperary, where Joseph grew up. She remembers that she was wearing a turquoise coat, and had a long pearl hat pin which made her feel better about the cheap blue beret.

They were walking around the mountain called Slievenamon, which means mountain of women, visiting Joseph's relatives and friends. Jean was used to rationing in England, where if someone offered a cup of tea, it was a treat to get a biscuit as well. But Joseph and his budding bride faced a generous spread at every stop. Every hostess insisted Jean have at least one boiled egg with her cup of tea.

Then they arrived at the home of the local gentry, who were looked up to because they had three or four more cows than everyone else. Jean knew her husband would be mortified if she declined an egg this time, and so she took another. It was her seventh. By this time she was bursting, absolutely busting. She was taken upstairs, expecting to find a toilet. Instead, two of her hostesses sat on the bed, chatting, while they waited for Jean to use the chamber pot in front of them. I've changed my mind, Jean said weakly. After seven eggs and umpteen cups of tea, the remainder of the walk was far from comfortable, to put it mildly.

When Jean told this story to one of Margaret's friends recently, the woman laughed. The seven eggs explained why Jean had another seven children after Margaret, she said.

The following Tuesday, 23 months to the day since Margaret's murder, dawns brisk and clear. The court is so crowded, there is hardly room for Jean and her brood, Damian, Mary Catherine, Bernadette and Helena. Deirdre looks anxious, Don is running late. Maud also arrives late, muttering 'pardon and sorree' as she finds her seat.

Kath Rowan, who has been a salt-of-the-earth friend to Jean, also squeezes in. She has been sharing the bus trip from Bacchus Marsh to Adelaide with Jean. In the evenings she sits with her friend, listening to her go over and over the events of the day in court. Kath likes a drink to relax; Jean's vice is chocolate. They have been christened the tippler and the nibbler. They also joke about themselves as Kath and Kim. Today Kath sits behind the Gassys. She feels sorry for them.

Brebner turns to the jury and explains that he is going to take a very long time to sum up the prosecution case. There is so much to cover, he says. He speaks slowly and patiently, and seems a different man from the one who cross-examined Gassy eleven days earlier. Gassy has his eyes down, taking notes, as Brebner argues that the accused had the motive, the means, the ability and the will to murder Margaret Tobin. He stresses that Gassy does not have to prove a thing, it is up to the prosecution to prove the charge and that there is no reasonable theory consistent with innocence.

For the first time, Brebner looks directly at the jurors. They must be independent, impartial and confine themselves to a completely dispassionate and clinical examination of the evidence presented in court, he says. 'You must determine the outcome without reference to any notions of sympathy to Dr Tobin and her loved ones; nor out of prejudice,' he says.

The prosecution case relies on circumstantial evidence; there is no eyewitness account to place Gassy at the scene of the murder. Nor is there conclusive forensics evidence – from the guns, DNA, or finger-prints – to pin the shooting on Gassy. Circumstantial evidence is not inferior to any other kind of evidence, Brebner tells the jury. It can be like a jigsaw; even though some parts may be missing, you can still determine the complete picture.

Brebner summarises the evidence that has been presented over the previous ten weeks, including the history of Gassy's deregistration, the Brisbane incident, the ballistics testing, handwriting evidence and witness identifications. As in his cross-examination of Gassy, Brebner relies on repetition of a few key phrases. He points out the many 'remarkable coincidences' involved in the case and argues that it is 'inconceivable' these are just coincidences.

It is a 'remarkable coincidence' that two men from the psychiatry congress in Brisbane recognised the identikit image of the shooter as similar to the man they had seen acting suspiciously. It is another 'remarkable coincidence' that the number plate of the car entered in the security log at the Brisbane Convention Centre was the same as the one Gassy hired in Sydney. There is also the 'remarkable coincidence' of Martin Smith at the Lindy Lodge Motel, seeing the identikit image and being reminded of the man he knew as David Paes. It can't be coincidence that Margaret Tobin was shot by a Glock pistol and Speer Gold Dot ammunition on the day the accused was in Adelaide under a false name . . .

At first Gassy's lips and cheeks betray no sign of tightness. The regular blinking is the only hint of his state of mind. But as Brebner continues, detailing another dozen or so 'remarkable coincidences', Gassy heats up. At times, it seems that his dark eyes are drilling holes in Brebner's back.

The jurors keep their faces carefully neutral, but some seem to have grown in stature. There is more consciousness in their bearing as they walk in and out of the jury box at breaks. Others, particularly Mr Vest, seem to have shrunk under the weight of responsibility. Early in the trial, one court watcher remarked at the resemblance between Gassy and this juror, a handsome man with a strong-boned, round, open face, dark olive complexion and short, dark hair flecked with grey. He often wears a white collared shirt with a vest and looks like a bank manager, an accountant, or perhaps an academic. Then again, Tom Young, the honorary consul for Mauritius, was no vicar – appearances can be so unreliable.

Brebner turns his focus to the only 'reasonable and rational conclusions' that can be drawn from the evidence. 'Do you really think . . .' he asks the jury repeatedly. They do not give any hint of their answer to his rhetorical question. There are no telltale nods or eye movements.

When the court breaks for lunch, Damian reaches for his mother and gives her a squeeze of utmost tenderness. Jean is upset that one of the young female jurors doesn't seem to be paying close attention. It is true that Ms Pert, a young blonde with a sassy wiggle, is having a terrible struggle to keep her eyes open. She yawns often, her lids drooping, and holds her head with one hand and then the other.

It is a shock to see Helena, Mary Catherine and Bernadette

standing together outside the court room. By themselves, they seem so unlike each other. Together, it is obvious that they are sisters. Only there is one sister missing.

Helena and Mary Catherine were nervous about their first days in court; each felt they bore a particular resemblance to Margaret and wondered if this would provoke some reaction. But when she came to it, Mary Catherine didn't find Gassy at all intimidating. He was more someone to be pitied, she felt. She had no trouble staring him down when he looked her way. Jean's children have more than a physical likeness in common; they also share a type of courage. They are not frightened to say what they think, even if it upsets others. One sister recently rang the *Advertiser*, which Don calls 'The Agoniser', to complain about the unflattering photograph it has been running. She is pleased that Margaret now looks much softer and nicer in the paper.

Brebner's voice begins to tire but still he speaks slowly, patiently. He cannot suppress all sarcasm, however. As he reviews Gassy's deregistration, he reaches the evidence given by Jill Floyd, the psychiatrist so warmly endorsed by the defendant. Brebner leans on the lectern in front of him. His watch sits there so he can see the time without having to glance at his wrist. There is also a pile of handwritten foolscap pages, with yellow highlighter illuminating sections of his small, neat writing. 'I will leave it to you to form your own assessment of Dr Floyd and her professional objectivity,' says Brebner. And then this little dry aside: 'As you will remember, she had a tendency to give rather long answers.'

Next day, proceedings are adjourned due to a sick juror. Three other juries in the building also are affected by sickness. When Gassy discovers which juror is missing – an older woman, 'Mrs Everymum' – he says he would prefer that she remain on the jury, rather than being discharged.

The following day is Thursday, 16 September 2004 and the thirty-ninth day of the trial. Don arrives in court with a 'Not happy John' sticker poking out of his top pocket. He doesn't think much of the Howard Government's line on the war in Iraq. Mrs Everymum is still unwell, so the judge proposes to discharge her. Gassy would prefer to adjourn until the juror returns, but the judge rules otherwise. She says: 'I did detect yesterday when speaking to the jury that some, at least, were extremely disappointed not to be proceeding immediately with the matter.' And so the only woman who was about Margaret Tobin's age is gone from the jury. One of the journalists doubts it will make a difference; he thinks the jury has made up its mind.

'Do you really think there is an innocent explanation . . .' says Brebner when he comes to the persons of interest list and railway ticket. He describes Gassy's 'non answers' to questions about why he compiled these lists as 'the last refuge of the desperate'. Elizabeth Gassy has her head on her father's shoulder, her eyes closed as Brebner says that Gassy's explanation for the lists – including that 'it seemed a good idea at the time' – were 'chock full' of implausibilities. When Elizabeth moves away, Xavier is left, very pale, with one arm tightly wrapped around his middle and the other hand holding his face. When Brebner turns to the ballistics evidence, rocking slowly from one foot to the other, Elizabeth holds her forehead tightly in her right hand, as if in agony.

Ms Pert is not the only one having trouble staying awake. Stevo rests his eyes as Brebner reviews the Brisbane evidence. 'It is my submission, firstly, you just can't accept what the accused tells you about anything,' says the prosecutor. Mr Vest is looking worried, a frown hovering constantly at his brows. Elizabeth sits between her parents, with her eyes closed and head down. It is the body language of someone who doesn't want to hear or see what is in front of her.

In the afternoon break, the tension releases in a spray of nonsense. Mary Catherine and Bernadette collapse in fits of laughter about nothing in particular. It is easy to picture them as giggling twelve-year-olds. Bernadette used to hide the vegetables she didn't want on Gerard's plate, under his mashed potato. The court room hums with silly chat. Helena wonders about the meaning of the Latin inscription on the coat of arms above the judge, *Dieu et mon droit* and *Honi soit qui mal y pense*. Brebner, who did Latin in grade 7, can't remember, and no-one else knows either. It means 'Port Power rules', says Stevo. Inevitably, the hysteria ends in tears. They were Helena's, later that night.

Next morning, the fortieth day of the trial, has the added anticipation that a Friday brings. The weather has changed suddenly, no
need for a jacket today. Just after 10 am, Brebner launches directly
into his home straight. Gassy stares sullenly at the floor; he seems less
assured. Mr Vest is holding his mouth; so anxious still. His forehead is
wrinkled and his eyes are lost in Brebner and his story.

In the morning break, one of the regular court watchers fronts
Jean and Kath at the volunteer's stand where refreshments are sold.
She is a retired psychiatric nurse and once worked at Glenside. People
who have delusions are so dangerous and difficult, she says. Jean and
Kath wish she would go away and leave them alone. Jean needs to
guard her remaining strength, not squander it on idle chat.

Brebner is back on his feet. The accused succeeded in doing what
he set out to do, to get close to Margaret Tobin without being recognised, Brebner says. He takes the risk that she might recognise him. It
is unlikely – his appearance has changed so much that he is virtually
unrecognisable as the doctor from St George Hospital. But if she
does, he will wait for another day.

Now Brebner comes to the defence argument that if a skilled
shooter like Gassy had fired the shots, they would have been placed
closer together. There is 46 cm between the highest and lowest entry
wounds. The horizontal spread between the shots is 4–5 cm. Maud
closes her eyes and holds her head with one hand as Brebner
describes the violent damage done to Margaret Tobin's body. 'So the
shooter hasn't done a bad job, has he, ladies and gentlemen?'

Even Ms Pert is paying attention as Brebner builds his final
momentum. He looks directly at the jury as he says there is just too
much evidence, just too many coincidences operating against the
accused. 'There is just one other thing that is INCONCEIVABLE,'
Brebner says, gesturing to Gassy angrily. It is 2.50 pm.

'And that is . . . that he didn't kill Dr Tobin.' Brebner sits down
with a flourish and a red face. The chatter of the jury floats back to
the court room as they file down the outside corridor to their private
room, which is littered with papers and notes.

In the break, Brebner holds court with the Tobin family. He offers
no false comfort. It's one of the hardest cases I have done, he says. If

there was a little bit more evidence, then Gassy would have gone. A little bit less, and we wouldn't have had a chance. Who can predict? He has seen certain cases lost and iffy cases won. Brebner is looking forward to his first work-free weekend in six months. He calls himself an appalling golf player, but intends to enjoy a hit this weekend. He has also bought a 'too expensive' bottle of red wine for tonight.

At 3 pm Gassy puts on his jacket, sips water, and launches forth into the defence summing-up. At first he seems a touch nervous, his voice is flat and occasionally hesitant. He refers to himself in the third person as Dr Gassy.

The prosecution has failed to produce a weapon or prove a motive, he says. They have relied on demonstrably biased witnesses. Learne Durrington's identification of Gassy as the man in the lift on the morning of the murder was false. Only Dr Gassy could have made that phone call from his parents' home on the evening of the murder. His sister was at work and his young nephew and niece were hardly likely to have been running around his parents' empty house at that time. 'The apparent thinness of his alibi is its strength,' Gassy says. 'It seems just too simple to have been a deliberate fabrication.' Dr Gassy does not answer calls to the house that evening because most phone calls are for his parents and he is not in the habit of answering calls for them. The jurors return Gassy's gaze as he says: 'So the fact that the phone wasn't answered on Monday evening doesn't mean that I wasn't home.'

Gassy's family embody misery. Xavier is wrapped in his own arms. Maud splays the fingers on her left hand across her face. Elizabeth, smartly dressed in a black-and-white checked skirt, is hitting her throat softly with a clenched fist. Xavier watches Gassy as he retells what is known about the shooting, but the mother and sister seem unable to place their eyes directly on him. Mr Vest gives Gassy the same frowning, worried concentration that he bestowed on Brebner.

All four shots must have been fired before the victim began to collapse, Gassy says. For some reason this point is important to him – he has emphasised it a number of times. He says that at a range of 3 metres, the victim would have been an easy target to a seasoned shooter. A relatively skilled shooter like Dr Gassy would have achieved a more accurate placement. As well, Dr Gassy had security firearms training, which included techniques for minimising the effect of fear and anxiety on accuracy. Maud holds her forehead with both hands as her son tells the jury: 'The only reasonable explanation for the shot placement is that the shooter was unskilled and untrained, which rules out Dr Gassy.' Gassy told the court some days ago that his mother hadn't known about his hobby, pistol shooting, nor his membership at various shooting ranges.

The shooting was inconsistent with a revenge killing, adds Gassy. Surely someone motivated by revenge would have wanted the victim to know who was killing her and why? The shooting has the hallmarks of a killing in which the shooter has little emotional investment. After speaking for an hour, Gassy asks to adjourn. The judge advises the jurors to bring an overnight bag on Monday in case they stay at a motel.

Outside, a police officer whispers to one of Margaret's sisters: 'He's a lying cunt. Gassy is a shitful shooter. We've got footage of him at a firing range and he is a very ordinary shooter. Plus even highly skilled and trained police miss marks.'

That night, Jean says that some family members have advised her to let out all her emotions. It might help, they say. But I am not like that, she says, I am a control freak. There have only ever been a few times that I have really lost it. She is referring to the deaths of her two children.

On a crisp, sunny Monday morning, day 41 of the trial, Stevo is shaking Barry's hand. 'What a team,' he beams. His voice has returned after being screamed quiet at the game on the weekend.

Jean is more uptight than usual. She and Kath were watching television in their rented apartment on the weekend when Jean saw a pair of feet run past on the wall outside the window. Kath thought Jean was joking until a second pair came scuttling past. Minutes later followed the tramp of police officers. When police later came to speak with the two women about the robbery of a nearby unit, Jean felt it was just too much.

Xavier is engrossed in a newspaper and Maud is doing a crossword as their son enters the court with a packet of pens and highlighter, and dark sunglasses hanging from his shirt pocket. After Gassy puts on his heavy dark jacket, he checks with a nearby sheriff's officer that his collar is correctly adjusted. Gassy is not a tall man and has to lift his chin slightly to speak over the screen in front of him. He looks directly at the jurors as he painstakingly rehashes the ballistics evidence. He says a number of times, 'As Dr Gassy told you . . .' His flat monotone drags on and on. When Stevo's chin nods onto his chest, the light bounces off his polished dome.

Brebner yawns and doodles with his biro. He tilts his chair back and sinks untidily into it, while his good-humoured junior, Emily Telfer, sits neatly upright. Brebs calls her Ebony because of her thick black hair, usually cleanly pinned back in a ponytail and accentuated by her pale, unadorned face. Brebner has been the front man of the prosecution but behind the scenes Telfer has been doing much of the legwork. She often has biro notes to herself on the back of her hand, and sometimes her hand shakes with nerves as she stands to address the judge.

Now Gassy turns to the handwriting evidence. 'I know it is a bit tedious but bear with me,' he urges the jury. Hours later, he is still on the subject. He suggests that his former secretary, Naomi Harry (as Naomi Sommers is now known), was suspiciously quick to recognise the handwriting on the receipt for the Edmonstone Motel in Brisbane. He notes that she was a friend of David Burke. Given that Burke is on the persons of interest list, 'she may well be motivated to testify to keep Dr Gassy in custody,' he says. Denise Conway, who identified Gassy as the man at the Shamrock Motel, had worked as a midwife and has a number of friends who are doctors. 'That may be a consideration in weighing up her evidence,' says Gassy.

Xavier nods encouragement to his son. He laughs loudly and looks indignantly at the jury as Gassy ridicules Learne Durrington's identification of the man in the lift. 'She is seeking retribution for the loss of her friend,' says the defence. Because Durrington works in the Health Department she could have obtained images of Gassy to assist her with the identification, he says.

The court rises at 3.30 pm for a break. One of Margaret's brothers-in-law, on his first day in court, thinks there might be a slim chance that Gassy didn't commit the murder. You haven't seen all the evidence, remonstrates his wife. The judge has previously intimated that she expects Gassy to be finished sometime this morning, but still he shows no sign of stopping. Margaret's family are strung out. 'I am going to grow roses,' says Don when Brebner asks how he is handling it. He means that Gassy is spreading manure thickly in the court room.

Gassy suggests there are many who might have wanted the victim dead. 'Being murdered is an occupational hazard as a psychiatrist,' he says. His summing-up is not finished when the court adjourns for the day.

The forty-second day of the trial is a beautiful turn-of-season Tuesday, with a soft, warm breeze and all the anticipation of spring in the air. On the way into court, Brebner tells the Tobin clan there are two things which can't be predicted: how long the jury will take, and what they will do. The problem is that, through no fault of anyone, it is not a cast-iron case, he says.

As Gassy resumes his summing-up, the jury watches blankly with not a hint of what they think, apart from Mr Vest, who looks as worried as ever. Gassy gesticulates with his arms and hands as he returns to the ballistics evidence. He seems to become more animated, more fluent and forceful when speaking about guns. He uses the jargon: GSR, to refer to the gunshot residue which was found in the car that he hired in October 2004. He has previously said this was because he put his shooting bag into the car when he was practising vehicle surveillance in Sydney, in case there was time to drop into a range for some practice.

Xavier watches his son like a hopeful old hangdog. His eyes follow his son's every movement, he waits on every word. Sometimes he turns his big brown eyes hopefully towards the jury. In the juror's box, Mr Jazz Bar, Mr High Pants and Mr Craggy are all sitting the same way – with their left knee up and their right arm across it. It is a body language which seems resistant to what Gassy is saying.

Gassy needs to speak to the judge in the jury's absence. He asks: Is it okay to tell the jury that Osman Ali (from whom he obtained a medical certificate in 1994) is deregistered? He wants to 'lay the foundation for saying that his evidence may be aimed at appeasing the Medical Board in pursuit of re-registration'. The judge points out that no evidence to that effect has been presented to the court. Then she adds, perhaps puzzled, I thought you relied on Ali's evidence.

When the jury returns, Gassy revisits the evidence of the various psychiatrists who examined him. Jill Floyd is 'a real therapist' and 'a real scientist', he says, and 'clearly a person of the highest integrity'.

'Woodforde, by contrast, is the Ellard practice whip and the henchman of the Medical Board. Phillips, the wearer of the hat and robe, revels in ceremony like the college functionary he is. They both prefer drug therapy and Phillips ECT as well,' he says. 'Phillips left a private practice in the Harley Street of Sydney to take up a government position in another state. You'd have to wonder why that is. Both spend large amounts of time in court and both are practised at giving evidence in the way that the side calling them wants.'

Gassy suggests that the entry of his hire car registration number in the Brisbane Convention Centre security log may have been a false entry. Perhaps it was made by someone from the centre who had a close association with a member of the medical fraternity who had a vested interest in seeing Dr Gassy in custody. He notes that Robert Champion, who recognised the identikit, knew the victim, 'so one has to wonder whether that has coloured his accounts'. The man who gave false details to a motel as David Paes may have simply have been seeking discretion when meeting a lover or engaged in something else of a sexual nature. Or perhaps he was en route to pick up cannabis at wholesale prices for resale in Sydney. Ms Sultry is the only juror who lets slip a smile at this.

He says Dr Gassy didn't want to use his own car to practise surveillance because people will report you if they think they are being followed. 'As a private investigator you really can't afford to get the police offside,' he says.

Xavier and Maud seem happier and more confident than they have been for weeks. Both are dressed more smartly than usual.

When the jury leaves the room, Brebner points out many areas where 'Dr Gassy hasn't put his evidence to the jury with complete accuracy'. The judge says she is not too troubled about some of these, and adjourns for the lunch break.

Back in her unit, Jean is dreadfully uptight and shows little interest in her salad roll. She spills coffee over her cream blouse. Helena reads the transcript of Jill Floyd's evidence. She remembers Margaret speaking of Floyd once.

Soon afterwards, Gassy tells the jury that one of the reasons he represented himself is to show them that he does not have a psychiatric disorder. 'You have observed me for more than two months,' he says. 'Do I give you the impression that I'm someone filled with anger or resentment or do I come across as someone who has faced adversity with calm and determination?' Mr Jazz Bar slides down in his seat but the other jurors remain expressionless.

At the end of his summing-up, Gassy peters out quietly: 'The prosecution's case is circumstantial which means you should acquit Dr Gassy if the circumstances, in your view, have any reasonably possible explanation consistent with innocence.'

Jean is pale, stricken. She stares ahead while the room waits to hear whether the jury wants to stay back late or to come back tomorrow morning for the judge's summing-up. At 3.38, the judge begins. In elegant prose, she sums up the evidence of the 160-plus witnesses. For roughly two hours, her voice goes smoothly, softly, steadily. She didn't want to list the inaccuracies in Gassy's summing-up to the jury, but corrects them in what she says now. Only an astute listener would detect this intent, however.

Then she asks the jury manager, an officious chap, to come forward. Thirteen jurors remain and one must be balloted off. The number of juror 103 is picked. What a strange, anticlimactic ending it must be for Ms Morticia, to be culled like this. After all these weeks, she has time only to retrieve her belongings from the jury room before being escorted from the building. There is barely time to whisper 'see you' to the remaining jurors as she walks out. The reality television show *Big Brother* treats its rejects better.

At 5.43 pm, at last, the judge asks the jurors to retire and consider their verdict.

On the seats outside the court room, the media pack waits

alongside Margaret's relatives. Don gives his home phone number to a couple of journalists but jokes later that he has no intention of returning their calls. The woman from ABC Radio hands out ice-creams.

At 8.30 pm, there is a sudden flurry of activity as the court reconvenes. The judge says the jury wish to retire for the night. It is a wise decision, after a very long day, she says.

Another long wait begins.

16

The twelve-headed monster

On the seventh day of the trial, it seemed somehow that a change came over the jury. It was a day on which Gassy asked, not for the first time, for Justice Vanstone to step aside from the case, arguing that she was biased. It's difficult to say exactly why it seemed there had been a change. Perhaps the jurors were not listening so carefully or critically. Perhaps it was the way they looked at the man in the dock. For whatever reason, it seemed as if at least some jurors had come to some judgement. Appearances are, of course, utterly unreliable. Perhaps familiarity had simply allowed them to relax a little. Perhaps it was simply the overactive imaginations of observers at work. Observation is inevitably a flawed process, often saying more about the observer's prejudices than anything else. Peter Brebner certainly wasn't reading anything into the vibe in the jury box. He thinks people who claim to be able to read juries are spouting nonsense and doesn't even bother trying himself. Nonetheless, it felt in the last few days of the trial as if there had been another shift in the jury dynamics.

Certainly, no-one is confident to make sweeping predictions as the little crowd gathers again outside Court Room Two, on the forty-third day of the trial, waiting for a verdict. Helena thinks the odds are

75–25 in favour of a conviction. We have to consider a strong possibility he won't be convicted, she says. Barry has brought in an extra helper in case family members need support at the crucial moment. The new sheriff's officer says she gave away nursing to work in the courts after sitting on juries herself. She became absolutely fascinated with the 'live theatre'.

But, as the hours drag by, there is little action on centre stage. Offstage, idle chat helps distract from the tension. 'Why do we have an English coat of arms in an Australian court?' one of the detectives asks no-one in particular.

'It's the Westminster system,' says the female sheriff.

'Are you getting nervous?' the slim, blonde television reporter asks the detective.

'We are cold, hard professionals,' he jokes back.

'They couldn't acquit him, could they?' she persists.

'Juries can do what they like,' he says. 'Unfortunately the trouble with the jury system is they don't get the whole picture. They get the version the judge allows them to have. But it's the system we have. Until a better one comes along, we are stuck with it.'

At 2.40 pm, there is a ripple of anticipation when a note is brought to Stevo. Don, lounging at the back of the court room, mops the sweat off his forehead. Stevo is on the phone: could you bring Dr Gassy up please? Deirdre rushes outside to ring for Jean to come to the court. Barry searches for the numbers to ring Brebs and the Gassys.

The journalists take their seats. Terry Anderson folds his long legs neatly. A line of square-shouldered, dark-suited detectives fills the back row. Brebner arrives in his gown. Stevo adjusts the judge's chair and papers. A stillness settles over the room's whispers and rustlings. Barry is being discreet and averting his eyes from the questioning stares.

At 2.50 pm, Justice Vanstone enters. The jury have no answer. Instead it is a question – can the judge please explain the meaning of 'beyond reasonable doubt' to them? The jurors look serious, uncomfortable with the pressure of the eyes on them. They listen closely to the judge's explanation, their eyes neutral.

Outside, Terry Anderson is surprised. He thought everyone realised the court was being recalled for a question, not a verdict. He hands around a bag of multicoloured snakes. People revert to the comforts of childhood at times like these. Barry says the reasonable doubt issue is one of the questions asked most often by juries. Don't read anything into the question, Brebner says, there is so much to cover in this case.

Helena has to leave later this afternoon to catch a plane home. She had hoped there would be a resolution before now. Helena made a mental note to herself earlier today when watching Learne Durrington speaking with Terry Anderson. Now she tells Learne what was on her mind: 'You know how you are vertically challenged, when you are talking to someone like Terry Anderson, I suggest standing back from him so it is not so obvious.' Durrington does not give the impression of someone who would give a rat's arse, as she might say, about her height. The interchange is so reminiscent of Margaret's determination to tell people when they are wearing the wrong colour, and either not realising or not caring whether such advice is appreciated.

The pretty television reporter – is there any other kind? – clearly remembers the day Margaret was killed. She was chasing the local angle on the Bali bombing. The other big story of the day was the start of the Snowtown trial. She couldn't believe it when news broke about Margaret's shooting. You never would have guessed that anything would push Bali off as the lead item on the bulletin, she says, confessing that she sometimes cries when doing death knocks. This is journalistic slang for the unpleasant task of seeking comment from the grieving family or friends of someone who has died. Another journalist says the *Advertiser* had to send a cadet to the CitiCentre Building because everyone else was at the airport, waiting for a local football club to arrive back from Bali.

Memory plays funny tricks. Jean remembers Don ringing her from the hospital to tell her of Margaret's death. Learne Durrington is sure she made the call. One policeman says it was raining on the day that Gassy's home was searched; another is sure that it was fine.

Just after 4 pm, Stevo calls for the court to reconvene. Barry, blinking, says there is a statement from the jury. Gassy stands controlled and still in the dock as the judge explains the jury have sent a note saying they don't believe they will be able to reach a verdict. She proposes calling them back in, to give them a 'Black direction', to take extra time to consider the issues. She explains to Gassy that this is a model direction for circumstances such as these. Gassy stares down, blinking rapidly, with no discernible expression on his face.

The foreman sighs as he walks in. The judge tells the jury that their deliberations have not been prolonged in view of the size of the case and number of witnesses. Experience has shown that juries can often reach agreement if given more time. 'You also have a duty to listen carefully and objectively to the views of every one of your fellow jurors,' she says. 'You should calmly weigh up and test every opinion. Calm discussion often leads to a better understanding and may lead you to believe that your original opinion was wrong. You should only join a verdict if you think it is correct . . . I ask you to retire again and see whether you can reach a verdict.'

At 5 pm, Helena leaves for the airport, and Bernadette breaks down. She sobs to Jean: 'I told you Mum I would sit with you to the end, and now we don't know if there will be an end.'

Don paces and sweats the hours away.

Over dinner at a nearby Chinese restaurant, Jean is almost in tears. She really misses Margaret, she says, because whenever Jean was in a strange place, Margaret was usually there with her. She always knew what to do, says Bernadette, describing the Chinese dinner set and chopsticks that Margaret once bought her. Jean consoles herself – she has a feeling in her bones that there will be a verdict tonight.

At 7.45 pm, the court reconvenes. There is a stranger in the chair where Barry usually sits. Barry is off duty but has stayed around, to see it through. At 7.50 pm, the jurors file in, as they have so many times before. They look the most serious yet. Even Ms Pert looks per-turbed. They wish to retire for the evening.

Many observers believe they know the source of the jury's difficulties in reaching a unanimous verdict. Such speculation cannot be mentioned here for legal reasons. The jury room is meant to be sacrosanct. An unusual exception to this occurred early in the trial, however, when the dynamics of juries were exposed in a documentary shown on SBS television, called *Secrets of the Jury Room*. It revealed that dominant personalities, emotions and speculation influenced the jurors' discussions as much as any examination of the actual evidence. Some jurors felt railroaded in the process.

The documentary followed the deliberations of two juries, comprised of volunteers, who participated in a mock trial of a young man charged with assisting the suicide of his partner. His partner, crippled by motor neurone disease, had previously planned on killing himself, but it was not clear whether he had done this unaided. The scenario was fictional, but the documentary was filmed in a court room with actual barristers, expert witnesses and a judge, which may explain why the 'jurors' took to their task as if it was real. The end result was that one jury acquitted the defendant, and the other could not reach a verdict.

Over the years, numerous inquiries have examined the pros and cons of trial by jury. One such report, by the Law Reform Committee of the Victorian Parliament, noted that the jury system originated from a misinterpretation of a famous clause in the Magna Carta of 1215, which provided that no person should be condemned 'but by lawful judgement of his peers, or by the law of the land'. The clause was taken in later centuries as enshrining a right to trial by jury, although this interpretation is no longer regarded as historically accurate. Yet the words of the clause, according to one author cited in the report, 'coined by a distant society in a half forgotten language, have been treasured by generations of men and women in the English-speaking world as a safeguard of individual liberty'.

Others have not been so kind about the merits of juries. 'It is an understatement to describe a jury . . . as a group of twelve men of average ignorance,' asserted one scholar cited in the report. The average jury comprised 'unusually ignorant, credulous, slow-witted, narrow-minded, biased or temperamental persons,' he said. Other, less acerbic critics, have raised concerns about the ability of jurors to handle complex information and lengthy cases. It is not difficult to appreciate, the committee's report says, that jurors will have forgotten a significant amount of the evidence by the time they retire to consider their verdicts. Many inquiries have, however, come to the conclusion that the jury system, though not without problems, cannot be bested.

Juries, in theory at least, force the law to make itself transparent and understandable to the community. The English jurist Lord Patrick Devlin wrote that: 'To refer a case for decision to a body of experts or even to men and women of superior mental powers would mean that the person accused might be imprisoned for ten or fifteen years or for life, for reasons which could not be made clear to the average citizen. This is not democracy. This is what trial by jury prevents.'

The judge who appeared in the SBS documentary was more blunt. Juries are a risk averaging process – you are less likely to get a loony result with twelve jurors than with a single judge, he said. Twelve people make a powerful organism which is greater than the sum of its parts, he added. One barrister interviewed for the documentary said she had not seen a jury convict an innocent man although she was sure that at times, guilty men had been acquitted.

It is the forty-fourth day of the trial. A Thursday. It is also 52 years to the day since Jean went into labour for the first time, and waited for Joseph to shave, and put on a collar and tie for the ambulance ride to the hospital.

Margaret was a Libran and a dragon, says Don. It was meant to be a good combination.

Waiting, waiting.

At 11.15 am, the court reconvenes. Another question. The jury want the judge to suggest how they might move forward.

Justice Vanstone – and yes, in answer to the question which inevitably arises, the judge's brother is married to the federal politician, Senator Amanda Vanstone – faces the jury. She advises them: 'Sometimes when you reach a difficult position and can't move on, it is good to go back to the beginning.'

Only a few jurors take notes as she speaks. Surely the force of will from the public gallery must be bearing on them. The jurors file out, faces down.

Brebner is on his feet immediately. Out of 'an abundance of caution', he asks the judge to make it explicit that her comments are merely suggestions for the jury to accept or reject as they see fit. The judge checks her words with the court reporter, and recalls the jury.

'There was a concern that I hadn't made it clear enough that what I have said are merely suggestions for your consideration. I thought I made that clear but that is all they are.'

Back outside the court room, questions are raised about the identity of the two men who have been hanging around for the past day or so. They are casually dressed in what Don calls 'surf wear'. One resembles a juror, perhaps they are brothers. He has a similar shaped face to Mr Teddy Bear, who has found it a major challenge to remain awake during the trial. Perhaps he suffers from sleep apnoea – he is on the tubby side.

Deirdre decides to take the initiative. She approaches the two men directly. 'What's your interest in the case?' she asks.

'We were wondering how long it would take until someone asked us who we were,' they reply. They are private investigators hired by a decidedly nervous New South Wales Medical Board to keep a close eye on proceedings. It is the first time the board has taken such a step. The board is waiting in Sydney, ready to swing into action if the defendant is acquitted, with contingency plans to protect doctors involved in Gassy's deregistration.

Others, too, have taken precautions. Many had a jolt on the day that Gassy told the court he had obtained the private addresses of various doctors from the Electoral Office. At least one police officer and one journalist subsequently demanded a silent listing on all such public registers. This case just shows that you never know what can happen, says the journalist. Perhaps he is not really joking when he says he has thought about moving overseas if Gassy is acquitted.

Meanwhile, Terry Anderson points out the sophisticated gent with crinkly-smooth grey hair, another recent arrival in court. It is Frederick Toben, the holocaust denier. Conspiracy theorists are all around.

At 12.10 pm, the knock, at last.

The jurors are deadpan as they walk in. Gassy is perfectly expressionless. Who can guess how he feels the pressure? There is no sign of a release valve.

The judge asks the foreman if the verdict is unanimous. Many hearts seem to stop beating in the moment before his response. People are listening so hard that they have difficulty hearing or comprehending.

The doctor in the dock has been found guilty. Gassy continues looking down as he hears the verdict. Not even a flicker moves his face.

Don feels no joy. Rather, he is overwhelmed by a feeling of absolute and utter relief. It leaves him feeling weak, as if his legs are made of lead. At last he can begin to relax, after what has begun to feel like the longest week of his life.

The proceedings move on quickly, almost before people have time to recover their breath. The judge thanks the jurors for their work. 'More has been asked of you than most jurors,' she says. 'I hope you will go away realising the level of care and effort to ensure justice is done. I wish you well for the future. You are excused from jury duty forever more.'

The jurors walk out for the last time, looking down.

Brebner springs to his feet, asking that the judge impose a mandatory life sentence and remand the prisoner without a non-parole period. Gassy continues to look down.

Dr Gassy, says the judge in a quiet, gentle voice. He looks at her. There is only one sentence, life imprisonment, she says. She suggests he may wish to seek legal advice about the sentencing.

'I won't be seeking any legal advice, your Honour.'

Xavier Gassy is composed as he leaves the court room. Jean rushes out, her first priority to reach Brebner with her thanks. It was about this time of the day, she says, that Margaret was born 52 years ago. Jean and Bernadette are whisked to a quiet place to gather their thoughts ahead of their encounter with the media pack, already waiting outside.

Don can't keep the lid on. Tears redden his eyes, the colour rises in his face. He thanks 'the boys', the square-shouldered detectives who are standing around awkwardly. Almost two years ago, some of these men were doing what they always do in such situations; checking whether the husband killed the wife. Don doesn't bear any grudges. He knows they were just doing their job, and they've been a great support since then. The big tough men look uncomfortable with Don's effusive thanks. One detective gives him a little smile and says, almost offhandedly, 'That's okay.' It's the Australian blokey way. No, says the detective later in the pub. He was just following protocol. It would not be professional for him to throw a hug in the court building. Over more than a few beers with Don later, however, the professional guard relaxes.

Barry leads the jurors past, on their way out of the building. Still the mother hen with his chicks. How strange they must feel, walking quietly down the stairs, with their little overnight bags. Research has shown that many jurors are stressed, sometimes even traumatised by their experiences. In one survey, jurors reported feeling fine during and immediately after the trial but then suffering sleeplessness, nightmares, depression and phobias in subsequent months. Some reports have recommended greater use of briefing and debriefing, as well as making counselling services available.

Within minutes of their big moment in court, the dozen are discharged onto the pavement. How will this experience mark them? Will they carry it with them, a burden until their deathbeds, the most momentous decision of their lives, or will they leave it behind, as just an amusing yarn to tell at a barbecue? What was it that finally brought them to a unanimous decision? Surely it was the judge's final direction. It was like 'join up the bloody dots, you mugs,' jokes Don.

Several of Margaret's former workmates and friends arrive at the court building. News has travelled fast. Rebecca Graham is in tears of relief. She is also angry. Xavier Gassy had been leaving the building by himself, a sad lonely figure, when Rebecca arrived with Learne Durrington. Rebecca thought she heard him hiss 'liar' at Learne.

Finally, Don, Jean and Bernadette are ready to face the wall of microphones and cameras outside. They tell of their relief and belief that justice has been well done, before being whisked away to unwind in a nearby pub popular with police. The mood of the gathering is confused; both celebratory and funereal. Jean speaks quietly in one corner with Learne, telling her how proud she feels of Margaret for writing to the Medical Board about Gassy, though it cost her her life.

'It was an ethical decision she made,' says Jean, 'and she was vindicated. I would have been so disappointed if there hadn't been a conviction because that would have meant that ordinary people didn't respect what she did.'

A policeman jokes to Deirdre that they should arrange to fill the public gallery with rows of short-haired women for Gassy's sentencing. The revenge of the 'lesbian underworld'.

The next week, Jean sends wine and chocolates to Peter Brebner and Emily Telfer. Members of the Major Crime Squad unwrap a crate of wine, biscuits, cheeses and chocolates. Someone rings Jean. We're not used to being thanked like this, he says.

Sometime later, a slim, attractive young woman, with fair hair falling straight to her shoulders, opens her mail to find a short letter from Gassy. He just wants to make sure that she realises his conviction was on Margaret Tobin's birthday. She is one of the *Advertiser*'s court reporters and thinks the letter is just another example of Gassy's bizarre behaviour. She had sensed that he enjoyed the media attention during his trial.

Exactly five weeks after the verdict, Gassy asks Justice Vanstone for a lenient sentence, in part because he said Tobin had 'suffered little' and the crime had no sadistic or financial element. The judge also hears victim impact statements from Jean and Mary Catherine before launching into her sentencing comments.

'Jean Eric Gassy, you have been convicted by verdict of a jury of the murder of Margaret Julia Tobin,' the judge begins. 'The killing was cool, calculated and clever. You could have got away with it. Only the most outstanding police work brought you undone.

'Your act robbed Dr Tobin's family of a loved and esteemed

member. You deprived the community of a gifted and respected medical administrator; someone with the training, intelligence and commitment to make a huge contribution.'

The judge says she is not satisfied that Gassy suffered from a delusional disorder at the time of his deregistration, although it seems likely that he suffered from some sort of paranoid disorder.

'But I am sure that your personality is flawed,' she continues.

Your response to your deregistration was to plan to kill those whom you saw as responsible. Your hatred for Dr Woodforde and Dr Phillips was palpable during their evidence, even though you tried to disguise it. There is no question in my mind that their lives have been in danger in the last eight years leading to your arrest. The surveillance tapes of Dr Nelson's rooms, of which the jury was not aware, are tangible proof that your ambitions extended beyond Dr Tobin.

In your very trial, you demonstrated a determination not only to brandish Dr Tobin's post-mortem photographs, but also to intimidate Dr Nelson by producing one such photograph to him. That act only tends to further confirm my own settled view that not only do you have no contrition for what you did, but you see the task as unfinished. That you have carried such a level of resentment for almost a decade indicates to me that you will never let it go. As well, I am satisfied that in your time in custody, new persons have been added to your list of targets . . .

On your side of the ledger, too, this is a tragic course of events. You are extremely intelligent. You have shown that you can bring that intelligence to bear on quite diverse fields of endeavour. You are plainly loved by your family. I cannot imagine how they will ever come to terms with what you have done.

There is really nothing that can be said in mitigation of your crime. That you do not accept the verdict of the jury is demonstrated by the fact that you have appealed.

The judge says she is satisfied beyond reasonable doubt that Gassy went to Brisbane in April 2002 in the hope of killing Dr Tobin there.

You had an opportunity to think again, or to seek help when your plans failed. You chose not to take it. It seems to me that this killing must rank in the worst category of murder. Only multiple murders could be more serious and many of those might be attended by circumstances of mitigation which are not present here.

In the end, I have determined that an extremely long non-parole period is called for . . . As I said, I think as long as you live, you will be profoundly dangerous. I recognise that by reason of the period I am about to set, you may well die in gaol. That is a consequence of the gravity of your crime. I forfeit to the Crown your handguns, ammunition and all associated firearm parts. I impose the mandatory sentence of life imprisonment.

The non-parole period I impose is 34 years. Your sentence will be backdated to 11 November 2002.

This is far from the last time, however, that Gassy will appear in court.

17

Inside madness

In a comfortable brick home in a leafy Sydney suburb sits a psychiatrist at his desk. These days he has trouble negotiating the stairs to his office on the second floor; it's one of the nuisances of time passing. At 75, he thinks it's just about time to give the working game away.

If he had the time or inclination, this slightly stooped, bespectacled man could tell many stories about what turns people to murder. During a distinguished career spanning more than five decades, Bill Barclay specialised in assessing murderers, amongst other things. He must have met several hundred murderers over the years. But most of the stories that he knows are banal. Most murders are domestic of some sort or a stupid, drunken brawl that escalated out of control. Most of the murderers he met were everyday people caught up in pitiful circumstances.

'Most often the homicide is very ordinary and tragic,' says Barclay. 'You go there expecting to meet a horrible person and you come out thinking, "You poor miserable bastard". You come out shaking your head thinking, "Why on earth did that happen?"'

He adds: 'I used to teach my students that a good way to get yourself killed is to say to someone with a gun – "You wouldn't have the guts".'

Cold-blooded executions, like that planned by Jean Eric Gassy, are rare. The question not fully answered in Court Room Two is why a man trained in the arts and sciences of healing became a killer. Sure, there was plenty of evidence about motive, that Gassy blamed Margaret Tobin, amongst other people, for his professional and personal downfall. But that could only ever be part of the explanation. Surely no normal person would spend many years brooding over such a loss, and plotting murderous revenge?

It is difficult, however, to draw a line which neatly separates pathology from personality. The crude question which usually arises in situations such as these – was he mad or bad? – leads only to crude answers. From the outset, Gassy was adamant that he was mentally fit to stand trial. Indeed, it often seemed that the primary aim of the proceedings, from his point of view, was to prove his sanity. Constantly he emphasised his intelligence – he told of receiving high marks while undertaking university studies in criminal justice in jail – as if someone so smart and highly functioning could not be mad.

During the 30 days of pre-trial hearings, the issue of Gassy's mental state was raised numerous times. The prosecution reported that a number of psychiatrists believed Gassy's delusional disorder was likely to have worsened since it was first diagnosed, and that there was a strong possibility it could impair his judgement, especially as he was representing himself. Peter Brebner also thought some of Gassy's statements during the voir dire, suggesting bias on the part of witnesses and the judge, were potential cause for concern, seeming to fit with the diagnosis of a delusional disorder. There was a risk that if Gassy became stressed during the trial, then his ability to make judgements and conduct his own defence might be impaired, Brebner told the judge. 'It is also my submission that, in this area, and particularly in the case of an unrepresented accused, one should proceed with the utmost caution, and caution suggests that attempts should at least be made to obtain reports,' he said.

Gassy, however, accused Brebner of being motivated to introduce psychiatric evidence that would be prejudicial to the defendant, rather than being concerned about justice. Gassy refused to be examined by a psychiatrist because it would be impossible, he said, for them to be impartial, given the history of the case. 'I would accede to any of your honour's requests other than to see a psychiatrist,' he said. 'The only fair way of establishing whether I have any kind of impairment is to proceed with the trial and to see whether, in fact, I am disadvantaging myself in in any way, in the way that I conduct my defence.'

The judge was sure Gassy was fit to stand trial. To meet the legal criteria, he simply had to be able to understand and respond rationally to the charge, to be able to exercise procedural rights during the trial, and to understand the nature of the proceedings and to follow the evidence. But during the voir dire, Justice Vanstone said she was less certain about the issue of mental competence at the time of the crime.

Again, Gassy was determined this should not be an issue. 'As I understood it as a practising psychiatrist, the issue of competence only really comes into the issue when someone was so psychotic that they really had no idea what their acts entertained,' he responded. 'In particular if someone is persecutory and they act against that person, they are still competent in that they still understand that their actions are wrong; it's only if someone is so delusional that their whole view of the world is wrong, like the person they are harming is like the devil, so they don't believe they are doing anything wrong at the time they commit the offence. They would not be competent. But simply having delusions about a person of a particular nature would not make that person incompetent even if they acted on their delusions, that's my understanding.'

The judge replied: 'I think what you just said was, as far as I understand it, just about right.'

Some days later, however, Brebner again returned to the issue – there were enough warning bells to oblige the judge to order a psychiatric evaluation, he said. Brebner argued that the judge had the power to do this against Gassy's will. However, the judge disputed this.

Instead an 'examination by transcript' was ordered. Forensic psychiatrists in Adelaide were reluctant to become involved – it was all too close to home for them – and so transcripts of the pre-trial hearings were sent to Bruce Westmore, in Sydney. In his interim reports, Westmore said he believed there were enough grounds for concern to warrant consideration being given to Gassy's scheduling in a psychiatric facility. But the prosecution doubted whether this was legally possible. Nor did the suggestion impress the judge, who decided that she was better placed to assess Gassy's condition than psychiatrists who had not seen him in action in court.

And there is no doubt that, as the weeks and months passed in the court room, Gassy often was in fine form as he cross-examined witnesses and debated points of law. His studies had paid off. But there also were times when observers gathered outside the court room in a break and muttered amongst themselves: he's mad; he's as nutty as a fruitcake; why on earth is he allowed to represent himself?

The mutterings grew louder on the days that Gassy cross-examined Tom Gottlieb and Stephen Adelstein, the two Sydney specialists who did not accept his self-diagnosis of AIDS. As these doctors endured Gassy's interrogation in the witness box, it became painfully clear that nothing they said – about his test results, about the usual course of HIV – could shake his conviction that he had AIDS. The whispers about madness surfaced again on the day that Gassy stood in court and declared he had been deliberately denied HIV treatment while in prison 'in a pre-emptive strike before the verdict'. He thought Jonathan Phillips and the prison medical staff were involved. 'It is not less than an attempted execution before the jury verdict in a country without the death penalty,' he said. 'It constitutes gross abuse of state power.' Gassy told the jury he had no motive to claim he was falsely suffering from AIDS. 'There really is no doubt at all that I have AIDS,' he said. 'I have had nine years to observe the course of my illness.'

He said the prison staff believed he had AIDS. 'For more than six months I was handing out hot water to the prisoners. I was the first worker to have this job to be coerced to wear gloves and when handing out bags of washed clothes to the prisoners.' Gassy accused an ophthalmologist that he saw at the Royal Adelaide Hospital, who had disputed his self-diagnosis of AIDS-related retinitis, of lying. He had been tested for HIV twice while in prison, and disputed the finding that his immune system was healthy. 'My CD4 count can only have been falsified because it is completely incompatible with the clinical picture,' he said.

For Scott Allen, the man at the Queensland Gun Exchange who took the unusual order for a spare slide for a Glock pistol, there was no question about Gassy's mental state. Allen prides himself on his ability to detect 'the crazies'; his shop tends to attract them. 'He should have pleaded that he was crazy, everybody would have believed him,' Allen said, some weeks after facing up to Gassy's court room cross-examination. Gassy had insisted that he had never been to Allen's shop but had ordered the slide over the phone and paid for it by money order.

Some days, it seemed that whenever anything happened that was not to Gassy's liking, he construed it as another sign of bias or malicious intent directed towards him. He suggested there was a sinister reason behind his difficulty in finding expert witnesses to testify. 'It just seems odd that none of these experts wanted to be involved,' he said. Another day, he asked the judge to order the *Advertiser* to publish a retraction on some errors in a story. He queried the journalist's motives: 'I would suggest his account is a deliberate vilification of the defendant in the pursuit of sensationalism and there should be some sanction.'

Gassy did not only bear grudges; he also remembered favours. He made a point of showing his appreciation for Detective Inspector Geoff Leonard, who had been in charge of the first search of his home. During the pre-trial legal argument, Gassy instructed Roger de Robillard to withdraw any allegations of improper behaviour that had been inferred against Leonard. 'Dr Gassy really does not wish to, in any way, say anything untoward towards Inspector Leonard because he was of a view that Inspector Leonard treated him in a decent manner when he told him about his HIV problem on that day,' de Robillard said.

Other days, it was not clear whether Gassy's statements were fed by delusion or cunning. Did he really believe that Margaret Tobin was a closet lesbian? Or was it just a strategy to create confusion and questions in the mind of the jurors? One hint emerged when Gassy said he had formed that view partly because of the victim's habit of calling herself Mrs Tobin, as if she wanted to emphasise her marital status. This clearly was an exercise in fiction. Margaret never went by the name of Mrs Tobin. Her husband was Don Scott.

Was it only a tactic to accuse his former secretary of conspiring with his former patient? Or did he really believe it? Did he really believe the police had used his mother as a 'human shield' on the morning they came to search his flat, beneath his parent's home? Did he really believe that the ballistics expert Peter Lawrence had been under political pressure in his investigations? Or was Gassy simply grabbing every available opportunity to weaken the prosecution case?

What did Gassy tell himself, in the internal voice safe from eaves-droppers, about Margaret Tobin's murder? Did he acknowledge to himself what he had done? Perhaps he could only hear the voice saying, she got what she deserved.

In Gassy's world, he was perfectly entitled to seek retribution from those he believed had ruined his life.

The public often has a vastly inflated view of the powers of modern medicine. This is partly as a result of the medical industry's skills in self-promotion. It is also comforting for people to believe that illness and suffering can be simply solved with miracle cures. And so it often comes as more of a shock and disappointment than it should to discover the fallibility of medicine. Absolutes and guarantees are not its usual currency. Psychiatry is even more prone to uncertainty and differences of opinion than other areas of medicine. There is no blood test for diagnosing madness. It is not uncommon for four or five psychiatrists to give four or five different opinions about a patient, as happened with Gassy. And there are plenty of prickly, difficult, suspicious characters who are not mentally ill.

At afternoon tea in many of the old mental hospitals, as they were called, staff would pour out cups of tea for the patients. Milk and two sugars were put in every cup. This simple action said much about the prevailing views towards the mentally ill: they were incapable even of deciding how they liked their tea. More recently, the comment of the judge in the SBS documentary, *Secrets of the Jury Room*, revealed something of contemporary attitudes when he suggested that a twelve-member jury would be less likely than a single judge to produce a 'loony' verdict. Madness has often been conflated with stupidity when any quick examination of history's great figures reveals the opposite. Many people with mental illness are extremely bright and creative. Even those of unexceptional intelligence, once they have knocked around the system for a bit, know what to say, and what not to say, if they want to persuade a doctor or someone else of their sanity. It is often said that doctors with mental illness get worse care because they are more likely to be able to disguise their problems and to avoid enforced treatment.

What is madness anyway? Everyone is out of touch with reality sometimes, even if only in our dreams or when we fall in love. All of us rely on delusions of some sort to get through life, perhaps believing that we are better, kinder people than we really are. One person's religious conviction is another's delusion. The eloquent and eminent Sydney psychiatrist John Ellard tells an amusing story from when he was a sleep-deprived intern at a Sydney hospital 50-odd years ago. He was woken to attend to a man who could not sleep because of 'the trumpeting of elephants'. Ellard blushes to recall that he prescribed a sedative injection. Next morning Ellard was himself woken by trumpeting – and realised that a circus was parked nearby. The lesson, he later wrote, was that when a patient told him something, it was to be accepted until there was clear evidence to the contrary and that 'it's not always easy to discover who has the delusions'.

Many of Gassy's 'fixed false beliefs' were not entirely implausible. Gassy's conviction that he had been the victim of political abuse of psychiatry might sound far-fetched, but such abuses have occurred. John Ellard notes that: 'A consideration of the history of psychiatry, both remote and relatively recent, makes it clear that there have always been psychiatrists who put their own interests, and the interests of the state – no matter how repressive – before the interests of their patients.' Ellard says a Sydney psychiatrist once managed to convince the courts that activities such as homosexuality and some criminal behaviour could be treated by psychosurgery.

One psychiatrist warns, however, that it is a mistake to focus on the content of Gassy's delusions and whether they were plausible or not. 'It's the whole pattern of his behaviour over a long period that's important,' he says.

Over the years, psychiatrists themselves have been unable to agree on definitions and classifications of mental illness. These vary between countries and cultures or can simply depend on the hospital or medical school where a psychiatrist trained. Ellard once wrote that law and psychiatry face similar problems 'for we both do our best to grapple with the difficulties of those who do not fit comfortably into the world we all share'.

The reasons for those discomforts stretch across an enormous range – from a wretched childhood, through harmful genes, to such things as the ingestion of lead as a child. There is no end to them. Just as complex are the results of those adversities, from carefully concealed internal suffering, through manifest schizo-phrenia to massacres in the street. The complexities of the human conditions are such that only those whose tidiness of mind exceeds their imagination can believe that every combination of feelings and of acts can be defined with precision, given a name and then placed it its own beautifully constructed pigeon hole.

The problem of paranoia has been especially controversial. Paranoid disorders can be particularly difficult to diagnose because a nugget of truth often lies at their heart. And often paranoid behav-iour encourages others to behave in a way that reinforces the paranoia. So it becomes a vicious circle, paranoia feeding itself. 'Paranoid people say people talk behind their backs, and they do,' says one psychiatrist. 'Why? Because if you talk to them, they will mis-interpret it. So you stop talking to them and you talk to others.' Or, as another psychiatrist puts it: 'Paranoia is built on truth but then it grows like a weed.'

And when does paranoia become pathological? Most normal people have paranoid thoughts at some times. Was it paranoid of the journalist and police officers who heard of Gassy's activities at the

Electoral Office to take their personal details off public registers? Or just sensible?

Some scientists argue that paranoia conferred a survival advantage in evolutionary terms. The ape who thought predators were lurking everywhere presumably took extra precautions as he or she went about daily life. Ian Dowbiggin, a Canadian academic who has written widely on the history of psychiatry, cites research showing that paranoia can be localised to the part of the brain involved in survival-related behaviours. These have been dubbed the 'four fs' – feeding, fighting, fleeing and fornicating. When individuals feel powerless and sense that those things and people central to their very existence – jobs, property, family, friends – are threatened, paranoid reactions often ensue. Dowbiggin argues that the delusional streak in human beings is unlikely to disappear as long as there is civilisation itself. There is, he says, something paranoid in the post-modern view which 'insists that nothing is what it seems, nothing should be accepted at face value, one should always read between the lines and doubt others' intentions and good faith'. The popularity of conspiracy theories also suggests the rise of paranoid thinking. 'Central to all these phenomena is the belief that our natural and human environments harbour malicious elements working to make people ill, while human agencies maliciously, intentionally try to suppress this information,' says Dowbiggin.

The nomenclature of paranoid disorders has changed since the early 1990s. Now, they fall under the label of delusional disorder, which encompasses several types of delusion. People can hold delusions that they are being persecuted (persecutory), that they have an illness (somatic), that someone is in love with them (erotomanic), or that involve grandiosity or jealousy. People can suffer from more than one type of delusion. There is debate about whether the content of delusions holds specific meaning. Some experts say this is not necessarily so; others believe that they hint at deep concerns. The content of delusions can be influenced by cultural factors; for instance, one text notes that delusions about vampires and poisoning are more common in Chinese patients. One psychiatric textbook cites the story of a man who was deluded that he had AIDS, in a case that has at least some shades of Gassy's story. The man's condom had come off during an encounter with a prostitute and a week later he noticed a discharge from his penis. A doctor diagnosed chlamydia but the man was convinced he had HIV. When the antibiotics caused thrush, he saw that as further evidence of AIDS, and tried to kill himself. A further examination of the man's history showed he was troubled long before the tryst. He was a high achiever, the child who had been chosen to redeem the family. At school he feared contaminating others with germs, and began to question the strict religion in which he had been reared, and became worried about his sexual orientation.

There have been three main schools of thought about delusional disorder: that it is a variant of schizophrenia; that it is a variant of mood disorder; or that it is a third form of psychosis distinct from both schizophrenia and mood disorder. It is this latter view which now dominates. Delusional disorder is distinguished from schizo-phrenia because the delusions are not bizarre, and are limited in scope, meaning the sufferer is usually able to maintain normal func-tioning in areas outside the delusion. In some of these individuals, notes one psychiatry textbook, the demarcation between normality, pathological behaviour, overvalued ideas and delusion may not be clear. Sufferers' lack of insight makes diagnosis and treatment difficult. People with paranoia rarely seek help. One journal article notes that these patients are notoriously reluctant to accept medical therapy. They are convinced that anyone who does not share their delusions is plainly and simply an enemy, part of the problem rather than part of the solution. It adds that treating them is a frustrating, thankless and sometimes dangerous job. Another text notes that patients often have enough insight to stay clear of speaking about the subject of their delusions with other people. They think that if they tell people what they believe, they will be punished further, as part of the conspiracy against them.

It is not surprising that Gassy was so well able to maintain control in court, says one experienced forensic psychiatrist. People with a delusional disorder are very, very single-minded, he says. While someone else might be drawn into the complexity of the court room situation and become overwhelmed, someone with a delusional disorder would be focusing on their belief 'that this is more proof', that the whole system is corrupt. If you know you are right and are utterly unshakeable in your belief that the system is conspiring against you, then everything you hear and see simply provides more evidence to confirm this belief.

When investigating patients with an apparent delusional disorder, doctors usually check whether there is an organic cause. Some conditions which affect the brain, such as Huntington's disease and epilepsy, can occasionally cause delusions. Persecutory delusions can sometimes be the first manifestation of a dementing illness. Some medications, herbal products and substances of abuse, such as amphetamines and cocaine, can also cause delusions. As for Gassy, explanations vary as to how and why he might have developed a delusional disorder.

Those mental health professionals from the psychoanalytic school see paranoid delusions as a protective psychological response. Paranoid people are highly sensitive to threats to their self-esteem but protect themselves from feelings of inadequacy by blaming disappointments on other people. As one researcher puts it, 'many patients have had to make a choice between something being wrong with them and something being wrong in the world'. Adverse experiences early in life may make people anxious and fearful of the dangerousness of others and the world. People who are depressed or have a low self-esteem may feel socially excluded and have a sense of being a target for others.

Psychoanalytic therapists ask about Gassy's early relationships with his mother and family, and whether these engendered a deep-seated lack of trust in the world. They wonder about the impact of the family's migration, and about Gassy's defensiveness about his background and skin colour. They speculate about the pressures and sense of entitlement that come with being the golden-haired son. The unwritten rules which govern family behaviour and dynamics can be difficult to uncover and decipher. In some families, writes John Ellard, they will be concealed or denied. 'For example, the parents may emphasise that their children are encouraged to grow up and become autonomous, but observations will reveal a thousand subtle pressures to ensure that they do not. Some of the rules which govern families are almost invariable – for example, the hierarchy of power descends from the parents to children – while others are more idiosyncratic, built up by years of negotiation or struggle between individual family members.' One can only speculate about the rules which shaped and influenced Gassy's development through childhood and adulthood.

But perhaps it is unfair to point the finger at the family. One policeman involved in the case thought so. 'How does a murderer come out of a family like that?' he was asked. 'It happens,' he replied. 'It's just like the best parents can have the worst kids and vice versa.'

Those who favour biological explanations for mental illness turn to the scientific literature examining differences – in brain chemistry, anatomy or function – between those with delusional disorders and control groups. It has been suggested that people with a delusional disorder have a biologically driven perceptual anomaly that gives them a more vivid and intense awareness of stimuli. People with persecutory delusions may be more likely to notice and recall potential threats, thereby reinforcing the delusional belief. They may tend to seek less information before reaching decisions, and thus be more likely to jump to conclusions on the basis of less evidence.

The biological and psychoanalytic views are not necessarily mutually exclusive. Biology and behaviour cannot be neatly separated; they interact and influence each other. Perhaps some people are born with a predisposition to delusional thinking, which may never manifest unless fertilised by life's experiences – whether their early upbringing, exposure to marijuana or physical or psychological distress. Similarly, there is no reason to supply a simplistic answer to the question about whether Gassy was mad or bad. Surely a person can be a mix of things.

The judge's early questions about Gassy's mental competency at the time of the crime were resolved by the end of the trial. 'There is absolutely no doubt in my mind that at the time you committed this crime you were mentally competent,' she said in her sentencing remarks.

You went to great lengths to cover your tracks and conceal your identity. You waited patiently until the opportunity to strike presented itself and you then acted calmly and efficiently. It might be thought that because of your unusual personality and your susceptibility to thoughts of persecution your responsibility for the crime is diminished. I do not accept that. And even if it were so, the reduction in non-parole period it could attract would come into collision with the need to protect the public from you and to deter you from future crime.

Delusions can be 'infectious'. Known sometimes as 'folie à deux', there have been cases where spouses, parents, siblings or children have adopted the beliefs of the delusional patient. In Gassy's case, his family gave no indication of accepting his diagnosis with a mental illness. 'In your opinion, have you ever felt that I was delusional or mad?' Gassy asked his sister Elizabeth in court. 'No,' she replied. Perhaps this is not so surprising; many families find it difficult to accept a mental illness in their midst. But the Gassys' denial went beyond this. During and after the trial, Gassy's parents told many people of the terrible conspiracy against their son. It wasn't possible for someone raised in a good Christian household to have done such a thing, said Maud. Xavier, in particular, made little attempt to hide his disdain for the judge and some of the witnesses. Was this a normal parental response in the face of knowledge that could be unbearably painful and shattering? Perhaps. But it may also give some insight into Gassy's upbringing. Some parents are able to accept that their children have done dreadful things, and to love them still.

Soon after Gassy's conviction, an anonymous email of about 2,500 words and displaying a detailed knowledge of the case was posted on a news chat site. Brilliante123@hotmail.com wrote that Gassy was innocent, that the police evidence had been unsound and that Gassy had never mentioned Dr Tobin's name to his family in the years following his deregistration.

'I doubt if he thought her the main reason for his deregistration,' wrote Brilliante123.

He probably had many more people he could prioritise for the event first if he was murderously inclined. All the evidence was

skewed to present a picture of a man who was delusional, dangerous and likely to do anything . . . There is no doubt in my mind
that he was set up in the workplace by certain persons, largely
nurses in the first instance on whom he was strict in order to give
the best service to patients. When Dr Tobin came onto the scene
as his superior she quickly made life very difficult for him and he
took extended sick leave on account of overwork and stress . . . A
bad man must have been a bad boy and a bad child. Gassy was a
good boy and good child who made it through the very bad State
School System in New South Wales to become a psychiatrist. In
one report I read his mother describing him as a 'quiet studious
boy'. His home background is spotless. His work history quite
long, quite honorable. The only stain on the whole thing was
when Gassy was deregistered after he had taken sick leave due to
stress and overwork . . . He was a victim of the system and still is I
believe . . . Did racism play a part in the choice of Gassy as the
culprit? One wonders . . . Gassy has been a model student, a
model son and a model uncle. I am sure he was a very good doctor
also otherwise he would have been sacked within the first few
years. You cannot last in the job of psychiatry in a hospital unless
you have the appropriate personality to do the job. People would
not opt to go to you. So what is it then? Perhaps someone out
there could tell me.

One researcher has described seven situations that favour the development of delusional disorders. These are an increased expectation of
receiving sadistic treatment, situations that increase distrust and
suspicion, social isolation, situations that increase envy and jealousy,
situations that lower self-esteem, situations that cause persons to see
their own defects in others, and situations that increase the potential
for rumination over probable meanings and motivations. These scenarios had much in common with Gassy's circumstances in the early
1990s, as he struggled at St George Hospital. He was out of his depth
in a difficult, demanding job. He worked in a unit with an uncertain
future, which had not been well supported by the hospital hierarchy

and which was plagued by poor staff relations. He needed to blame someone for the problems he was experiencing. When Margaret Tobin arrived, stirring the pot noisily and vigorously, she presented an obvious target. As subsequent events unfolded – the changes at the hospital, the dealings with the Medical Board – Gassy also grew suspicious about other people. He was incapable of seeing that much of the cause of his downfall lay in his own hands. If he had followed the recommendations of the Impaired Registrants Panel, or the Professional Standards Committee, or the Medical Tribunal, he could have continued practising. But this was impossible, due to the nature of his delusional disorder. The eight years of social and professional isolation which followed his resignation from St George can only have fed the delusions.

Try, for a moment, to imagine what it was like to live in Gassy's world – sitting in the flat beneath his parents' home, preoccupied by thoughts of his enemies. Brooding over how they had won. They had taken everything that mattered. Being a doctor was so important to him, not just for the monetary reward and status that it brought. It was the core of who he was. Without it, he was no-one, nothing. He was no longer even independent, but had reverted to a childhood dependence on his parents. The humiliation, the degradation of it all. Not only that, he had a terminal disease, and now his enemies were preventing him from getting the treatment that might prolong his life. A look into this world might help explain the gratification that Gassy found in shooting Margaret Tobin. In the court room, he tried not to let this show on his face, but it was obvious in how he continually referred to Margaret Tobin as 'the victim'. This phrase seemed to give him a particular pleasure.

It is human nature to look for someone to blame whenever there is a tragedy, to assume that every mishap or disaster might have been prevented if only someone had done something other than what they did. We can never know whether Margaret Tobin's life might have been saved if Gassy had been appropriately treated early in his illness, or if his application for a gun licence had been disallowed, or if a thorough investigation had been made of the suspicious disturbance at the Brisbane Convention Centre, or if the medical profession did a better job of looking after its own, or if the Medical Board of New South Wales went to greater efforts to monitor the wellbeing of deregistered doctors, or if . . .

'Isn't it frightening to think that help can't find its way to a psychiatrist?' says a psychiatrist, a friend of Margaret's from her Victorian days. 'There is a man behind this and he didn't get treatment.' Even in retrospect, however, it's difficult see how this might have happened, given the differences in opinion about Gassy's diagnosis in the 1990s – even at the end of his lengthy deregistration process, the Medical Tribunal was unable to come to a clear finding about Gassy's psychiatric state. Under such conditions, it was not legally possible to enforce treatment. Even if his family had thought him unwell and supported him having treatment, this would have been almost impossible to arrange without his consent. The pendulum has swung so far, in reaction to the days when patients were routinely treated without being asked their consent, that it is extremely difficult to ensure treatment for someone who resists it. If Gassy had been treated with antipsychotic medication, however, this may have taken the edge off his delusions and dampened his desire for retribution.

Should the experts have predicted that Gassy could become so dangerous?

Consider what John Ellard has to say about some of the varieties of dangerousness.

First we encounter the very dangerous, those capable of setting in train widespread killing, raping and destruction. They are, of course, national and religious leaders and captains of industry. If you doubt what I say, then reflect upon the Crusades, which killed millions of people over some centuries, upon any war of national expansion you care to choose and the casualties caused by, say, the manufacturers of cigarettes or those who controlled the industries which discharged huge quantities of mercury into the sea. The very dangerous rarely figure in discussions of this kind, for often they are the pillars supporting the social structures in which they exist and to give them a psychiatric diagnosis would be likely to amount to blasphemy, heresy or criminal libel depending upon where you happen to live.

Regarding the category of psychotically dangerous, Ellard says:

. . . if the brain is sufficiently diseased then its owner may begin to make serious mistakes about the world, believing, for example, that innocent civilians are out to kill him. Such a person may well defend himself, as many of us would. Confronted by such a dire threat, he gets in first . . . Here again social forces are important. Since deinstitutionalisation is the order of the day, it is important to those implementing that policy to assert that people with psychotic illnesses present no more danger than is presented by a random sample of the population. The facts are not quite like that; most psychotic people are perfectly harmless, but there is a small subset who are very dangerous indeed.

Now it seems obvious that Gassy belongs to this small subset. Whether that could have been predicted early in the course of his illness is not clear. In 1997, John Woodforde warned in an affidavit there was a risk of 'aggressive or violent behaviour' if Gassy acted in response to his delusional beliefs. But many people with persecutory delusions never enact violence. The New South Wales Medical Board deals regularly with cases involving delusional doctors. It is extremely rare for such cases to involve murder.

On 11 February 1993, Gassy gave a lecture to staff at Pacific House. The subject was the management of violent patients. He began it with a quiz. The first question was: psychiatrists cannot predict violence – true or false? His answer, according to notes taken by a colleague at the time, was that violence is very difficult to predict. It is more likely when the patient has a history of recent violent acts, talks of violence or makes threats, or their family has a fear of violence.

On the basis of Gassy's own words, in this lecture, it is clear that the people on Gassy's hit list have good reason to be fearful, as indeed many are. So long as Gassy lives, they will have reason to feel uneasy.

The other thing that could be safely predicted, on the basis of what is known about delusional disorder, is that Gassy would not accept the jury's verdict.

The disorder, according to one psychiatric text, is often marked by a determination to succeed against all the odds, a tendency to identify barriers as conspiracies, an endless crusading spirit to right a wrong, and the belief that defeat is unacceptable. Rather than surrender, the paranoid person appeals as often as the legal system permits.

By their very nature, rare and unusual disasters are more difficult to prevent than everyday tragedies. But that doesn't mean that they are not worth inspecting for possible lessons.

In October 2000, a 34-year-old psychiatrist in London called Daksha Emson picked up a knife to stab first her three-month-old baby Freya, and then herself. She then covered them both in accelerant and set it alight. Freya died of smoke inhalation; her mother survived another three weeks in a burns unit but died without regaining consciousness. At the time of her death, Daksha was in the grips of a psychosis associated with her bipolar affective disorder. It had been triggered by her postnatal condition and aggravated by psychosocial stresses, including family tensions.

The response of the National Health Service (NHS) and the psychiatric profession was not to close their doors and shut down debate. Instead, a full inquiry was held, with the aim of drawing broad lessons and understanding. It investigated everything from the impact of Daksha's cultural background – she was the eldest child of Indian parents who emigrated to England when she was nine – to the fear of discrimination which discouraged her from being open about her condition and getting appropriate help. It noted the stigma within the psychiatric profession towards mental illness, both with regards to patients and to unwell colleagues. 'If the NHS cannot look after a psychiatrist with manic depression what hope is there for anyone else?' the inquiry asked in its report.

'Inevitably Daksha was seen first and foremost as a doctor, a psychiatrist and a colleague leading to an underestimate of the level of risk indicated by her personal history, the nature of her enduring mental illness and her current circumstances,' the report continued.

'This tragedy deserves the attention of all of those in the NHS, the medical profession, medical education and social care who could have organised things differently and thereby might have saved the life of this young doctor and her baby and others like her.'

The inquiry recommended action to reduce the stigma associated with mental health problems, to improve the care for doctors with mental health problems and to improve occupational health services for NHS employees.

Will Australian health services and psychiatrists go to similar lengths to examine the lessons from Gassy's story? Unlikely, judging by the reluctance of the Royal Australian and New Zealand College of Psychiatrists to draw attention to the Gassy case. They are too scared. Scared of Gassy, scared of doing anything which might further inflame prejudices about psychiatry. It is now many years since the late William Dibden, a former college president and a former director of South Australia's mental health services, wrote: 'It is a striking thing that psychiatrists are extremely ambiguously regarded in our society and that being referred to a psychiatrist is still a matter of shame or humiliation.' All these years later, psychiatrists still seem to find it somehow shameful that one of their own should develop a mental illness. Surveys suggest they would rather self-prescribe than reveal their problems to a colleague.

The irony, of course, is that such attitudes and behaviour only re-inforce the stigma which surrounds mental illness. When psychiatrists are reluctant to acknowledge mental illness in their own ranks, how can they expect the rest of society to do any better at tackling it?

Surely Gassy's story highlights the need for better support gener-ally for health professionals who often work under stressful, difficult conditions. Surveys have documented high rates of stress among psy-chiatrists, many of whom face verbal and physical abuse as part of the job. One survey of trainee psychiatrists found about one-third reported that at least one patient under their care had killed them-selves in the previous year.

Ian Hickie, Margaret's friend and colleague, believes his profession has been reluctant to examine the story of Gassy's terrible down-fall. Amongst other things, he believes psychiatry should be actively discussing whether Gassy should be forced to have treatment in prison.

'It's collective denial,' Hickie says. 'It's, "We understand it but we won't discuss it with anyone else in case you misunderstand it".'

'Where is the learning? The thing is already a tragedy but it is a total tragedy if there is no learning out of it. We don't know if this could have been prevented, this is a very unusual case. But the issues raised by the case shouldn't be ignored. The danger is that it will be seen as a one-off, odd case of no further relevance, and yet there are many unresolved issues.'

18

Perils of leadership

It is telling that the ancient linguistic root of 'to lead' means 'to go forth, die', according to Ronald A. Heifetz, a man with broad perspectives on the subject of leadership. A psychiatrist and accomplished cellist, Heifetz is cofounder of the Centre for Public Leadership at the John F. Kennedy School of Government at Harvard University in the United States. He has researched, taught and written widely on the challenges and difficulties facing leaders. One of his books, *Leadership Without Easy Answers,* has been reprinted at least a dozen times since 1994.

The fatalistic origins of the word reflect more than its military associations. Leadership can also be dangerous outside war zones, warns Heifetz. In a chapter with the chillingly prescient title 'Assassination', he explores the costs to leaders of challenging the status quo. 'Leaders and authority figures get attacked, dismissed, silenced, and sometimes assassinated because they come to represent loss, real or perceived, to those members of the community who feel that they have gotten, or might get, the bad end of a bargain,' he wrote. The severe distress associated with change can make people cruel, he says. Leaders are always failing somebody. '. . . someone exercising leadership will be shouldering the pains and aspirations of a community and frustrating at least some people within it,' he says. 'Adaptive work often demands loss. Even a bright new innovation or scientific discovery will meet resistance from those who feel threatened.'

As a young woman, Margaret Tobin chose to specialise in a particularly difficult field. The mental health sector was then, as it is now, stigmatised, demoralised, overwhelmed by demand, underwhelmed by resources, and unable to boast of many political or powerful champions. At a relatively early stage in her career, Margaret set her sights on becoming a leader in her chosen field. It was a considered decision. She knew there would be some price to pay. Indeed, she wrote of the personal and professional costs involved in leaving behind clinical work to become a manager. Your medical peers will regard you with suspicion, she often told other doctors contemplating such a move. Running mental health services is a spectacularly relentless and thankless job, removed from the satisfaction that a clinician can derive from contact with patients and their families, and vulnerable to political and bureaucratic knee-capping. But Margaret thought she could achieve more, influencing resource allocation and policy, than by caring for individual patients. It was also a choice which appealed to her personality and skills. She was used, from early in her life, to setting the pace and mobilising the troops.

Margaret lost her life because she did not resile from difficulty or from tough decisions. She would not turn a blind eye when confronted by a colleague with problems. Many others in a similar position would have thought twice – or not at all – about contacting the Medical Board about Gassy. They would have taken the easier option; traditionally that has been the way in the health system and medical culture, both of which struggle to confront problems in health professionals' behaviour or practice. John Ellard has written of knowing of several instances in large hospitals in which a health professional's illness was discussed widely – but never with the affected person. But that was not part of Margaret's personal or professional character. For her, dealing with Gassy was just one of many difficult decisions to be made.

Music, according to Heifetz, teaches that dissonance is an integral part of harmony. 'Without conflict and tension, music lacks dynamism and movement. The composer and the improvisational musician alike must contain the dissonance within a frame that holds the audience's attention until resolution is found.' Margaret, who loved classical music and opera, deliberately pushed people beyond their comfort zones. It was how she worked, trying to force individuals and groups to re-examine longstanding behaviour and beliefs, in order to make changes. Heifetz advises leaders to keep a clear demarcation between their personal and professional roles, to avoid internalising conflict. 'Exercising leadership and bearing personal responsibility requires seeing the difference between oneself and one's role. A person who leads must interpret people's responses to his actions as responses to the role he plays and the perspective he represents.' However, many people were unable to make that distinction between Margaret and her professional role. They attacked the woman herself. Gassy was not the first nor the last to assassinate Margaret; the others, however, were inflicting character assassination. 'The negative views of her were often formed with little knowledge,' says John Brayley, an Adelaide psychiatrist whom Margaret mentored in leadership and management. 'By dismissing the person they could dismiss any need to change what they were doing. At the time, every group you would speak to would say change was necessary, but it was other parts of the system that needed to change and what they were doing was fine. By being so critical of Margaret, they didn't really have to account for what they were doing.'

Margaret knew something of the antagonism directed her way. She was stung by a critical letter sent by members of the South Australian branch of the Royal Australian and New Zealand of College of Psychiatrists. On a selection panel in Adelaide, she argued once against employing a particular person because she thought he might be a bully. 'I am going to be the only bully in mental health,' she joked. 'Everyone else has to be nice.' But sometimes her close colleagues hid the magnitude of the maligning from her. They thought she had enough else on her plate to worry about. Undoubtedly, the attacks were also encouraged by Margaret's own style. She was in a hurry; she had a sharp tongue, and little tolerance for fools, pomposity or roadblocks. She could make mistakes. She was far from being a perfect leader, as human beings generally are. 'Each of us has blind spots that require the vision of others. Each of us has passions that need to be contained by others,' says Ronald A. Heifetz. Margaret knew that she needed offsiders who could act as foils.

Doubtless her gender played a role in the antagonism. Heifetz warns that challenging people to face harsh realities can be brutal work. Men who take on such jobs are often called strong, powerful leaders. Women in such positions are often called something else altogether. Teresa Heinz Kerry, wife of the US presidential candidate John Kerry, once noted that a woman who has opinions is called opinionated, while a man who has opinions is called smart and well-informed. Helen Garner's book about a young man killed by his girlfriend, *Joe Cinque's Consolation*, was published during the Gassy trial. The girlfriend's conviction of manslaughter rather than murder and her relatively short jail term didn't particularly surprise Emily Telfer, Peter Brebner's offsider and a keen reader. Her response to the book was: 'I have seen many cases where women seem to get an easier deal or a more sympathetic ear.' Society expects women to be kind and gentle, and this can be a double-edged sword.

The terrible irony of Margaret's death is, of course, that it only reinforces everything she worked so hard to combat – the stigma of mental illness and community fears of the mentally ill. It was a double whammy when news broke that a former psychiatrist had been arrested. All those jokes about psychiatrists being madder than their patients were given another opportunity for an airing. Tragically, Margaret's murder also exemplified the failure of the health system to direct mental health care to those who need it. In the years after his deregistration, Gassy attended dozens and dozens of medical appointments. He must have cost Medicare a small fortune. But not one of these appointments led to him getting the care that he really needed.

For many, the tragedy is that a life which still had so much to offer was cut short. Margaret was in her prime, both personally and professionally, at the time of her murder. We shall never know what impact she might have been able to achieve in South Australia, or nationally. Many expected that she might end up as an international player, working for the World Health Organization or some such agency.

Discussing a possible job advising the WHO on mental health services for Pacific rim countries, she had joked wickedly with one colleague about having the title 'director of the Pacific rim'. Margaret had achieved so much in a short time, but there was so much more to do, wrote Janice Wilson, a friend and psychiatrist from New Zealand, in an obituary. 'She was on a roll, she was going to continue to make a significant difference to the lives of people. Her death is such a loss and such a waste. I will miss her terribly for her support, her clear thinking about and analysis of complex social issues, her ability to articulate the way forward, but mostly I will miss her for her passion, her humour, her forthrightness, her sense of fun and her sense of the absurd.'

In another obituary, Ian Hickie wrote that Margaret's family and close friends thought her 'determined, bossy and uncompromising'. He said:

She loved being in charge and relished the opportunity to put into action the skills she had developed in specialist psychiatry, medical administration and business leadership. It is difficult to describe Tobin in the past tense. Her focus was always on the future, the work that was yet to be done. She prided herself on the development of genuine, at times frank and tense partnerships between leading professionals, service managers and key consumer and carer representatives. Often in health the emphasis is on the generation of new ideas rather than their implementation. Tobin made it clear that ideas that were never implemented were useless . . . The greatest tragedy to arise out of these sad events will be if Tobin's life is remembered not for who she was, the relationships she formed or the careers she fostered but for the disturbing way in which she was taken from us.

Three months before she died, Margaret was interviewed by the *Advertiser*. She told the journalist that positive progress was being made in mental health reform in South Australia, and she expected better services would become available in the next three to five years. In the wake of her death, however, progress came to a crash-stop.

Eventually, Jonathan Phillips was appointed to pick up the reins of leadership. But it was not a happy arrangement, and he quit after much soul-searching in May 2005, believing the state still was not ready for serious mental health reform. At this stage of his career, he did not have time to waste beating his head against the wall. John Brayley, the acting deputy general manager of the Flinders Medical Centre and one of Margaret's former protégées, was then appointed to the job. And so the revolving door syndrome continued.

Margaret's name lives on in a number of awards for young psychiatrists and medical administrators. Her work helped lead to the development of courses for trainee psychiatrists in leadership and management. But for many, her real legacy lies with those people whom she influenced into taking leadership roles in the public sector.

Sitting in her office at the Prince of Wales Hospital in Sydney, Florence Mansfield keeps her voice quiet and struggles to control the tears rising up in her brown eyes as she describes how Margaret pushed and extended her, personally and professionally. 'I don't think I would have progressed in my career if I hadn't met Margaret Tobin,' says Mansfield, who is now a senior manager of mental health services. She began her career as a nurse. It was something she wanted to do from when she was a young girl visiting her uncle in a psychiatric hospital. He was suffering from his time as a prisoner of war during World War II.

'Margaret had a huge impact on my life. She had the ability to single out people who had an open mind and could use vision, and would challenge them, in a constructive way. It wasn't that she liked people who would just do what she wanted. Because she always questioned, she made you question too. She enjoyed watching people better themselves. I think she got a lot of satisfaction out of that. A lot of people don't know that about her.

'She gave me a vision for mental health care. It wasn't a matter anymore of just going to work and doing x, y, z. It was doing that but also thinking about how it could be done better. She was absolutely after the best mental health care that you could provide.

'A lot of people didn't like Margaret Tobin. I accept that, but I thought they didn't know her. I think probably Margaret believed the higher she got, the more she could do. A lot of people just saw her as being ambitious. She upset a lot of people, let's face it. She brought about change and a lot of people don't like change; she looked for the positives in change. You can't do that sort of a job and not have enemies; that is the way it is.'

Lucy Chen, a medically qualified health services researcher who worked with Margaret at St George Hospital, was another who felt a huge personal loss from the death of her friend and mentor. 'I had been working in the health system for more than ten years when I met her,' says Chen. 'She was the only executive who would give me the time and advice, who would think about things from my viewpoint, about my future development. I still miss her. When I am stuck in an issue, I wish I could pick up the phone and talk to Margaret.'

This sentiment is shared by Rae Conway, a nursing manager who often turned to Margaret for advice about career and work issues at St George Hospital. Margaret's death changed some of Conway's attitudes. She decided that life was too short to spend so much of it on work, and made a conscious effort to put more time into connections with family and friends. Conway keeps close the goodbye note that Margaret wrote when leaving Sydney. 'It has been a real pleasure getting to know you,' Margaret wrote neatly on stationery illustrated by little blue birds. 'I have been grateful for your unfailing good humour, support for my endeavours, hard work and huge contribution to what has been achieved. You have been a very valuable member of the team. I shall watch your career with interest.' About eighteen months after Margaret's death, Conway's career took a leap forward when she was appointed to run a Sydney hospital. She wished Margaret could have seen her progress, and thought back to how Margaret used to tell her, you could manage anything you want. Margaret had meant that if you can manage mental health services, you can manage anything because mental health is so hard.

Margaret gave her life to work – literally, in the end – but it is her personal qualities that many remember. 'I have a sense of her tremendous zest for life, and her energy, and her commitment,' says Cristina Thompson, a manager who worked at St George Hospital at the same time as Margaret. 'You don't meet people that often in life who have a passion. One of the things I remember fondly about her is that she wasn't lukewarm.'

When Di Skene first struck up a friendship with 'the queen of mental health', she was quite nervous about it. Di worked at a hospital in Adelaide and knew of the strong feelings Margaret aroused, and didn't want to get caught up in the politics of it all. They were careful to keep their friendship separate from work. When Di thinks of Margaret now, she remembers the woman with a daggy sense of humour and the day they made a train excursion with their husbands. Margaret struck up a conversation with a young woman on the train who was clearly finding life difficult. She had left home young and was working in a supermarket to put herself through study. Di watched Margaret tuck the teenager under her wing, and bring her along on their day – chatting, looking at shops and having lunch. Margaret was genuinely interested in the woman's life and how she had overcome various hardships. But she was not the type to wear her heart on her sleeve.

In his book, Ronald A. Heifetz also writes of the need for leaders to have sanctuaries where they can restore their sense of purpose, put issues in perspective, and regain courage and heart. 'When serving as the repository of many conflicting aspirations, a person can lose himself in the role by failing to distinguish his inner voice from the voices that clamour for attention outside. Partners can help greatly, as can a run, a quiet walk, or a prayer to break the spell cast by the frenzy on the floor. Just as leadership demands a strategy of mobilising people, it also requires a strategy of deploying and restoring one's own spiritual resources.' Margaret chose for her partner someone able to provide that sense of sanctuary. When Don Scott speaks of his time with Margaret, he returns again and again to the image of her arriving home exhausted on Friday nights. His job was to pour red wine and food into her, and tuck her into bed. Another of his jobs was to buy fresh flowers every Friday, so Margaret could enjoy them over the weekend. Don also remembers how she sometimes laughed so hard at the television show, *The Glass House*, that tears ran down her face. Sometimes she would literally fall off the lounge with laughter. It was infectious. Margaret's death deprived Don of more than his wife, lover and best friend. He also lost the person who helped bring meaning and stability to his days. Counselling might have helped, but he didn't feel comfortable seeking therapy from South Australian psychiatrists in case they'd been his wife's adversaries. He tried to be philosophical – that is life and you just have to deal with the hand you get – but it wasn't easy.

When Gassy was convicted, Margaret's brothers and sisters hoped this would mean they could begin to put the tragedy behind them. 'We will all miss her in our own way,' Margaret's sister Mary Catherine wrote in a victim impact statement read to the court.

> To some of us she was a mentor or a figure head; to others, she was a fashion consultant, a relationship guide or a friend. Waiting for the trial, it could be said that part of all our lives had been frozen in time, put on hold, unable to move forward until some resolution had been obtained . . . now that the matter has been resolved, I expect that most of us will move on and gain some semblance of normality in our lives. For my mother, though, I imagine that it will be the hardest, because when it is your child, even time doesn't heal.

Jean has felt freer since seeing the news of Gassy's conviction in writing. Finally, she has felt able to return to Mass. She has re-entered the life of her community and the various clubs with which she is involved. She has rediscovered the joy of gardening, and delights in the chatter of bright parrots outside her windows.

September and October are always particularly difficult for Jean. The twenty-third of September brings the anniversary of Margaret's birth, and three days later it is Gerard's birthday. And there is no respite from the anniversary of that dreadful day in October.

She dreams a lot.

'In all my dreams, wherever I am, I am lost,' Jean tells a friend on the phone one day. 'I can't get back to where I want to be. Psychologically, I will never get back to where I was.'

Update

In the second half of 2005, three men spent long hours poring over the thousands of pages of transcript documenting the Gassy trial. They examined the facts, as they had been presented during the voir dire and then the trial before the jury, and they considered the points of law that had arisen along the way. The deliberations of the three men, who presumably were of similar intelligence, training and experience, took them to quite different destinations. One became convinced there had been a miscarriage of justice. The other two thought otherwise.

During a two-day appeal hearing in June 2005, Gassy had argued a number of grounds for appeal against his conviction, including:

- That the two warrants issued for the searches of the Oyster Bay home were invalid and that the evidence then obtained should therefore have been excluded.
- That he had been wrongly denied access to legal representation during a part of the voir dire because Justice Vanstone had ruled that counsel were unable to appear at the voir dire unless they were also briefed to appear at the entire trial.
- That a number of Justice Vanstone's statements to the jury,

especially her final comments shortly before the guilty verdict was returned, had been prejudicial.

Justice Bruce Debelle, one of the three judges in the Court of Criminal Appeal who considered Gassy's appeal, concluded that it should be upheld on two grounds. In summary these were that:

- Justice Vanstone's final comments to the jury were seriously flawed and clearly spelt out a line of reasoning to the jury which would lead to a guilty verdict. She had given the jury a prejudicial resumé of the prosecution case rather than objective, impartial assistance. 'In the result, the appellant lost a fair chance of an acquittal,' he held. 'The errors associated with the supplementary direction are so fundamental and have caused such a miscarriage of justice that there has not been a fair trial according to law,' he wrote.
- Justice Vanstone had erred in holding that Gassy could not be represented during the voir dire unless he was for the rest of the trial also. This led to a miscarriage of justice as the defendant was not aware of the extent to which he could test evidence on the voir dire. A counsel might have persuaded the judge to exclude some of the evidence. 'Had the evidence of a number of identification witnesses been excluded, the prosecution case would have been that much weaker,' Justice Debelle said. 'There is a real possibility that exclusion of that evidence would have had a material effect upon the reasoning of the jury. That conclusion is reinforced by the fact that the jury took some time to reach its verdict . . . In my view, the fact that the appellant was denied legal representation when he had legal representation available constituted a grave miscarriage of justice in this trial . . . In my view, the refusal to permit the appellant to be represented at this important stage of the voir dire hearing dealing with evidence capable of having a critical bearing on the trial was so grave that the trial was fundamentally flawed. If it be said that this is to adopt an unrealistically high standard for the proper conduct of a fair trial, I would conclude that the failure to allow representation had the consequence that the appellant lost a chance fairly open to him of being acquitted.'

Justices David Bleby and Richard White, however, entertained little sympathy for the view that the trial judge's final comments had been prejudicial. They felt it was appropriate for her to have suggested how the jury could approach the evidence. She was not suggesting a line of reasoning leading to a guilty verdict, they said, but merely an orderly approach to decision-making in what was a circumstantial case of some complexity. 'All the judge did was to suggest a process to the jury. At no stage did she suggest the conclusion that should be reached at each stage.'

The two judges also dismissed Gassy's complaint that Justice Vanstone had undermined his case by telling the jury that he had made mistakes in his summing up, but not detailing them.

Justice Vanstone had told the jury in her summing up: 'In Dr Gassy's address to you he has not always been accurate in his reference to evidence, and I say that not to criticise him because, as I said to you before, his task is a daunting one. But in addition he has sometimes put submissions for which there is no evidentiary basis. In what I am about to say I will be very careful to be accurate and you will know that you can rely on my statements of the evidence. If I am inaccurate, after you have retired Mr Brebner or Dr Gassy will correct me and then I will bring you back to correct what I said.'

Rather than undermining Gassy, the appeal court judges felt Justice Vanstone was helping him by alerting the jury to the fact that his errors could be due to the enormity of his task representing himself. If Justice Vanstone had explained each error to the jury it would have been prejudicial to Gassy's case. 'Such a lengthy exercise would have focused the juror's attention on the weaknesses in the appellant's case and his credibility would have been compromised. There would be a risk that instead of remaining neutral, the overall balance of the summing up would have tilted in favour of the prosecution.'

The judges also dismissed Gassy's contention that Justice Vanstone's statement to the jury – 'well, if you believe that Telstra cannot get it wrong then you will have to consider who might have been in the Gassy household at that time to have made that call' – destroyed his alibi in the eyes of the jury. The trial judge was entitled to raise a range of possible scenarios, they said.

But the two appeal court judges agreed with Justice Debelle that Justice Vanstone had erred in ruling that Gassy could not have legal representation for only a part of the voir dire. They felt it was understandable that someone might want to be legally represented on preliminary legal arguments but still conduct their own defence at trial. There was no good reason why the appellant should have been denied that right to limited representation. But this did not necessarily mean the appellant had been denied a chance of acquittal. The two judges noted that the ruling related to only eleven of the voir dire's 30 sitting days, when Gassy was without representation but required it and was prepared to pay for it himself.

While some important issues were heard during this period, the judges noted that Gassy continued to have access to his counsel, the Mauritian-born Roger de Robillard, inside and outside of court during this time. They also noted that when Gassy was later given leave to have de Robillard appear in the voir dire, it was Gassy himself who subsequently chose to terminate those services and to then represent himself. The two judges noted that Gassy had shown a clear grasp of legal principles during his trial and appeal and had been articulate in arguing them. 'In all the circumstances it is not possible to find that the appellant lost a chance fairly open to him of being acquitted by virtue of his failure to be represented by counsel at the relevant time,' they held. 'Although he was wrongly denied representation when he wanted it, there has been no miscarriage of justice.'

Justices Bleby and White also disagreed with Justice Vanstone about the search warrants executed on the Gassy residence. They held that both were invalid: the first because of the incorrect address (replacing its first page with the correct address did not make it valid); and the second because the paperwork had not been properly completed. However, the judges said this did not mean the evidence obtained during the two searches should have been excluded, as the contravention of the law by the police was not deliberate.

In conclusion, Justices Bleby and White dismissed the appeal, confident there was no reasonable possibility of an unsafe or unsatisfactory verdict. 'The prosecution case, although circumstantial, was a strong one.'

Their decision was delivered three days before Christmas. By then Gassy was already planning other legal forays.

In the first weeks of 2006, he initiated proceedings alleging that the Department for Correctional Services in South Australia was trying to kill him. ABC Radio reported from the Adelaide District Court that Gassy was using the *Freedom of Information Act* to gain access to documents which he claimed contained evidence that prison health staff were attempting to murder him by depriving him of lifesaving treatment for AIDS. He was also busy preparing an application to seek leave to appeal over his conviction to the High Court of Australia.

So long as he remains delusional, Gassy will find no end of opportunity for feeding his paranoia. Anyone who has dealings with him, whether prison staff, doctors or fellow prisoners, may fall into his focus. Gassy will continue to nurture his grievances and to put his case before the courts for as long as he is able. A bleak future awaits. He has few visitors, save his loyal elderly parents, who regularly make the trek from Sydney to South Australia. They continue to tell people that their son has been the victim of a conspiracy, and worry about who will care for him when they are gone.

Epilogue

One story of how I came to write this book begins at the breakfast table, when I picked up the newspaper and couldn't believe what I was reading about a murder in Adelaide.

I had met Margaret Tobin for the first time just five days earlier, at a workshop at the Hilton Hotel at Melbourne Airport. She was one of about 50 eminent health and medical experts asked to come up with some clever ideas for how to encourage systematic use of reliable evidence in health care policy and practice. I was the scribe hired to provide an account of the day. As is usual with these sort of things, the organisers had a pretty good idea of what they wanted out of the workshop before it even began.

I was pleased to meet Margaret in person because it was a chance to arrange an interview with her for an article I was researching for *The Bulletin* magazine on workplace-based screening for depression. We had previously chatted by phone when I was researching a profile of her close friend, Ian Hickie, for the magazine *Australian Doctor*. Then I had thought her comments refreshingly direct for a bureaucrat. But it was only with the benefit of hindsight that I realised later, looking back on those notes, just how upfront she had really been.

I can clearly picture the quizzical look Margaret gave me when I introduced myself that morning in Melbourne. She looked up from the papers on the table in front of her, offered half a smile, and seemed almost to look right through me. I was not sure whether she was taking my measure and having a bit of a chuckle about it too, or whether she was simply distracted and thinking of something else altogether.

The next day, with me back in Sydney and her in Adelaide, we exchanged emails about interview times, and settled on the following Monday afternoon as one possibility. When this didn't eventuate, I assumed she must have been busy in the fallout from the Bali bombing. I missed the news that she was dying at about the time I was hoping she might call.

The other story behind this book is that Margaret died three days and eighteen months after my brother Jeff. He was 34, with a gorgeous young daughter, when he killed himself, in the grip of a terrible depression and anxiety which had followed an incredible high. I had been dreading that phone call for years.

Jeff had bipolar. In our last telephone conversation, a few days before his death, he said he had never really understood what that meant. Jeff was a classic case of someone who slipped through all the cracks – in family, in health services, in workplaces, in community. When he was manic, he had little insight into his condition or his need for treatment. The terribly irony is that his death occurred during a time when he understood that he needed treatment and care. I wish that I'd known then about the mental health first aid booklet produced by Margaret and Karin Myhill in South Australia. Amongst other things, it gives advice for dealing with people suspected of being suicidal. I wish I'd known to ask 'are you safe?', as the booklet suggests, in my last conversation with Jeff. I had sensed he wasn't but didn't know how to broach the subject.

When you are grieving yourself, you are more sensitive to other people's losses. Margaret's death came as such a shock. As I spoke to some of her colleagues and friends, I became more curious and wanted to find out more about this woman with an interesting, powerful personality. It soon became clear that Margaret's life also told a larger history, of the changes that have occurred in mental health care and of the struggles faced by change agents in deeply conservative health systems.

As I interviewed Margaret's former colleagues and friends, many choked up or broke down in tears as they told what her loss meant for them personally. While I knew that more than a few people hadn't liked her at all, it also became clear that Margaret had a vast network of colleagues and friends, and made time in her hectic schedule to mentor many.

Her own commitment to public mental health services inspired many others to remain in what is often a difficult and thankless task. Greg Aldridge, who worked closely with Margaret at St George and went on to a senior management position elsewhere, was not alone in saying: 'She made me whatever I have become.' Her murder was all the more shocking for him because he had at one stage been a close friend of Eric Gassy, with whom he worked at both Bankstown and St George hospitals.

Margaret's family – her husband Don, her mother Jean and her brothers and sisters – were extremely generous in sharing their memories, despite the pain this involved. Jean has a thing about blue wrens and, over the years, Margaret gave her many cards and paintings featuring the dainty little birds. Whenever Jean sees parrots now, their bright colours and chatter remind her of Margaret. She takes such joy from the birds who gather in her colourful garden. The warble of magpies makes Don think of Margaret. She loved the sound.

For me, it is pelicans. Jeff once told me, when he was staying with us while in an extreme mania, that he was one. When I later gave him a Christmas card with a black and white photo that I had taken of a pelican, he rewarded me with a look of real appreciation. He felt that, just once, I understood.

Some of Margaret's colleagues and friends, including Christine Charles, John McGrath and Mick Reid, also described their own experiences watching family members struggle with a mental illness. More than a few times, I learnt about other young people who had reached a place where they felt their only option was to take an early exit.

All of these stories helped me feel my own grief. Sometimes I treasured the sadness that arrived with someone else's sadness because it brought me closer to Jeff. He was not forgotten. And sometimes, it was easier to watch others grieve than to live it myself. Like many journalists, I prefer to tell other people's stories than my own. It is easier, perhaps even cowardly, to question and to listen than to speak and reveal.

As I watched Don agitate and irritate various bureaucrats in his determination to have memorials appropriately dedicated to Margaret, I thought of how this book helped fill my own need to make a memorial to Jeff. I was also reminded that grief can be destructive. It can illuminate differences, and push people apart as well as bring them closer. The effects of tragic loss can take years, perhaps even lifetimes, to be understood. How many lives have been shaped by the griefs, often unspoken, of their parents or grandparents?

Margaret learnt earlier than most that life is a perishable gift with an invisible use-by date. So many times I asked the question of Margaret's friends and colleagues – why was she so driven? Mostly they could only hazard a guess. My own guess, for what it is worth, is based on my own experience of losing a brother. When her brother Gerard died, Margaret was at an age when most people have no real appreciation for life's fragility. The Catholic sense of duty to commu-nity already ran in her veins, and perhaps Gerard's shortened life strengthened a resolve to make the most of her time. Margaret's col-leagues often spoke admiringly of her energy and ability to eat up long days and come back hungry for more. But those who knew her best also knew this was not as easy as she tried to make it look. Her impatience for change often left her bone weary.

Sitting in court, those many long weeks in Adelaide, I watched the utter devastation of the Gassy family. Whatever else he is and has done, Eric is a son and brother, too. Instead of enjoying a peaceful retirement, Xavier and Maud Gassy spent long months in Adelaide, exhausting their finances and last years of life in aid of their son. Court rooms are more used to seeing defendants whose family are not able or willing to provide that level of care and support.

Xavier and Maud chatted often with me during the trial. They were friendly and, when I told them about this book, initially agreed to be interviewed. It became clear, however, that they did not really understand what would be involved when Maud suggested that surely the book could be written without using anyone's names. Later, she was unhappy to break the news that they could not help with the book after all. She did not like to go back on her word, but her son had told them not to speak to me. My son, he has been through so much, said Maud, he doesn't trust anyone. I could say nothing to reassure them, knowing that this book would only heighten Gassy's paranoia.

One Friday afternoon I was uncomfortably reminded of the memorable opening lines of a slim book called *The Journalist and the Murderer*, which is fat with insights into my trade. 'Every journalist who is not too stupid or too full of himself to notice what is going on knows that what he does is morally indefensible,' wrote the New York-based author, Janet Malcolm. 'He is a kind of confidence man, preying on people's vanity, ignorance or loneliness, gaining their trust and betraying them without remorse.' Journalists quote these lines so often, they must sense a truth to them. Malcolm, the daughter of a psychiatrist, has also written widely on what she once called 'the decrepit mansion of psychoanalysis'.

On this Friday afternoon, I was standing outside the court building asking Mick Standing why Gassy, after putting so much careful planning into the murder itself, had let his guard drop so much that he was caught by the cameras at the Renmark servo. The detective thought that Gassy had been done in by his own adrenaline. 'He got cocky,' he said. 'That is why people like me catch people like him.' It was an awkward moment when Xavier and Maud suddenly emerged behind us. Had they heard Standing's speculation? Evidently not. Maud put one hand on his shoulder and another on me as she wished us a good weekend. And give your husband a hug, she told me. As they walked away, I realised the TV cameras had been waiting to pounce. The elderly couple scurried along the footpath, holding newspapers over their head as the cameramen pursued them. I followed the Gassys into the Central Market, apologising on behalf of my industry. Don't worry, they said, they are just doing their job.

Only later was I struck by my hypocrisy. Of course, this book can only add to the grief of the Gassys and for that I am sorry.

In May 2005, after a long magazine article on the case, Tom Young, the honorary consul for Mauritius, was moved to write a letter to the editor, stating that Xavier and Maud Gassy were among the victims of the crime. During their son's trial, he had developed a profound sympathy for 'these distraught but very supportive elderly people'. Once they must have been so proud of their son's medical achievements. Now they would live with his actions for the rest of their lives. 'How sad,' wrote Young.

As I researched Margaret's history, the questions I asked about her work were also helping with the questions I wanted answered for myself. Why is it so difficult to get good care for people with mental illness? Why are so many Australians with mental illness killing themselves? Why doesn't mental health rate amongst the politicians?

As I pondered Eric Gassy's absolute belief in his own sanity, I was reminded that my brother held, at some stages, a similar conviction. When he was manic, Jeff had little insight into his condition. He was convinced he was fine, and that the problem lay with the rest of us. He managed to convince at least one psychiatrist that this was the case. One of the reasons it is so difficult to get good care for the mentally ill is that they often are adamant they don't need it. And their families are often locked in denial. Anything else can seem like betrayal. The stigma and ignorance which surround mental illness make it even more difficult for friends and families to reach out for help.

Margaret's career tells the story of the huge changes which have occurred in mental health in recent decades. There have been so many good intentions, so much rhetoric. But still there is so much suffering, so much loss. We do not have the tools to prevent or effectively treat much mental illness. But with the knowledge that already exists, it should be possible to do a much better job than currently occurs. The number of recent reports that have documented the failings in care for people with mental illness would fill an old-fashioned phone box. They all tell a similar tale – of a system so over-stretched in trying to meet the demand for crisis and acute services that it has little capacity to focus on early intervention and rehabilitation, much less prevention. As one report puts it, the focus of consumer rights has 'moved from open human rights abuses to problems of neglect'.

It turns out that my brother, with his cheeky grin and ratbag laugh, who was such a one-off character to us, was not so special at all. His story – of falling between the cracks of fragmented systems of care, of long hours waiting in emergency departments, of ending up in police custody when he needed medical care, of hating the side effects of his medications, of adverse experiences which engendered a profound mistrust of the medical system, of despair and confusion – is far too common.

The history of mental health teaches that when reformers dream of a better future, they are reaching for the stars. Translating visions into reality is complex, difficult and unpredictable work. So many variables are involved, there are bound to be failures as well as successes. It is unfortunate that 'deinstitutionalisation' is the one tag that sticks in the community's mind about mental health policies of recent decades. It was only ever meant to be one part of the equation – and arguably the least important part, given that the institutions only saw a relatively small proportion of those with mental illness. There has never been the equivalent catchphrase to describe the need for community-based services to provide for the full range of peoples' needs, from acute and chronic health care to housing, rehabilitation and other support. If there was such a catchphrase, it might have helped capture the imagination of the people and their politicians. As it was, reformers underestimated the immensity of their task. Closing powerful institutions was to prove so difficult that it was unevenly accomplished. Building up strong, effective services in the mainstream health system and broader community has proven far more difficult. One disappointed mental health advocate laments that community-based care is a nice idea – assuming 'the community gives a shit'. Community-based services, involving disparate professional groups and a multitude of sectors and layers of government, will never wield the political power of monolithic institutions. Meanwhile, people with mental illness are less able than many others to fight for their fair share in a health system where resources often are allocated, not according to need or equity, but according to who can capture the most headlines and political attention.

One of the most telling medical investigations of recent times comes from a study linking the hospital, cancer and death records for people treated for a mental illness in Western Australia between 1980 and 1998. It found they died, on average, two to three decades earlier than other Australians. Their suicide rate increased during the period of the study, but was not the major reason for life expectancies more often seen in Africa. This was instead due to their poor physical health, with the findings suggesting they were not as well treated for heart disease and cancer as other Australians. This is such a revealing report because it says that the underfunding and poor state of mental health services is only one part of the story of how we fail the mentally ill. We also fail them at so many other levels.

In Adelaide, I was much struck by the comment of a journalistic colleague, who had met Margaret briefly and been unimpressed by her persona and policies. 'There was a view that she was too soft on people with mental illness, that she didn't put the community first, she put them first,' this colleague said over coffee one day, as if a line can be so neatly drawn between 'them' and 'us'. It is a view which conveniently overlooks that the mentally ill are 'us' and 'ours'. I was reminded so many times when researching this book that few families are untouched at some stage in their history. As Margaret told a journalist a few weeks before her death: 'People need to stop thinking about mental illness as a rare and worrying condition important to somebody else and start thinking that mental health is everybody's business. A person in your family or circle of friends is absolutely certain to get a mental illness of one sort or another and, therefore, it is urgent that the community understands and is sympathetic to mental illness.'

Ultimately, my colleague's comment was helpful because it revealed so much about our views about mental illness. We fear madness. It is the ultimate in loss of control and loss of self. We are so frightened by the thought of losing our minds that we would prefer not to know or to see those who do. We would rather blame them for their problems than look at ourselves. The tragic death of the former high flier Rene Rivkin was widely seen as reflecting the failings of one man. What about the failing of health services and the broader community to care for someone who was so desperate that he was reported to have spent his last days lying in a darkened room crying?

One senior health department executive explains his observation that crises involving mental health patients do not receive the same weight of bureaucratic or political concern as crises involving other patients: 'It's partly because of discriminatory attitudes. The patients aren't seen as being as important as other patients. Someone can be waiting for six hours in an emergency department and it's a bigger scandal than a mental health patient in an acute crisis waiting for four days.'

It seems that little has changed since 1993, when Human Rights Commissioner Brian Burdekin wrote of the mentally ill: 'They suffer from widespread systematic discrimination and are constantly denied the rights and services to which they are entitled. The stigma and suspicion directed at people affected by mental illness is the major barrier to their full and equal enjoyment of life, creating fear and isolation when people are most in need of tolerance and understanding.'

As I read about the depressions, psychoses and other troubles which have developed in the men, women and children who came to this country in search of asylum but instead were locked in immigration detention centres, I cannot help but wonder: if they were developing cancer as a result of their detention, would there be community outrage? Would people care then? Yet their mental health troubles may be just as likely as cancer to cut their lives short.

One evening I listened to Ian Hickie speak on the radio about the shocking case of Cornelia Rau, who was wrongly locked in an immigration detention centre, and who was failed by so many individuals and systems and bureaucracies. It occurred to me that hers is the modern-day version of what happened routinely to psychiatric patients years ago. Many families have stories, whether they know it or not, of relatives with mental illness who were locked away, out of sight and out of mind.

Too often, a similar fate awaits the mentally ill today. They are confined, if not behind bars or walls, then in isolation and hardship by the indifference of the broader community and our political leaders. We have moved so far from a widespread acceptance of the principle that in a civilised society, the strong take some responsibility for the less fortunate. The marginalised and disadvantaged are the inevitable losers when the broader culture and health system promote individualism and self-reliance. We live in a time when compassion is out of fashion. As Brian Burdekin told a journalist from the *Sunday Age* newspaper in late 2004, the mentally ill are 'the forgotten people of the 21st century'.

In 2004, a GP called Andrew Gunn wrote angrily in a medical magazine of his frustrations and difficulties in obtaining psychiatric care and support services for his patients with mental illness. 'Prosperity and pleasantness are common casualties of severe mental illness,' he said. 'The poor, smelly, irritable and homeless are losers in our competitive, dog-eat-dog society, and they know it. They deserve more support, not a death sentence.'

In the months before and after Margaret's murder, the Mental Health Council of Australia conducted a national consultation with over 400 organisations and individuals. When the council published its report, titled *Out of Hospital, Out of Mind!* in 2003, it concluded that:

Despite the efforts of many committed politicians, government officials, service providers and community advocates, we do not have a system of effective or accessible mental health care . . . To simply continue with the current inadequate pace of reform, perpetuate the same inadequate resource base, utilise the same governance structures and fail to invest in innovation and disease prevention, is to condemn many of the most disadvantaged and ill members of our community to many more years of abuse, neglect and very poor mental and physical health.

On the third anniversary of Margaret's death, on 14 October 2005, Don Scott picked a bright pink rose from his garden, slipped it into his lapel, and headed into the centre of Adelaide for a memorial service marking the unveiling of a plaque for Margaret. Many of the guests who mingled on the grassy square in front of the CitiCentre Building were wearing bright clothes as they had been asked. A didgeridoo played, and guests took it in turns to drop red roses and blue irises on the plaque. Don stood out in a lipstick-pink tie which matched his green shirt with pink stripes. 'If I'd known you were wearing that, I mightn't have come,' Mick Standing joked to him.

The following week, another damning report on the state of Australia's mental health services hit the national headlines. Called *Not for Service: Experiences of injustice and despair in mental health care in Australia*, it detailed a 'broken and failing system'.

Its 1,008 pages described many personal tragedies, including numerous reports of patients harming themselves or others after being unable to access appropriate care, as well as systemic problems, such as underfunding and workforce shortages. The available evidence suggested, it concluded, that people with mental illness 'still struggle on a daily basis to access appropriate health care or be treated with respect or dignity when they do enter our health care systems'.

Margaret Tobin's death was a tragedy at so very many levels.

For further information about mental illness, contact:

beyondblue: <www.beyondblue.org.au>
Lifeline 13 11 14 (local call)
Kids Help Line 1800 551 800 (free call)
SANE Mental Health Information Line 1800 688 382 (Monday to Friday, 9 am to 5 pm)
New South Wales Rural Mental Health Support Line 1800 201 123.

To find out what mental health services are available in your area call Lifeline's Just Ask information line on 1300 13 11 14 (Monday to Friday 9 am to 5 pm EST).

References

Chapters 3 and 4

Andrews, G., *The Tolkien Report: A description of a model mental health service*, New South Wales, privately published, 1991.

Anonymous, 'Structural reform of the state psychiatric services. Case study: Lakeside Hospital, Ballarat', DRAFT: Not for release or file, Office of Psychiatric Services, Victoria, 12 September 1990.

'Aradale Hospital scandal, claim MPs', *The Courier*, Ballarat, 15 November 1991, p. 4.

'Aradale horror', *The Courier*, Ballarat, 20 November 1991, p. 1.

'Aradale to face huge shakeup', *The Courier*, Ballarat, 21 November 1991, p. 3.

'Aradale charges', *The Courier*, Ballarat, 29 November 1991, p. 1.

Ashton, Seaton, 'Taking razor to Lakeside puts mentally ill at risk', *The Courier*, Ballarat, 1 June 1991, p. 2.

Ashton, Seaton, 'Is Aradale a wrinkle in time?' *The Courier*, Ballarat, 18 November 1991, p. 2.

'Assault claims at Lakeside', *The Courier*, Ballarat, 18 October 1990, p. 1.

'Audit of standards of treatment and care in psychiatric hospitals in the State of Victoria', March 1992, Department of Human Services, Victoria, 1992.

Australian Medical Workforce Advisory Committee (1999), *The Specialist Psychiatry Workforce in Australia*, AMWAC Report 1999.7, Sydney.

'Bans lifted at psychiatric hospital', *The Courier*, Ballarat, 28 September 1990, p. 5.

'Base Hospital helps Lakeside to cope', *The Courier*, Ballarat, 26 September 1990, p. 7.

Brothers, C.R.D., *Early Victorian Psychiatry 1835–1905*, A.C. Brooks, Govt Printer, Melbourne, 1957.

Cunningham Dax, E., *Asylum to Community: The development of the mental hygiene service in Victoria, Australia*, World Federation for Mental Health, F.W. Cheshire, 1961.

Editorial, 'Lakeside report demands action', *The Courier*, Ballarat, 18 April 1991, p. 6.

Editorial, 'Psychiatric care moves premature', *The Courier*, Ballarat, 24 June 1991, p. 6.

Editorial, 'Major improvements at Lakeside', *The Courier*, Ballarat, 10 October 1991, p. 8.

Faulkner, Peter A., 'Changing the paradigm in psychiatric services', A thesis submitted to the Royal Melbourne Institute of Technology in partial fulfilment of the requirements for the award of Master of Business in Health Administration, 1991.

'Government plans for more support for psychiatric patients', *The Courier*, Ballarat, 18 October 1991, p. 5.

'Health dispute worsens as nurses stood down', *The Courier*, Ballarat, 18 December 1990, p. 4.

Hill, Kendall, 'Lakeside marked to go in health reform', *The Courier*, Ballarat, 24 May 1991, p. 2.

Hill, Kendall, 'Half Lakeside beds to go in restructure', *The Courier*, Ballarat, 29 May 1991, p. 3.

Hill, Kendall, 'Lakeside staff in limbo says union', *The Courier*, Ballarat, 1 June 1991, p. 9.

'Lakeside stop work', *The Courier*, Ballarat, 14 December 1990. p. 3.

'Lakeside wards left unattended', *The Courier*, Ballarat, 17 December 1990, p. 5.

'Lakeside volunteers keen to give further support', *The Courier*, Ballarat, 21 December 1990, p. 5.

REFERENCES

'Lakeside death leads to trial. Nurse contributed to death, says coroner', *The Courier*, Ballarat, 4 July 1991, p. 2.

'Lakeside move', *The Courier*, Ballarat, 31 August 1991, p. 1.

'Lakeside care improved says Minister', *The Courier*, Ballarat, 9 October 1991, p. 4.

'Male nurse on kill charge', *The Courier*, Ballarat, 25 September 1990, p. 4.

Morgan, Morris, 'Lakeside wards left unattended', *The Courier*, Ballarat, 17 December 1990, p. 5.

Murphy, Shane, 'Living the experience: an oral history. Study of life in a large Victorian psychiatric hospital', Research project, Graduate Diploma of Psychiatric Nursing, Ballarat University College, Division of Life Sciences, School of Nursing, October 1992.

Murphy, Shane and Hodges, Lawrence, *Lakeside Hospital Centenary 1893–1993*, Grampians Region, Victorian Government Department of Health and Community Services, October 1993.

'New director faces challenge at Lakeside', *The Courier*, Ballarat, 13 May 1989.

Nicholls, Brenda, 'Bringing mental ills in from the medical cold', *The Courier*, Ballarat, 20 October 1990, p. 36.

'No surprise, says Mayor', *The Courier*, Ballarat, 21 November 1991, p. 3.

'Nurse jailed for assault at Lakeside', *The Courier*, Ballarat, 3 October 1991, p. 2.

'Nurse was drinking, court told', *The Courier*, Ballarat, 3 July 1991, p. 2.

'Open Mind', a newsletter about the Investigative Task Force's Report on the Aradale Psychiatric Hospital and Residential Institution, published by the Office of Psychiatric Services, Health Dept Victoria, vol. 2, no. 2, Supplement, No. 2, November 1991.

'Patient died after dispute, court told', *The Courier*, Ballarat, 27 September 1991, p. 2.

Paton, Michael, Tobin, Margaret and Hudson-Jessop, Pamela, 'Integrating public and private psychiatric practice: from national agenda to personal experience', *Australasian Psychiatry*, June 1999, 7 (3), pp. 143–146.

317

'Rolling stoppages to hit Lakeside staff', *The Courier*, Ballarat, 13 December 1990, p. 15.

Rubinstein, W.D. and Rubinstein, H.L., *Menders of the Mind: A history of the Royal Australian and New Zealand College of Psychiatrists 1946–1996*, Oxford University Press, Melbourne, 1996.

Shorter, Edward, *A History of Psychiatry: From the era of the asylum to the age of Prozac*, John Wiley & Sons, New York, 1997.

Social Development Committee, 'Inquiry into the future use of Willsmere Hospital', Parliament of Victoria, 1985.

Stanford, Anne, 'Assault claims at Lakeside', *The Courier*, Ballarat, 18 October 1990, pp. 1–3.

Thornicroft, G. and Tansella, M., *The Mental Health Matrix*, Cambridge University Press, Cambridge, 1999.

Tobin, M.J., 'Inquiries at Lakeside and Aradale Hospitals: lessons and advances?', *Australian and New Zealand Journal of Psychiatry*, 27, 1993, pp. 333–340.

Tobin, M.J., 'Transition from clinician to manager – a case study', *Australian Health Review*, 16 (1), 1993, pp. 51–59.

Tobin, M.J., 'Rural psychiatric services', *Australian and New Zealand Journal of Psychiatry*, 30, 1996, pp. 114–123.

'Union bans lifted in psychiatric hospitals', *The Courier*, Ballarat, 20 December 1990, p. 4.

'Union attacks government over Aradale', *The Courier*, Ballarat, 21 November 1991, p. 5.

'Urgent call for volunteers in Lakeside Hospital strike', *The Courier*, Ballarat, 15 December 1990, p. 1.

Victorian Government, Investigative Task Force's Findings on the Aradale Psychiatric Hospital and Residential Institution, November 1991.

Whiteford, Harvey, 'Can research influence mental health policy?', *Australian and New Zealand Journal of Psychiatry*, 35, 2001, pp. 428–434.

'Willsmere project working paper no. 1: Principles and strategies for staff redeployment', Report prepared by working party no. 1, June 1986.

'Willsmere project working paper no. 2: Principles and strategies for relocation of patients and services', Report prepared by working party no. 2, June 1986.

'Willsmere project working paper no. 3: Draft principles and models for psychiatric services for elderly people', Report prepared by working party no. 3, June 1986.

Chapter 5

Carberry, B. and Poulton, C., 'Wide Open 1973', *The Journal of Sydney Technical High School*, 1973.

Duyker, Edward, *Of the Star and the Key: Mauritius, Mauritians and Australia*, Australian Mauritian Research Group, Sydney, 1988.

Fogarty, R. and Grimison, L., *The Journal of Sydney Technical High School*, 1970.

Poulton, C.J. et al., 'Wide Open', *The Journal of Sydney Technical High School*, 1972.

The Editorial Committee, 'Senior Year Book', Faculty of Medicine, University of Sydney, 1979. 1979 Year Book Committee, Sydney University Medical Society, 1979.

Chapter 6

Letter from Dr Margaret Tobin, Area Director Mental Health, Southern Sydney Area Health Service, to Ms Sharon Payne, New South Wales Medical Board regarding Dr Eric Gassy. Dated 13 July 1994.

Ritchie, L., *A Hundred Year History of the St George Hospital 1892–1994: The healing saint*, St George Hospital, 1998.

Robotham, Julie, 'It's duelling professors as drugs row gets personal', *Sydney Morning Herald*, 26–27 June 2004, p. 1 and p. 6.

Tobin, M.J., 'Public sector psychiatry towards 2000, New roles and challenges: technician or clinician?', *Australasian Psychiatry*, 4 (1), 1996, pp. 18–23.

Tobin, Margaret and Boyce, Philip, 'Defining the role of the consultant psychiatrist in a public mental health service', *Australian and New Zealand Journal of Psychiatry*, 32, 1998, pp. 603–611.

Tobin, Margaret and Hickie, Ian, 'Outcomes focused service delivery: developing an academic–management partnership', *Australian and New Zealand Journal of Psychiatry*, 32, 1998, pp. 327–336.

Tobin, Margaret and Wells, Jane, 'Pscyhiatrists managing change: lost control or at a loss', *Australasian Psychiatry*, 7 (4), 1999, pp. 194–198.

Chapter 7

Details of Gassy's consultations with Drs Floyd, Woodforde, Phillips and Ali were taken from evidence given in court or from documents before the court, which were released to the author by the South Australian Courts Administration Authority.

Gassy, J.E., Comments on Woodforde's report of 30.8.94. Document not dated.

Gassy, J.E., Summary of events leading to my appearance before the Impaired Registrants' Panel (Medical Practice Act 1992). Dated 29 January 1995.

Internal Southern Sydney Area Health Service Memorandum from Sarah Ashton to Dr W.G. Troy regarding future of Pacific House. Dated 26 August 1992.

Letter from Noel M. Wilton for NSW Health Director General to Dr J.D. Campbell, Chief Executive Officer, Southern Sydney Area Health Service. Dated 11 December 1992.

Letter from Dr John Woodforde to The Registrar, Medical Board of New South Wales regarding Dr Jean Eric Gassy. Dated 30 August 1994.

Letter from Dr Jonathan Phillips to Mr Edson Pike, Legal Services Manager, New South Wales Defence Union Ltd regarding Dr Eric Gassy. Dated 17 October 1994.

Letter from Dr John Woodforde to The Registrar, Medical Board of New South Wales regarding Dr Jean Eric Gassy. Dated 21 November 1994.

Letter from Dr Jill Floyd regarding Dr Eric Gassy. No Addressee given. Dated 10 March 1995.

Letter from Dr Osman Ali to Whom it may concern regarding Dr Eric Gassy. Dated 1 April 1995.

Letter from Dr J.E. Gassy to Ms L. Rogers, New South Wales Medical Board regarding decision not to practise. Dated 7 July 1995.

Letter from Dr J.E. Gassy to Ms Elizabeth Tydd, Medical Board of New South Wales regarding Board's concern for his health. Dated 9 September 1996.

Letter from Dr J.E. Gassy to Ms A. Harvey, Legal Officer, New South Wales Medical Board regarding lost certificate of registration. Dated 24 September 1997.

Reasons for Determination in The Medical Tribunal of NSW. No 40000 of 1997 re Dr Jean Eric Gassy. Dated Friday 1 August 1997. Plus transcript of some of the hearing in the Medical Tribunal of New South Wales, June 1997.

St George Hospital Internal Memorandum from Dr J.E. Gassy to Bruce Cross regarding Director of Psychiatry position. Dated 15 June 1992.

Trollope, Anthony, *The Eustace Diamonds*, Penguin Books, Middlesex, 1969.

Chapter 8

Adams, Rob, 'Historical walk: notes from a guided tour of Glenside. A short History of mental health services in SA 1846 to 1995', Royal Adelaide Hospital Glenside Campus Mental Health Service, 2003.

Beringen, Helen, 'Probe into hospital restraint on patient', *The Advertiser*, 1 January 1993, p. 2.

Brennan, Peter, *A New Millennium, A New Beginning: MCSPS The Mental Health Services Review*, MA International Pty Ltd, Management Consultants to the Health Industry, May 2000.

Clark, Fiona, '"Mafia" culture of fear at hospital', *The Advertiser*, 26 September 1997, p. 9.

Coorey, Phillip and Foster, Michael, 'Glenside closure backdown', *The Advertiser*, 14 October 1998, p. 14.

Cornwall, Deborah, 'Hospital's staff cuts "dangerous"', *The Advertiser*, 29 September 1989, p. 8.

Cross, Neil, 'Glenside slammed over patient', *The Advertiser*, 6 January 1993, p. 2.

Dibden, W.A., A biography of psychiatry [electronic resource]: the story of events and the people involved in the development of services for the psychiatrically ill in South Australia 1939–1989. [Adelaide], Adelaide University Library, 2001, <http://www.library.adelaide.edu.au/digitised/Dibden/index.html>.

Donovan, Zac, 'Patient charged over Hillcrest doctor's death', *The Advertiser*, 4 December 1992, p. 1.

Douglas, Mark, 'Backlash fears for mentally ill', *The Advertiser*, 22 October 1992, p. 26.

'Escapee caught', *The Advertiser*, 17 July 2002, p. 5.

Ferguson, John, 'Hospital staff cheated death: secret memo', *The Advertiser*, 14 December 1993, p. 3.

'Glenside security upgraded', *The Advertiser*, 23 August 2002, p. 24.

Hackett, Peter, 'Abuse of mentally ill patients in SA claimed', *The Advertiser*, 20 July 1991, p. 15.

Hailstone, Barry, 'Bans "interfering" with welfare of patients', *The Advertiser*, 14 August 1986, p. 11.

Hailstone, Barry, 'Mental health to be under new board', *The Advertiser*, 21 November 1987, p. 2.

Hailstone, Barry, 'Glenside, Hillcrest merge not favoured', *The Advertiser*, 19 July 1988, p. 10.

Hailstone, Barry, 'Crisis for mental services', *The Advertiser*, 13 April 1991, p. 3.

Hailstone, Barry, 'Doctors fear mental health plan will fail', *The Advertiser*, 23 November 1991, p. 14.

Hailstone, Barry, 'Patients now pawns in struggle', *The Advertiser*, 19 March 1992, p. 23.

Hailstone, Barry, 'Mental health warning', *The Advertiser*, 8 December 1992, p. 3.

Hailstone, Barry, 'Mental health revamp backdown', *The Advertiser*, 10 December 1992, p. 2.

Hailstone, Barry, 'Mental health board and chief sacked', *The Advertiser*, 11 December 1992, p. 3.

Hailstone, Barry, 'Hospitals let care status lapse', *The Advertiser*, 20 February 1993, p. 19.

Hailstone, Barry and King, Melissa, 'Hospital assaults shock', *The Advertiser*, 12 December 1992, p. 1.

Hailstone, Barry and King, Melissa, 'Nurses "in constant fear of violence"', *The Advertiser*, 12 December 1992, p. 6.

Haynes, Peter, 'Hospitals merger "may lead to reduced services"', *The Advertiser*, 23 November 1987, p. 4.

Hellaby, David, 'Mental health reform headache', *The Advertiser*, 20 September 1993, p. 5.

'Hillcrest Hospital to become leading psychiatric centre', *The Advertiser*, 24 March 1989, p. 11.

REFERENCES

Hogben, Bruce, '"Hundreds" to walk out in hospital row', *The Advertiser*, 13 March 1986, p. 3.

Hogben, Bruce, 'Investigate Glenside: Govt', *The Advertiser*, 15 March 1986, p. 16.

Hogben, Bruce, 'Nurses to march in prelude to 24-hour strike', *The Advertiser*, 3 July 1986, p. 15.

Hogben, Bruce, 'Intimidation alleged as nurse unions fall out over strike', *The Advertiser*, 4 July 1986, p. 10.

Hogben, Bruce, 'Psychiatric nurses return to work', *The Advertiser*, 5 July 1986, p. 11.

'Hospital help appeal', *The Advertiser*, 4 July 1986, p. 3.

'Hospital sale plan angers unions', *The Advertiser*, 6 March 1991, p. 16.

Hughes, David, 'Advanced training in adult psychiatry', *Australasian Psychiatry*, 10 (1), 2002, pp. 6–11.

Humphreys, Bernard, 'Hillcrest Hospital closure to go ahead', *The Advertiser*, 24 June 1991, p. 3.

James, Colin, 'Family not told of man's death', *The Advertiser*, 8 March 1989, p. 12.

Jory, Rex, 'Psychiatric hospitals may amalgamate', *The Advertiser*, 3 April 1987, p. 3.

Jory, Rex, 'Glenside Hospital land may be sold', *The Advertiser*, 11 December 1987, p. 13.

Jory, Rex, 'Hospital to sell land for synagogue', *The Advertiser*, 25 March 1989, p. 13.

Jory, Rex, 'Psychiatric merger plan overturned', *The Advertiser*, 1 April 1989, p. 11.

Kay, H.T., *1870–1970 Commemorating the Centenary of Glenside Hospital*, The Griffin Press, Adelaide, 1970.

Kemp, Miles, 'Mental health care critic now the boss', *The Advertiser*, 1 August 2000, p. 1.

King, Melissa, 'Mental health system slammed', *The Advertiser*, 15 November 1995, p. 10.

Magarey, Joel, 'Service "pitiful" for mentally ill', *The Advertiser*, 9 March 1994, p. 8.

Male, Andrew, 'Solving a mental block', *The Advertiser*, 16 April 1992, p. 15.

'Mental health body set up', *The Advertiser*, 17 October 1988, p. 16.

'Mental health nurses' roster row resolved', *The Advertiser*, 23 August 1996, p. 5.

Murrie, John, 'Fears of $3m health blow-out', *The Advertiser*, 25 March 1994, p. 10.

'New steps to curb attacks in hospitals', *The Advertiser*, 26 January 1993, p. 3.

'Nurse slated over man's death', *The Advertiser*, 14 March 1992, p. 13.

'Nurses threaten to escalate bans', *The Advertiser*, 16 August 2000, p. 27.

'Patient still at large after fleeing Glenside', *The Advertiser*, 16 July 2002, p. 10.

Pengelley, Jill, 'Walking out the door', *The Advertiser*, 18 July 2002, p. 28.

'Police report patient over hospital killing', *The Advertiser*, 15 July 1988, p. 3.

Power, Bill, 'Police raid hospitals', *The Advertiser*, 12 April 1994, p. 1.

'Psychiatric nurses strike over rosters', *The Advertiser*, 27 July 1996, p. 5.

'Shake-up fails to cure mental health crisis', *The Advertiser*, 18 September 1993, p. 3.

'State's mental health funding under fire', *The Advertiser*, 22 October 1991, p. 5.

'Talks ordered on Glenside troubles', *The Advertiser*, 14 March 1986, p. 13.

Tichy, Noel M., *The Leadership Engine*, HarperCollins, USA, 2002.

Tobin, Margaret and Edwards, Julie, 'Are psychiatrists equipped for management roles in mental health services?', *Australian and New Zealand Journal of Psychiatry*, 36, 2002, pp. 4–8.

Tobin, Margaret et al., 'Consumer participation in mental health services: who wants it and why?', *Australian Health Review*, 25 (3), 2002, pp. 91–100.

Tobin, Margaret et al., 'Clinical Practice Guidelines: a tool to measure variance', *Australasian Psychiatry*, 11 (1), March 2003, pp. 26–28.

Tobin, Margaret et al., 'Improving the safety of mental health services', *Australasian Psychiatry*, 11 (2), June 2003, pp. 176–179.

Turner, Jenny, 'RAH staff train for violent patients', *The Advertiser*, 12 August 1991, p. 2.

'Two escape Glenside as two others surrender', *The Advertiser*, 15 July 2002, p. 4.

Weidenhofer, Michelle, 'Doctor slain "because of medication"', *The Advertiser*, 10 March 1994, p. 8.

Weidenhofer, Michelle, 'Stabbing victim a vampire, court told', *The Advertiser*, 12 March 1994, p. 3.

Weidenhofer, Michelle, 'Killer psychotic, court told', *The Advertiser*, 15 March 1994, p. 7.

Weidenhofer, Michelle, 'Coroner criticises health services over man's death', *The Advertiser*, 12 July 1996, p. 6.

Chapter 9
Mitchell, Susan, *All Things Bright and Beautiful: Murder in the City of Light*, Pan Macmillan Australia, 2004.

Chapters 14–16
Chronology – prosecution case. R v Jean Eric Gassy (document presented in court).

Letter from Dr Craig Raeside to Mr Peter Brebner, Director of Prosecutions. Dated 22 May 2004.

Report of the Judges of The Supreme Court of South Australia to the Attorney-General Pursuant to Section 16 of the Supreme Court Act 1935 for the Year Ended 31 December 2004 (accessed at: <http://www.courts.sa.gov.au/courts/supreme/judges_report/judges_report_2004.htm>).

Transcript of R v Jean Eric Gassy in the Supreme Court of South Australia, including voir dire hearing, sentencing remarks by Honourable Justice Vanstone on 28 October 2004 and various documents presented in court.

Victoria, Criminal Justice Statistics and Research Unit, Report, Survey of Victorian Jurors, Department of Justice Victoria, Melbourne, Vic., 1998.

Victoria, Parliament, Law Reform Committee, Law Reform Paper, Jury Service in Victoria, Volume 1, Law Reform Committee of Victoria, Melbourne, Vic., 1996.

Victoria, Parliament, Law Reform Committee, Jury Service in Victoria, Final report: Volume 3: report on research projects, Law Reform Committee of Victoria, Melbourne, Vic., 1997.

Chapters 17 and 18

American Psychiatric Association, *Diagnostic and Statistical Manual of Mental Disorders*, Fourth edition, Washington, 1994.

Andreasen, Nancy and Black, Donald, *Introductory Textbook of Psychiatry*, Second edition, American Psychiatric Press, Washington, 1995.

Bentall, R.P., *Madness Explained: Psychosis and human nature*, Penguin Books, England, 2003.

Dowbiggin, Ian, 'Delusional diagnosis? The history of paranoia as a disease concept in the modern era', *History of Psychiatry*, xi, 2000, pp. 037–069.

Ellard, John, *Some Rules for Killing People: Essays on madness, murder and the mind*, Edited by Gordon Parker, Angus & Robertson, Sydney, 1989.

Ellard, John, *The Anatomy of Mirages: A psychiatrist reflects on life and the mind*, University of New South Wales Press, Sydney, 1994.

Feeman, Daniel et al., 'A cognitive model of persecutory delusions', *British Journal of Clinical Psychology*, 41, 2002, pp. 331–347.

Freeman, Daniel and Garety, Philippa, 'Connecting neurosis and psychosis: The direct influence of emotion on delusions and hallucinations', *Behaviour Research and Therapy*, 41, 2003, pp. 923–947.

Garner, Helen, *Joe Cinque's Consolation*, Picador, Sydney, 2004.

Hales, Robert and Yudofsky, Stuart, American Psychiatric Press Synopsis of Psychiatry, Washington, 2005.

Heifetz, Ronald A., *Leadership Without Easy Answers*, Harvard University Press, USA, 1994, pp. 6, 235–236, 263, 268, 273. Reprinted by permission of the publisher, Cambridge, Mass.: The Belknap Press of Harvard University Press, Copyright © 1994 by the President and Fellows of Harvard College.

Interview with Senator John Kerry and Teresa Heinz Kerry by Paula Zahn, CNN, aired 5 January 2004. Accessed at: <http://transcripts.cnn.com/TRANSCRIPTS/0401/05/pzn/00/html>.

Lott, Deborah, 'Physician – treat thyself?', *Psychiatric Times*, vol. XVIII, issue 12, December 2001.

North East London Strategic Health Authority, Report of an Independent Inquiry into the care and treatment of Dr Daksha Emson and her daughter Freya, October 2003.

Rey, Joseph, Walter, Garry and Giuffrida, Michael, 'Australian psychiatrists today: proud of their profession but stressed and apprehensive about the future', *Australian and New Zealand Journal of Psychiatry*, 38, 2004, pp. 105–110.

Sadock, Benjamin James and Sadock, Virginia Allcott, *Kaplan & Sadock's Synopsis of Psychiatry*, Lippincott Williams & Wilkins, Philadelphia, 2003.

Spitzer, Robert et al., *DSM-IV Case Book: A learning companion to the diagnostic and statistical manual of mental disorders*, Fourth edition, American Psychiatric Press, Washington, 1994.

Walter, Garry, Rey, Joseph and Giuffrida, Michael, 'What is it currently like being a trainee psychiatrist in Australia?', *Australasian Psychiatry*, vol. 11, no. 4, December 2003.

Update

Supreme Court of South Australia Court of Criminal Appeal. R v Gassy (No 3). Judgment of The Court of Criminal Appeal (The Honourable Justice Debelle, The Honourable Justice Bleby and The Honourable Justice White), 22 December 2005.

Epilogue

Andrews, G. et al., *The Mental Health of Australians*, Mental Health Branch, Commonwealth Department of Health and Aged Care, Canberra, 1999.

Auditor General Victoria, Mental Health Services for People in Crisis, Victorian Government, October 2002.

Australian Institute of Health and Welfare (AIHW), *Mental Health Services in Australia, 2003–04*, AIHW Canberra, (Mental Health Series no. 6), 2005.

Australian Medical Workforce Advisory Committee, *The Specialist*

Psychiatry Workforce in Australia, AMWAC Report 1999.7, Sydney, 1999.

Bloch, Sidney and Singh, Bruce, *Understanding Troubled Minds: A guide to mental illness and its treatment*, Melbourne University Press, Melbourne, 1997.

Buchanan, Jo, *Wings of Madness: A mother's journey*, New Holland Publishers, Sydney, 2004.

Ellingson, Peter, 'The shame of our "forgotten people"', *Sunday Age*, 12 December 2004, p. 1.

Evaluation of the National Mental Health Strategy, *Final Report*, Prepared for the Australian Health Ministers Advisory Council by the National Mental Health Strategy Evaluation Steering Committee, December 1997.

Groom, G., Hickie, I. and Davenport, T., *Out of Hospital, Out of Mind! A report detailing mental health services in 2002 and community priorities for national mental health policy for 2003–2008*, Mental Health Council of Australia, Canberra, 2003.

Groom, Grace, 'Primary mental health care reform in Australia: The vision and the reality', submitted in fulfilment of the requirements for the degree of Doctor of Health Science at Deakin University, June 2002.

Gunn, Andrew, 'Down a deadly path', *Australian Doctor*, 15 October 2004, p. 24.

Hickie, I. and Groom, G., 'Primary care-led mental health service reform: An outline of the better outcomes in mental health care initiative', *Australasian Psychiatry*, 10 (4), 2002, pp. 376–382.

Lawrence, D., Holman, D. and Jablensky, A., *Duty to Care: Preventable physical illness in people with mental illness*, University of Western Australia, Perth, 2001.

Malcolm, Janet, *Psychoanalysis: The Impossible Profession*, Vintage Books, New York, 1980.

Malcolm, Janet, *The Journalist and the Murderer*, Vintage Books, New York, 1990.

Malcolm, Janet, *The Purloined Clinic*, Vintage Books, New York, 1992.

Not for Service: Experiences of injustice and despair in mental health care in Australia, Mental Health Council of Australia, Canberra, 2005.

REFERENCES

Safe, Mike, 'The enemy within', *Weekend Australian* magazine, 30 April–1 May 2005, pp. 20–25.

The National Mental Health Plan Steering Committee, Consultation Paper on the National Mental Health Plan 2003–2008, March 2003.

Acknowledgements

My thanks go first and foremost to Mitchell, my sweetheart, for his wonderfully constant love, support and understanding. My grandmother Lorna Cameron is also a true and dear friend, always there to provide some wit and wisdom.

I am also extremely grateful to Margaret's family for their generosity and courage in sharing their lives and their memories, in spite of the pain this has cost them. To Don Scott, Jean Tobin, and Margaret's brothers and sisters, Helena, Bernadette, Patrick, Mary Catherine, Peter, and Damian – thank you so much. Many of Margaret's colleagues and friends were also of great help, and I would like to particularly acknowledge Reta Creegan, Ian Hickie and Jonathan Phillips. Thanks also to Brendan Kelly for his contributions.

In Adelaide, a number of people helped me survive those long weeks away from home and husband. Thanks to the McInerney Clements household for their warm hospitality and dark humour; to Terri Curtis, Ruby, Marsden and Bobbie for sharing their home with me; to Alex Kennedy and Kerry Wakefield at the *Independent Weekly* for helping keep me solvent; to Emily Telfer for her cheerful, efficient help; and to my mother Jan Sweet. Thanks also to Margot Storer for helping acquaint me with Adelaide.

Many people generously gave of their time, providing feedback on drafts and for this I thank Daniel Clements, Jenny Cooke, Reta Creegan, Linda Doherty, Miranda Harman, Ian Hickie, Lesley Hopkins, Marie McInerney, Bronnie Marshall, Mark Ragg, Don Scott, John Sweet, Matt Sweet, Jean Tobin, and Patrick and Natalia Tobin. The (amateur) detective work of my friends, the Tully Waggons, also assisted enormously. My appreciation also to Ginny Stein for her help.

Thanks also to Deborah Callaghan for helping me find a publisher, and to everyone at Pan Macmillan for their help and support during what sometimes has seemed like the never-ending book. Thanks also to Karen Ward for her meticulous copy-editing.

A number of institutions and organisations also assisted with my research, and I would like to acknowledge: Victoria's Mental Health Library; University of Sydney libraries; the University of Melbourne; *The Courier* newspaper at Ballarat for the use of their library; the State Library of South Australia; and the South Australian Courts Administration Authority, in particular Terry Anderson and Barry the sheriff.

Writers have a vested interest in making their subjects seem more interesting than they may actually be in real life. That is the nature of story-telling. Nonetheless, there can be no doubt that Margaret Tobin was a particularly interesting person at many different levels, and that the story of her career also helps tell a much broader history, and one which should be of concern to us all.

Many times, I was reminded of the difficulty of trying to tell someone's story without being able to speak with them directly, instead having to rely on the perceptions and memories of others. Not many of us would feel ourselves satisfactorily represented by a portrait drawn from second-hand impressions. Sometimes different people's recollections were in competition, if not outright conflict. Sometimes it felt like I was trying to put a jigsaw together without the benefit of the picture on the jigsaw box to guide me. No doubt some pieces have been put together wrongly and there are also likely to be some gaps in the picture or mistakes in its detail. And perhaps the jigsaw analogy is not so helpful anyway, implying a static picture when people are more like moving pictures, in a constant state of change. Overall, however, I hope the portrait is broadly true and fair. For that, I must thank the many people who gave so generously of their time and energy to assist with interviews and other research. Some sources did not want to be named in any way but amongst the interviewees, I would like to thank Rob Adams, Greg Aldridge, Jennifer Alexander, Pam Allen, Scott Allen, Jeremy Anderson, Terry Anderson, Gavin Andrews, Vera Auerbach, Bill Barclay, Kate Barclay, Lesley Barclay, Elizabeth Benson, Jenny Beutel, Annemaree Bickerton, Warwick Blakemore, Rob Bonner, Darren Bowd, Phil Boyce, Michelle Bradley, John Brayley, Peter Brebner, Peter Brennan, Dean Brown, Peggy Brown, Bill Buckingham, Terry Burke, Tom Callaly, John Campbell, Eileen Casey, Kaye Challinger, Bob Champion, Christine Charles, Lucy Chen, Denise Conway, Rae Conway, Tony Cotter, Katy Cottrill, Chris Crawford, Rocco Crino, Andrew Crowther, Matthew Cullen, Tim Daly, Jim Davidson, Julia Davison, Paul Debenham, Angela Dell'Olio, Michael Diamond, Helen Dornom, Charles Doutney, Learne Durrington, Ed Duyker, Judith Dwyer, Fred Ehrlich, Peter Eisen, John Ellard, Keith Evans, Scott Fanker, John Farhall, Peter Faulkner, Russell Firmin, Peter Fitzsimmons, Jim Fletcher, Stephen Freiberg, Gavin Frost, Glen Fuller, John Gallichio, Val Gerrand, Chris Gibbs, Kate Giles, Bryan Gillard, Michael Giuffrida, Kieran Gleeson, Maureen Gleeson, Darty Glover, Jill Gordon, Des Graham, Rebecca Graham, Gerald Graves, Grace Groom, Lee Gruner, Judy Hardy, Naomi Harry, Suzanne Heath, Bronwyn Hendry, Barbara Hocking, Mary Anne Holland, Lesley Hopkins, Shelley Horne, David Hughes, Norman James, Sandy Jeffs, André Jenkins, Tom Jones, Adrian Keller, Brendan Kelly, Alex Kennedy, Jeff Kennett, Priscilla Kincaid Smith, Andrej Knez, Beth Kotze, Claudie Larose, Geoff Leonard, Geraldine Leslie, Sandy Lester, Cas Liber, Pam Limbert, Maren Lorentzen, Liz Mackenzie, Peter McArdle, Christine McBride, Chris McDowell, Rocky McEwin, Pat McGorry, Chris McGowan, John McGrath, Moira McKinnon, Michael McMahon, Mary Malone, Florence Mansfield, Kae Martin, Mike Melino, Phil Mitchell, Maria Mithen, Matt Moss, Paul Mullen, Shane Murphy, Robyn Murray, Karin Myhill, Craig Nelson, John O'Neill, Annie Paton, Michael Paton, Craig Patterson, David Pearce,

Deirdre Pearsall, Bill Pepplinkhouse, Carlyle Perera, Jenny Phillips, Jonathan Phillips, Deb Podbury, Vince Ponzio, Geoffrey Prideaux, Mary Pryor, Roxanne Ramsay, Beverley Raphael, Mick Reid, Val Reilly, Jennifer Relihan, Dal Retallack, Colin Riess, John Rimmer, Bruce Robinson, Ann Roche, Alan Rosen, Grant Sara, Alan Scarborough, Elizabeth Scott, Robyn Shiels, Bruce Singh, Yvonne Skarbek, Di Skene, Tim Smyth, Jeff Snars, Tony Spriggins, Fred Stamp, Mick Standing, Lynda Stephens, Mark Stevens, Just Stoelwinder, Robyn Stringfellow, Tom Stubbs, Cynthia Stuhlmiller, Sue Tait, John Taylor, Chris Tennant, Owen Thomas, Cristina Thompson, Sally Tideman, Carolyn Tobin, David Tofler, Ruth Vine, Michael Walsh, Garry Walter, Merrilyn Walton, Victor Wasylenko, Max Watson, Bob Wells, Harvey Whiteford, Barbara Wieland, Simon Willcock, Anne Sved Williams, Grant Williams, Michele Willis, Andrew Wilson (Queensland), Andrew Wilson (New South Wales), Frances Wilson, Ian Wilson, Murray Wright, Tom Young. Apologies to anyone inadvertently omitted.

And last, but certainly not least, thanks to dearest Jas for the joy you bring. Your dad would have been so proud of you.